LIBYA

This book examines the socioeconomic and political development of Libya from earliest times to the present, concentrating in particular on the four decades of revolutionary rule which began in 1969. Focusing on the twin themes of continuity and change, Ronald Bruce St John emphasizes the full extent to which the revolutionary government has distorted the depth and breadth of the post-1969 revolution by stressing policy change at the expense of policy continuity.

Following a brief look at pre-independence Libya, the author explores the way in which the fragility of the post-independence state, unable to contain rising Arab nationalist struggles and growing economic expectations, opened the way for the Free Unionist Officers led by Muammar al-Qaddafi to seize power. He then traces the progressive development of the revolutionary state through four stages:

- the consolidation of power to 1973;
- the projection of power to 1986;
- withdrawal and retrenchment to 1999;
- the redefinition of the state after 1999.

Highlighting the issues facing the contemporary state and providing possible solutions, this book will be an indispensible text for students of current affairs, history, North Africa, and the Middle East.

Ronald Bruce St John is an independent scholar and consultant for Associated Press, *National Geographic, New York Times,* ABC's 20–20, the Department of State, the National Intelligence Council, and Fortune 500 companies. An analyst for Foreign Policy in Focus, he has served on the International Advisory Board of the *Journal of Libyan Studies* and the Atlantic Council Working Group on Libya, and has published a large number of books, articles, and reviews on Andean America, North Africa and the Middle East, and Southeast Asia.

THE CONTEMPORARY MIDDLE EAST

Edited by Professor Anoushiravan Ehteshami

INSTITUTE FOR MIDDLE EASTERN AND ISLAMIC STUDIES, UNIVERSITY OF DURHAM

For well over a century now the Middle East and North Africa countries have formed a central plank of the international system. **The Contemporary Middle East** series provides the first systematic attempt at studying the key actors of this dynamic, complex, and strategically important region. Using an innovative common format – which in each case study provides an easily digestible analysis of the origins of the state, its contemporary politics, economics and international relations – prominent Middle East and North Africa experts have been brought together to write definitive studies of the MENA region's key countries.

Books in the series

Jordan
A Hashemite legacy
Beverley Milton-Edwards and Peter Hinchcliffe

Syria
Revolution from above
Raymond Hinnebusch

Israel
Challenges to identity, democracy and the state
Clive Jones and Emma C Murphy

Turkey
Challenges of continuity and change
Meliha Benli Altunışık and Özlem Tür Kavli

Sudan
Abdel Salam Sidahmed and Alsir Sidahmed

Saudi Arabia
Tim Niblock

Jordan
A Hashemite legacy, 2nd edition
Beverley Milton-Edwards and Peter Hinchcliffe

Morocco
Challenges to tradition and modernity
James N. Sater

Tunisia
Stability and reform in the modern Maghreb
Christopher Alexander

Libya
Continuity and change
Ronald Bruce St John

LIBYA

Continuity and change

Ronald Bruce St John

Routledge
Taylor & Francis Group

LONDON AND NEW YORK

First published 2011
by Routledge
2 Park Square, Milton Park, Abingdon, Oxon OX14 4RN

Simultaneously published in the USA and Canada
by Routledge
270 Madison Ave, New York, NY 10016

Routledge is an imprint of the Taylor & Francis Group, an informa business

Typeset in Bembo and ITC Stone Sans by Prepress Projects Ltd, Perth,
UK
Printed and bound in Great Britain by CPI Antony Rowe, Chippenham

British Library Cataloguing in Publication Data
A catalogue record for this book is available from the British Library

Library of Congress Cataloging in Publication Data
St. John, Ronald Bruce
Libya : continuity and change / Ronald Bruce St John.
p. cm. – (Contemporary Middle East ; 10)
Includes bibliographical references and index.
1. Libya–Politics and government–1969- 2. Libya–Economic conditions.
3. Libya–Foreign relations–1969- I. Title.
JQ3345.S75 2011
961.204–dc22
2010035109

ISBN 978-0-415-77976-0 (hbk)
ISBN 978-0-415-77977-7 (pbk)
ISBN 978-0-203-83068-0 (ebk)

To Carol

CONTENTS

PREFACE

This book focuses on contemporary Libya, especially the four decades since the Free Unionist Officers, led by Captain Muammar al-Qaddafi, overthrew the monarchy and seized power on 1 September 1969. To tell this story accurately and completely, it is necessary first to examine the earlier history of the country because the evolution of its economy and society in the colonial and post-colonial eras strongly influenced the socioeconomic and political policies of the present regime. In so doing, I will argue that much of the current scholarship on Libya has been too narrowly focused on Qaddafi and his often seemingly idiosyncratic policies at the expense of a broader and deeper analysis of the influences and considerations behind contemporary regime policies.

In common with most revolutionary governments, the Qaddafi regime from the outset of the One September Revolution has emphasized change at the expense of continuity in its official ideology and public policy statements. In the process, it has understated the extent to which the policies it developed and implemented borrowed from the past as they sought to change the future. Over time, the official emphasis on change has continued when in fact the revolutionary government in many areas has been increasingly guilty of looking backwards toward the future.

The emphasis in this book on the twin themes of continuity and change represents a notable departure from the past. Most students, journalists, scholars, and other observers of Libya have tended to focus on change at the expense of continuity in their analysis of the actions and policies of Libya, in part because they are not familiar with the country's history. A central argument of this book is that continuity as much as change has characterized the foreign and domestic policies of the Libyan government since independence in 1951, and most especially since the revolutionary government seized control in 1969. In concentrating on the dual themes of continuity and change, a central objective of this book is to assist readers to understand why Libyans think and act as they do and why the actions of the Libyan elite have generated more support among the Libyan citizenry than many Western observers have acknowledged.

Chapter 1 details the history of Libya from earliest times to the end of the Italian occupation, examining the impact of the many peoples that have conquered, occupied, and administered the region over the last 3,000 years. Many of these early civilizations built impressive cities and monuments, the ruins of which are still visible today. Because the remains of these early occupiers are so spectacular, the ruins themselves are often considered the prime legacy of the past when the social, economic, and political inheritance of past administrators has been far more important. Successive waves of Arab invaders brought the Arabic language and the Islamic religion to Libya, and they also reinforced tribal structures and nomadism as a form of social organization. In turn, the Ottoman Empire brought an element of political stability, limited economic development, and nascent state formation to Libya, reinforcing local, tribal, and regional identities in the process. As for the Italians, their short but harsh rule had very important economic, social, and political consequences that impacted on Libya well into the independence era.

Chapter 2 covers the emergence of contemporary Libya, exploring the continuity that linked the past with independent Libya. The discussion examines the forces which shaped the emergence of a precarious statehood, highlighting the general absence of state formation at the end of the Italian colonial period, the conflicted Four Power negotiations immediately after World War II, and the subsequent role of the United Nations in the independence process. The focus then turns to the socioeconomic and political forces, inside and outside Libya, which impacted on the policies and institutions of the Idris regime and eventually led to the overthrow of the monarchy in 1969. In addition to continuity and change, central themes in this chapter include the absence of an overarching ideology during the monarchical period, the fragmented nature of the polity, and the absolutist political system that characterized the monarchical government.

Chapter 3 details the organization and operation of the system of direct democracy, centered on a national network of congresses and committees, implemented by the revolutionary government. The direct democracy system was introduced in the Third Universal Theory and later codified in the three slender volumes of *The Green Book*, Qaddafi's socioeconomic and political manifesto. The Libyan leader has used this formal system of government, known as the people's sector, to mask an informal system of rule, known as the revolutionary sector, which is centered on himself and a coterie of close advisors. The revolutionary sector is largely based on family and tribal ties and is buttressed by the security services and the armed forces. The discussion in this chapter centers on the evolution of both the formal and informal systems of government in the context of continuity and change. It also explores the legal and religious policies of the regime, and examines reforms in other areas, including education, health care, and housing.

Following the discovery of oil, Libya was accurately described as a *rentier* economy, and after four decades of revolutionary experimentation it remains one. The discussion in Chapter 4 focuses on economic developments after 1969, highlighting the various stages of economic reform implemented – or not implemented – over the last four decades. In so doing, it pays special attention to hydrocarbons as the economic base for the country's political entity. It also looks at the interplay of economic, social, and political forces with an aim to frame the repeated economic crises suffered by Libya in the context of the country's overall political economy. The discussion concludes with thoughts on the Libyan economy in the post-hydrocarbon era.

With the overthrow of the monarchy, the revolutionary government undertook an aggressive and wide-ranging foreign policy, notable for the depth and breadth of its objectives and activities. It continued its pursuit of related goals into the 1980s, when a series of foreign policy setbacks caused Qaddafi to rethink and moderate some of his early initiatives while continuing to pursue others. Following a short decade in which the UN sanctions regime constrained external initiatives, the goals and methods of Libyan foreign policy in the post-1999 era changed as Qaddafi sought to integrate Libya into a fuller participation in the international community. In the process, he pursued an activist foreign policy in Africa, expanded relations with Europe, and normalized relations with the United States.

The concluding chapter, Chapter 5, draws together the themes pursued throughout the book, ending with a tentative assessment of post-Qaddafi Libya.

ACKNOWLEDGMENTS

This book is the product of well over three decades of research and study which began before I first visited Libya in 1977. Over time, a large number of people have encouraged and assisted my research and writing, and I want to acknowledge their generosity and support. I will not attempt to name them here as it would take far too much time and space and, in any case, most of them prefer to remain anonymous.

Some of the material in this book has appeared in one form or another in the four books and dozens of articles on Libya which I have published since 1981. With the intent to cast more fully the contemporary Libyan experience in the context of continuity and change, all of the material herein has been thoroughly revised and updated, condensing it in some cases and expanding it in others.

On a personal level, I would like to thank my wife, Carol, and our two sons, Alexander and Nathan, for their counsel and support over our many years together and offer a special thanks to Nathan for drawing the sketch map of Libya.

NOTE ON TRANSLITERATION AND USE OF NAMES

In the case of Libya, the transliteration of personal and place names from Arabic into English is especially frustrating and imprecise because the Latin spelling of people and places was never standardized. On the contrary, diplomats, explorers, travelers, and others, most of whom were not linguists, often fixed the spelling of Arabic names and places in the Latin alphabet. Consequently, many of the Latin spellings in widespread use today are a mixture of English, Italian, and French adaptations. In the interest of clarity and with the needs of the lay reader in mind, I refer to people and places in this text according to general international usage, employing conventional, contemporary spellings whenever possible.

CHRONOLOGY

644–646	Arabs occupy Cyrenaica and Tripolitania.
1517	Ottomans occupy Cyrenaica and later Tripolitania.
1711	Karamanli dynasty rule begins.
1835	Second Ottoman occupation begins.
1911	Italian occupation begins.
1951	King Idris al-Sanusi proclaims Libya an independent state.
1961	Oil exports begin.
1969	Free Unionist Officers overthrow the monarchy.
1971	Qaddafi announces the formation of the Arab Socialist Union.
1973	Third Universal Theory marks beginning of the Popular Revolution.
1976	Part one of *The Green Book* is published.
1977	Declaration of the Establishment of the People's Authority is issued.
1980	United States closes its embassy in Tripoli.
1981	United States orders Libya to close its diplomatic mission in Washington.
1984	Libya and Morocco sign the Treaty of Oujda, declaring their union.
1986	United States bombs targets in and around Benghazi and Tripoli. Morocco withdraws from union with Libya.
1988	United States accuses Libya of building a chemical weapons plant. Pan Am flight 103 explodes over Lockerbie, Scotland.
1989	Algeria, Libya, Mauritania, Morocco, and Tunisia form the Arab Maghrib Union. UTA flight 772 explodes over Niger.
1991	Libya opens the first stage of the Great Manmade River.

1992	United Nations imposes economic sanctions on Libya. Libya demands compensation from Italy for its 32-year occupation.
1995	Islamists clash with Libyan security forces in Benghazi.
1997	Vatican establishes full diplomatic relations with Libya. South Africa bestows Order of Good Hope on Qaddafi in recognition of his support in the fight against apartheid.
1998	Libya and Germany sign an economic cooperation agreement.
1999	Libya remands two suspects in Lockerbie bombing. UN Security Council suspends economic sanctions on Libya. Qaddafi calls on African nations to create a United States of Africa.
2000	Libya abolishes most central government executive functions, devolving responsibility to the 26 municipal councils making up the General People's Congress. Widespread racial violence breaks out in Libya with mobs attacking African migrant workers. Libya contributes officers to a UN peacekeeping mission for the first time in a decade.
2001	Three Scottish judges sitting in a special court in the Netherlands find one of two defendants guilty in the Lockerbie bombing. Libya pledges $2 billion in development assistance to several Caribbean island states. Germany asks Libya for compensation for victims of La Belle discothèque bombing. Libya occupies seat on UN Social and Economic Council.
2002	Libya launches an internet website offering a $1 million reward for information on individuals, mostly regime opponents affiliated with Islamist movements, wanted by Libyan officials. Libya rejects a US report that it has a poor human rights record. The African Union replaces the 39-year-old Organization of African Unity.
2003	Libya elected chairman of the UN Commission on Human Rights. Libya agrees with Great Britain and the United States to accept responsibility for the Lockerbie bombing and to pay compensation to the families of the victims. The UN Security Council lifts Libya sanctions. Libya abandons unconventional weapons programs and related delivery systems.
2004	Libya restores diplomatic relations with the United States. The European Union lifts arms embargo on Libya. Libya sends peace-keepers to the Philippines to oversee implementation of ceasefire with Moro Islamic Liberation Front. Libya announces it will abolish $5 billion in subsidies on electricity, fuel, and foodstuffs in a move to liberalize the economy.
2005	Libya abolishes People's Courts. Qaddafi argues that pending UN reforms should abolish the Security Council. The General People's Congress approves a measure allowing foreign banks

	to open branches and to contribute as shareholders in local banks. Libyan opposition organizations, meeting in London to discuss plans to remove Qaddafi from power, reject foreign military support.
2006	The General People's Committee creates a human rights office. The United States removes Libya from its list of state sponsors of terrorism. The World Bank says that Libya ranks among the least diversified oil-producing economies in the world. Libya announces that 1.2 million students will receive inexpensive computers as part of One Laptop per Child project.
2007	Libya announces plans to make 400,000 government workers redundant in order to ease public spending and stimulate private sector. Qaddafi criticizes US plans to deploy AFRICOM, a newly created American military command for Africa. Libya releases six foreign medics charged with the deliberate HIV infection of children in a Benghazi hospital.
2008	Libya elected to a two-year term to the UN Security Council. Qaddafi abolishes several ministries, complaining of graft and corruption, and hands power to the people. Italy apologizes to Libya for damage inflicted during the colonial era and signs a $5 billion investment deal by way of compensation. Qaddafi convenes a meeting of African kings, tribal chiefs, and traditional leaders, who crown him "King of Kings." Libya and the United States sign an agreement calling for compensation for the victims of attacks by either party on the other.
2009	Qaddafi threatens to nationalize the hydrocarbon sector in response to current low oil prices. Qaddafi reiterates earlier proposal for a one-state solution to the Israeli–Palestinian imbroglio. Qaddafi elected to one-year term as chairman of the African Union, promising to push for a United States of Africa. With the death of the president of Gabon, Omar Bongo Ondimba, Qaddafi becomes the longest serving head of state in the world, excluding monarchies. The Scottish government releases Abdel Basset al-Megrahi, the only person convicted in the Pan Am 103 bombing, on compassionate grounds. Libya celebrates the 40th anniversary of the One September Revolution. Libya elected president of the UN General Assembly. In his first ever visit to the United States, Qaddafi addresses the UN General Assembly in New York. Saif al-Islam al-Qaddafi is appointed head of the People's Social Leadership Committee system, his first official government position. The Qaddafi Foundation, a non-governmental organization (NGO) headed by Saif al-Islam al-Qaddafi,

releases its initial human rights report, which is highly critical of the government's human rights record. Two days later,
Human Rights Watch, for the first time, holds a press conference in Libya to announce the mostly critical findings of its
most recent report on human rights in Libya.

2010   The Libyan stock exchange opens to foreign investors.
Qaddafi declares that there is no place for a civil society in
Libya. Russia announces a $1.8 billion arms deal with Libya,
which includes fighter airplanes, tanks, and other sophisticated weapons systems. Qaddafi fails in a bid to be reelected
chairman of the Africa Union. Libya releases more than 200
political prisoners, including several former members of the
Libyan Islamic Fighting Group, but hundreds more detainees
remain imprisoned. Qaddafi suggests that the best solution to
ethnic violence in Nigeria is to divide the country into separate
Christian and Muslim states, a proposal widely denounced in
Nigeria. The head of the privatization board says that Libya's
long-term goal is to have 100 percent of the economy in private hands, with half the economy expected to be controlled
by private investors within 10 years. Saif al-Islam al-Qaddafi
calls for democratic reforms in Libya, including a formal
constitution. Libya and the United States sign a bilateral trade
agreement. Libya ends a two-year dispute with Switzerland
sparked by the July 2008 arrest in Geneva of one of Qaddafi's
sons. Four US senators call for a probe into the release of
Abdel Basset al-Megrahi, the only Libyan convicted in the
Lockerbie bombing. Israel forces a Gaza-bound aid ship sponsored by the Qaddafi Foundation to divert to an Egyptian port.
The Sudanese president, Omar Hassan al-Bashir, indicted by
the International Criminal Court for genocide, war crimes,
and crimes against humanity, meets with Qaddafi in Libya.

LIST OF ABBREVIATIONS

AFRICOM	US Africa Command
AGIP	Azienda Generale Italiana Petroli
AIDS	acquired immunodeficiency syndrome
AMU	Arab Maghrib Union (also Union du Maghreb Arabe or UMA)
AQIM	Al-Qaeda in the Islamic Maghrib
ASU	Arab Socialist Union
b/d	barrels per day
bcm	billion cubic meters
BP	British Petroleum
BPC	basic people's congress
CEN-SAD	See COMESSA
CNPC	China National Petroleum Company
COMESA	Common Market for Eastern and Southern Africa
COMESSA	Community of Sahel-Saharan States (also Communauté des Etats Sahélo-Sahariens or CEN-SAD)
EMP	Euro-Mediterranean Partnership
EPSA	exploration and production-sharing agreement
EU	European Union
FDI	foreign direct investment
FROLINAT	Front for the National Liberation of Chad (also Front de Libération Nationale du Chad)
GDP	gross domestic product
GMR	Great Manmade River
GNP	gross national product
GPC	General People's Congress
HIV	human immunodeficiency virus

IAEA	International Atomic Energy Agency
ICJ	International Court of Justice
ILSA	Iran and Libya Sanctions Act of 1996
IMF	International Monetary Fund
LIA	Libyan Investment Authority
LIFG	Libyan Islamic Fighting Group
LIPETCO	Libyan General Petroleum Company
LNG	liquefied natural gas
NATO	North Atlantic Treaty Organization
NOC	National Oil Company, National Oil Corporation
OAU	Organization of African Unity
OECD	Organization for Economic Cooperation and Development
OPEC	Organization of the Petroleum Exporting Countries
PLO	Palestine Liberation Organization
POLISARIO	Popular Front for the Liberation of Saguia el-Hamra and Rio de Oro (also Frente Popular para la Liberación de Saguia el-Hamra y Rio de Oro)
PSLC	people's social leadership committee
RCC	Revolutionary Command Council
SADR	Saharan Arab Democratic Republic
TMC	Transitional Military Council
TSCTP	Trans-Sahara Counter-Terrorism Partnership
UMA	See AMU
UN	United Nations
WLGP	Western Libya Gas Project
WTO	World Trade Organization

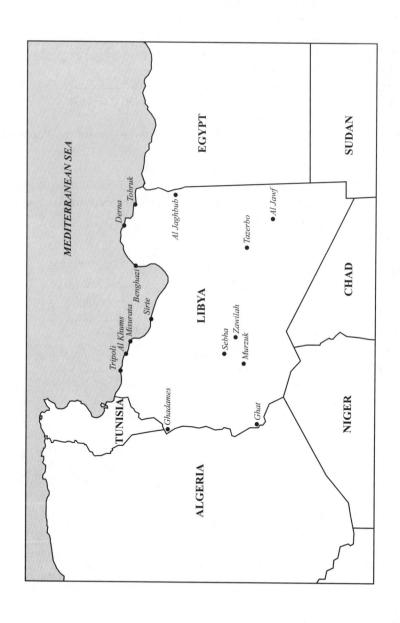

1

INTRODUCTION

Libya is a relatively new state situated on a land that has been conquered, occupied, and administered by outsiders for centuries. The ancient Egyptians applied the name Libya to a desert people living beyond their western frontier, and the early Greeks applied it to all non-Punic Africans living west of the Egyptian border. From the time of the Punic Wars, both Greeks and the Romans applied the term "Libya" to Africans living on Carthaginian territory. When Italy invaded in 1911, it applied the name "Libya" to the provinces of the Ottoman Empire it targeted for occupation as part of a policy aimed at justifying its aggression by linking it to the former North African territories of the Roman Empire. No one applied the term "Libya" to what is now the Great Socialist People's Libyan Arab Jamahiriya before the last century, and the Italians did not do so in a formal sense until 1929, when the separately administered territories of Tripolitania, Cyrenaica, and Fezzan were joined under a single governor. Following independence in 1951, the United Kingdom of Libya became the Kingdom of Libya in 1963, the Libyan Arab Republic in 1969, the Socialist People's Libyan Arab Jamahiriya in 1977, and the Great Socialist People's Libyan Arab Jamahiriya at a later date. For the sake of convenience, the country generally will be referred to as Libya throughout this book.

In the beginning

The names Tripolitania, Cyrenaica, and Fezzan were first used during the Ottoman period (1551–1911) to define the three geographical areas making up Libya. Tripolitania consists of the fertile Jifara Plain in the northwest and the Jabal Tarabulus (Jabal al-Nafusha), which extends south to the great stony plateau of the Hamadah al-Hamra. The oases of Fezzan lie below the Hamadah, stretching from the Wadi as-Shatti to the Murzuk Depression. In the eastern half of the country, Cyrenaica encompasses the fertile region of the Jabal al-Akhdar, and to the south the oasis systems of Awjilah, Jalu, Jaghbub, and Kufrah, together with the Great Sand Sea. Tripolitania and Cyrenaica are separated by almost 500 kilometers (310 miles) of desert, known as the Sirte Plain, which stretches to the Mediterranean coast. This natural barrier has long divided the country into east and west, fostering regionalism as an important influence on the country. Drainage systems accommodate seasonal rainfalls in various parts of Libya, but the country has no permanently flowing streams or rivers (Goudarzi 1970: 6–18; Rivlin 1949: 36).

From at least 7000 BC, it would appear that the coastal plain of Libya shared in the Neolithic culture common to the Mediterranean littoral. In the south, in what is now the Sahara and Sahel, a savannah people flourished until changing climatic conditions around 2000 BC caused the region to desiccate. In the process, most of the area's rivers disappeared, with sediment filling the alluvial valleys and driving the remaining water into underground aquifers, the source for the Great Manmade River project in the modern era. Retreating from the approaching desert, nomadic herdsmen and hunters migrated to the Sudan or were absorbed by local Berbers. Egyptian inscriptions dating from the Old Kingdom (*c.* 2700–2200 BC) constitute the first recorded testimony of Berber migrations as well as the earliest written record of Libyan history. Berber speakers now constitute a minority in North Africa as a whole and also in Libya, but the magnitude of the geographical area in which they are found testifies to the size of the original population (Brett and Fentress 1996: 1–25; Raven 1993: 6–7; Dupree 1958: 33–6).

The Garamantes were a tribal confederation of Saharan peoples who lived in what is now Fezzan. Little is known of them, including what they called themselves. The name Garamantes was Greek in origin and was later adopted by the Romans. The Garamantes were a local power for almost 1,000 years (500 BC to 500 AD). Confined to a chain of oases only 400 kilometers (250 miles) long, they were situated on a direct route from central Africa to the Mediterranean. Consequently, the Garamantes largely controlled trans-Saharan trade from Ghadames south to the Niger River, east to Egypt, and west to Mauritania (Daniels 1970; Liverani 2000).

Classical period

After founding the colony of Carthage in what is now Tunisia around 814 BC, the Phoenicians or Punics extended their influence along the north and west coast of North Africa. In Tripolitania, they built three large coastal cities, Oea (Tripoli), Labdah (Leptis Magna), and Sabratha, known collectively as Tripolis (three cities). The Punics established good trade relations with the Berbers of Tripolitania, teaching and learning from them, and in the process, the Berbers became somewhat Punicized in language and custom. Carthage and Tripolis drew support from Berber tribes in both the first Punic War (264–241 BC) and the second Punic War (218–202 BC). Even after the Romans sacked Carthage at the end of the third Punic War (149–146 BC), Punic influence on the region remained significant (Aubet 1993; DiVita *et al.* 1999: 146–61).

Greek influence

The region of Cyrenaica takes its name from Cyrene. Founded in 632 BC, it was the first Greek city in North Africa and one of the foremost cities in the Greek world. Over the next 200 years, the Greeks established four more cities on the North African shore: Ptolemais (Tolmeita), Euesperides (later Berenice and now Benghazi), Teuchira (later Arsinoe and now Tukrah), and Apollonia (later Susa, the port of Cyrene). Known as the Pentapolis, these five cities eventually became republics and experimented with a variety of democratic institutions. Libya would not again experience democratic experimentation for almost 2,000 years. The cities constituting the Pentapolis traded together and shared a common coinage, but intercity rivalries limited other forms of cooperation, even when faced with a common foe. Owing to this weakness, they were conquered in 525 BC by the Persian king, Cambyses III, and for the next 200 years they constituted the westernmost province of the Persian empire (MacKendrick 1980: 117; DiVita *et al.* 1999: 184–239).

In 331 BC, Cyrenaica returned to Greek rule under Alexander of Macedonia, and it remained so until the last Ptolemaic king, Ptolemy Apion, bequeathed it to Rome in 96 BC. In 67 BC, Cyrenaica was joined with Crete as a Roman province, and in 115–17 AD Cyrene suffered considerable damage during an insurrection by its Jewish community, a revolt brutally suppressed by Emperor Trajan (ruled 98–117) (De Felice 1985: 1–2). In 300, Emperor Diocletian (ruled 284–305) separated Cyrenaica from Crete, forming the provinces of Upper Libya and Lower Libya and marking the first time that the term "Libya" was used as an administrative designation in the country. With the partition of the Roman Empire in 324, control of Cyrenaica passed to Constantinople and the Byzantines while Tripolitania was attached to the western empire (MacKendrick 1980: 121).

Roman Empire

In the third century BC, Carthage and Rome began to compete for control of the central Mediterranean, an epic struggle that concluded with Rome's destruction of its rival at the conclusion of the third Punic War in 146 BC. At the time, the Roman provinces of Africa approximated the territory earlier controlled by Carthage, but by 27 BC the Romans had expanded their influence to include virtually all of the coastal areas of contemporary Tunisia. Systematic Roman colonization of North Africa, including Tripolitania, did not begin until one century later (Raven 1993: 33–48). In the process, the region became an important granary for Rome as well as a significant trading center for consumer goods, such as ivory, ostrich feathers, and salt. Ancient trading routes from the interior of Africa to the Mediterranean coast included routes from Tripoli in the north-west to Ghadames, Ghat, Air, and Kano in what is now northern Nigeria; from Tripoli to Murzuk, Fezzan, and Bornu, west of Lake Chad; and from Benghazi in the northeast to Awjilah, Kufrah, Wadai, and Abeche in what is now eastern Chad (Wright 1989a: 16; Ahmida 2005: 3–4).

Following the destruction of Carthage, the Romans occupied the three trading posts of the Tripolis. Roman culture in North Africa was largely urban, and one of them, Leptis Magna, later developed into the finest example of a Roman city in Africa (MacKendrick 1980: 143–75). The economic and political importance of Leptis Magna rested on its geographical location in relation to the Mediterranean and the well-watered littoral of Tripolitania (DiVita *et al.* 1999: 44–143). The city prospered from the first to the early third centuries; however, following a serious economic crisis in the second half of the third century, attacks by Berber tribes, especially the Austuriani, were increasingly frequent (Warmington 1954: 9–10).

In 238, the increasingly heavy tax burden imposed by Rome sparked a revolt in North Africa which left many of the important towns of the region devastated. For a time, the economic center of the area shifted to the smaller towns of the interior which were spared the worst effects of the Roman suppression of the revolt. The projection of imperial power into the hinterland antagonized already tenuous relations between Romans and native Berbers as the autonomy of the latter was increasingly circumscribed. The Emperor Diocletian granted the region autonomy in 294–305, but some time in the early fourth century Tripolitania was made a Roman province (Rinehart 1979: 10).

The spread of Christianity into Africa in the first and second centuries complicated an already an explosive situation. With Christianity seen as a vehicle of dissent, Berbers converted to the faith not out of conviction, but as a challenge to Roman rule. Adding to the mix, the Donatists, a North African sect holding strict views regarding sanctity and purity, split with the mainstream Catholic Church around 312. Thereafter, Berber revolts flared for more than a century under the banner of Donatism. In 405, Emperor Honorius (ruled Roman Empire 393–5 and Western Roman Empire 395–423) declared Donatism a heresy, and in 411 he made it a criminal offense. In the interim, persistent religious conflict progressively undermined Roman authority throughout the region (Warmington 1954: 76–102; Raven 1993: 150–61, 168–81, 190–4).

Vandals

The Vandals, a group of Germanic tribesmen, crossed into North Africa from Spain in 429 (Warmington 1954: 14, 51). After the Teutonic onslaught left only a few North African towns in Roman hands, Emperor Valentinian III (ruled 425–55) in 435 concluded a treaty with Gaiseric, the Vandal leader, in which Rome retained Carthage but surrendered the surrounding provinces to the Vandals.

Four years later, Gaiseric reneged on the agreement, capturing Carthage in 439. Valentinian III concluded a new agreement with the Vandals in 442, in which he ceded to them North Africa from Tripolitania to eastern Numidia, a former Berber kingdom overlapping present-day Algeria and Tunisia. Thirteen years later, the Vandals crossed to Italy and sacked Rome itself (Raven 1993: 196–200). Fourteen centuries would pass before Italy again ruled even a part of Libya.

Although they occupied North Africa for almost a century, the territory ruled by the Vandals was smaller than the old Roman provinces and gradually ringed by independent Berber kingdoms. Gaiseric used bribes and other forms of patronage to exercise some authority over these smaller fiefdoms, but after his death in 447 the efforts of his successors were less successful. With the Vandal Kingdom slowly disintegrating from within, Emperor Justinian I (ruled 527–65) sent an army to North Africa in 533 to reassert Roman rule. His army succeeded in defeating the Vandals in 534, but the Byzantine Empire never reached the full extent of the old Roman Empire (Raven 1993: 205–20).

Early Arab influence

With the death of the Prophet Muhammad in 632, Arab armies initiated a campaign of proselytism that eventually led to the conquest of half the known world. The Byzantine provinces of Egypt, Syria, and Persia proved the more attractive early prizes, with the remote and less wealthy regions of North Africa a secondary target. Alexandria was not occupied until 643, followed by Cyrenaica in 644. Two years later, the Arabs moved into Tripolitania, overrunning isolated Byzantine garrisons on the coast and consolidating Arab control of the region. Almost two decades then passed before the Umayyad general, Uqba bin Nafi, invaded Fezzan in 663, forcing the capitulation of Germa, capital of the Garamantes. Stiff Berber resistance in the Tripolitanian hinterlands later delayed the Arab advance, but Arab armies in 670 surged into present-day Tunisia. By 715, the Arab Empire stretched north to the Pyrenees in Spain, and in North Africa it conformed to the limits of the old Roman Empire (Laroui 1977: 79–81; Raven 1993: 224–30).

Libya has been subjected to a long history of invasion and occupation; however, it was the arrival of the Arabs in the seventh century which had the most lasting impact. Islam and the Arabic language, backed by a social system well suited to pastoral nomadism, were easily absorbed by a North African people whose lives were still structured to some degree by the ethos of Punic civilization. In the process, the often confusing, even contradictory, message of sectarian Byzantine Christianity was gradually cast off (Hardy 2002: 19). In its place, Cyrenaica and Tripolitania were systematically organized under the political and religious leadership of the Umayyad Caliphate (661–760). Successful in extending their power and influence into North Africa, Spain, and southern France, the Umayyads imposed a degree of Arab sovereignty, if not Arabization or Islamization. The process of Arabization required many more centuries to complete whereas Islamization was largely the work of the Berbers themselves (Laroui 1977: 87).

Abbasids, Aghlabids, and Fatimids

In a period of turmoil, the Abbasid dynasty (750–1258) replaced the Umayyads and relocated the caliphate to Baghdad. Recognizing the difficulty of governing their North African domains from afar, the Abbasids accepted the autonomy of military officers and regional governors as long as they recognized the spiritual leadership of the caliph and paid an annual tribute. In 800, the Abbasid caliph Harun al Rashid (ruled 786–809) appointed Ibrahim ibn Aghlab the amir of a significant part of the contemporary Maghrib. Establishing a hereditary dynasty at Kairouan in northeastern Tunisia, the Aghlabids ruled Tripolitania and present-day Tunisia, largely functioning as an autonomous state (Laroui 1977: 115–22, 127–8).

In the late ninth century, missionaries of the Ismali sect of Shi'i Islam converted the Kutama Berbers of the Kabylie region of Algeria to a militant brand of Islam and led them on a crusade against the Sunni Aghlabids. With the fall of Kairouan in 909, the Fatimids (910–1171) ruled over much of North Africa, including Tripolitania. The Fatimids were the only important Shi'i caliphate in Islamic history, and the Abbasids were their principal enemy, although the Umayyads also recognized the danger they posed. Coastal merchants were the foundation of a Fatimid state founded by religious enthusiasts and imposed by Berber tribesmen (Rinehart 1979: 15–16).

With the Islamic world divided into three caliphates, North Africa became a battleground in a competition mostly contested by surrogates and local allies. Initially, the Fatimids looked west, threatening Morocco with invasion, but they eventually turned east, completing their conquest of Egypt by 969. Relocating their capital to Cairo, they established a Shi'i caliphate to rival the Sunni caliph in Baghdad. The Fatimids left North Africa in the hands of their vassals, the Zirids, a Berber dynasty that ruled the northern parts of present-day Algeria, Libya, and Tunisia from the late tenth to the mid-twelfth century (Brett and Fentress 1996: 131–5; Laroui 1977: 138–47). The Fatimid Caliphate later assumed a renewed importance in the early twentieth-first century when Muammar al-Qaddafi , the Libyan leader, called for a new Fatimid state in North Africa as part of his ongoing efforts to project Libyan influence south into the Sahara and Sahel regions.

Hilalian migration

In the middle of the eleventh century, the Zirids rejected Shi'i Islam, broke with the Fatimids, and initiated a Berber return to Sunni orthodoxy. In response, the Fatimid Caliphate invited the Bani Hilal and Bani Salim, Bedouin tribes from Saudi Arabia known collectively as the Hilalians, to migrate to the Maghrib. First in Cyrenaica and later in Tripolitania, the Hilalians imposed their Islamic faith and nomadic way of life on the indigenous population. Tripoli was sacked, and life in once great Greek and Roman cities was snuffed out. Assimilating or displacing coastal Berbers, the Arabs ravaged settled agricultural life, converted farmland to pasturage, and perpetuated nomadism as the dominant form of social organization. Other socioeconomic factors, such as a weak central state, nomadic migration, and a long process of climate change prior to the Hilalian migration, contributed to and facilitated the decline in settled agriculture and the spread of pastoralism at this time (Ahmida 1994: 16–17).

The Hilalian migration initiated a prolonged Arab occupation of Libya that endured to the present. Cyrenaica was occupied mainly by the Bani Salim while the Bani Hilal settled in Tripolitania and beyond. The Cyrenaican tribes divided according to their status into two categories. The *Sa'adi* tribesmen were the descendants of the Bani Salim and owned the land whereas their clients, the *Marabtin*, were the descendants of earlier Arab invasions. This association did not exist in Tripolitania and Fezzan; however, a patron–client relationship developed between the tribesmen of the Bani Hilal and the Berber and earlier Arab settlers (Peters 1990: 40–58; Evans-Pritchard 1949: 29–61, 84–111). After 1969, the revolutionary government sought first to abolish the tribal system, but later it accepted the existence of tribes and integrated them into the ruling network (Obeidi 2001: 108–35).

From the eleventh to the twentieth centuries, tribal life remained the dominant pattern of existence in Libya. All tribes had their own homeland, soil, pasture, and wells, and a dependable water source was the principal concern of every tribe. Libyan tribes were mostly semi-nomadic, combining herding, cereal cultivation, and date collection in a cycle of annual migration. Private property existed in towns and oases, but collective ownership of land and water was the norm in the hinterland. Among the semi-nomadic tribes, personal ownership was necessarily limited to movable goods such as animals and equipment. Given the scarcity of resources in pre-modern Libya, intertribal conflict was common, with land and water the normal sources of dispute (Peters 1990: 40–59).

Tribal dynasties

In the eleventh and twelfth centuries, two Berber dynasties arose in Morocco, the Almoravids (1073–1147) and the Almohads (1147–1267). Founded by religious reformers, they dominated the western Maghrib, including Tripolitania, for over 200 years. The state apparatus of the Almoravids rested on a militant version of Sunni Islam's Maliki school of jurisprudence and an administrative and military elite recruited among the Sanhaja Berbers of the middle Atlas and western Sahara. In 1146, Abd al-Mu'min bin Ali al-Kumi (ruled 1130–63), the founder and first military chief of the Almohad dynasty, captured Marrakesh, signaling the end of the Almoravids. The centralized, theocratic government of the Almohads went well beyond the Berberism, tribalism, and simple legalism of the Almoravids. The Almohad Empire later split off into three competing dynasties: the Marinids (1244–1420) in Morocco, the Zayinids (1236–1318) in Algeria, and the Hafsids (1228–1574) in Tunisia and Tripolitania (Laroui 1977: 157–208; Brett and Fentress 1996: 99–119).

With their economic strength and political support residing in coastal towns such as Tripoli, the Hafsids ceded the hinterland to indigenous tribes who made only nominal submission to the sultan. The Hafsid era spanned more than 300 years; however, a combination of tribal states, theocratic republics, and coastal enclaves progressively defied the sultan's authority. In 1460, the merchant oligarchy of Tripoli declared the city an independent city-state. After the Spanish captured Tripoli in 1510, Emperor Charles V (1500–58) offered the island of Malta and the outpost in Tripoli to the Knights of the Order of St. John of Jerusalem. The Order accepted his offer in 1530, but Ottoman troops later drove the Knights from Tripoli in 1551 and invaded Malta in 1565 (Joffé 1990: 69–70). In the interim, Draughut Pasha, a Turkish pirate named governor by the sultan, restored order in the coastal towns of Tripolitania in 1552. By the end of the sixteenth century, North Africa was divided into several Ottoman provinces approximating the modern states of Algeria, Libya, and Tunisia (Laroui 1977: 201–18, 236–59; Rinehart 1979: 17–19).

From the twelfth to the sixteenth centuries, Cyrenaica largely remained outside the orbit of the Maghribi dynasties that sought to control Tripolitania. Cyrenaica was oriented to the east, where a succession of Egyptian dynasties claimed suzerainty over the region even though they exercised at most only nominal political control. The Bedouin tribes of Cyrenaica readily accepted authority from no one other than their own chieftains. In the fifteenth century, merchants from Tripoli revived some of the markets in the region, but the principal source of income for Cyrenaican Bedouins remained the tribute paid by caravans and pilgrims traveling between Egypt and the Maghrib (Rinehart 1979: 18).

In Fezzan, the tribal chieftains of the Beni Khattab, operating from their capital at Zawilah, dominated the region. Like the Garamantes, they derived their power from control of the oases situated on the trading routes from Africa to the Mediterranean. Around 1550, the Moroccan Muhammad al-Fasi displaced the last of the Beni Khattab and founded a new line at Murzuk, which continued as the undisputed rulers of the region under Ottoman suzerainty. In the 1580s, the rulers of Fezzan pledged fealty to the Ottoman sultan; nevertheless, the Ottoman administration in Tripoli wisely refrained from attempting to exercise any real authority in the region (Rinehart 1979: 18–19).

Ottoman rule (1551–1911)

By the mid-sixteenth century, the regions east of Morocco were provinces under the direct control of the Ottoman Empire. The Sublime Porte, as the Ottoman government was known, divided them into three regencies, Algiers, Tunis, and Tripoli. The term "regency" was meant to convey their semiautonomous position within the empire; however, the Turkish term by which they were known within the empire, *ocaklar* (garrisons), better suggested the nature of the empire's relations with its hinterlands (Anderson 1986a: 40). The territory controlled by the Regency of Tripoli approximated northern Libya today. The Ottomans governed Libya through a pasha appointed by the sultan, who was dependent upon the *janissaries*, a military caste. Originally, the janissaries were an elite military force; however, by the eighteenth century, they had become a self-governing military guild.

The Barbary corsairs provided the treasury of the Regency of Tripoli with a steady income from corsairing or privateering, a practice widely but wrongly described as piracy. Interested in booty and ransom for profit as opposed to murder or assassination for political gain, the corsairs took a businesslike approach and operated under a formal set of rules that the European powers accepted and honored. The Barbary corsairs also constituted a significant extension of Ottoman naval power in the Mediterranean, often contributing manpower and ships to the Ottoman fleet (Parker 2004: 6).

Although the socioeconomic life of the Regency of Tripoli has not been explored in detail, it largely consisted of two parallel societies that operated side by side but separately. The ruling elite, small in number and mostly foreign, focused its attention on the urban areas and coastal regions. The economy of the state was oriented toward trade and corsairing, and its survival was contingent on the collection of revenue by means other than local taxation. Therefore, officials resident in Tripoli were most concerned with events around the Mediterranean and in Europe. The indigenous population, on the other hand, naturally looked inward, concerned with commerce, trade, and pastoralism, along with local issues and concerns (Abou-El-Haj 1983; Pennell 1989: 216–17).

Karamanli dynasty (1711–1835)

In 1711, Ahmad Karamanli overthrew the pasha appointed by the sultan and founded a dynasty which governed Libya for the next 124 years. Recognizing nominal Ottoman suzerainty, Ahmad Pasha created a quasi-independent, dynastic military garrison with a government largely Arab in composition. In power until 1745, he pursued aggressive, often enlightened, internal and external policies. As he expanded commercial and diplomatic relations with Europe, Ahmad Pasha strengthened the armed forces to increase the power and prestige of Tripoli. Extending his political authority into Cyrenaica and Fezzan, he unified the country, suppressing rebellious Arab and Berber tribes in the interior. By 1745, Fezzan had become a tributary to Tripoli and the rest of the country was largely pacified, facilitating the trans-Saharan trade which had long constituted an important source of revenue for Tripoli (Folayan 1979: 1–4).

The decline of the Karamanli dynasty began immediately after the death of Ahmad Pasha in 1745. His successors were men of inferior talent and industry, and the issue of dynastic succession led to repeated power struggles within the ruling family. As the weakness of the regime became obvious, the Arab and Berber tribes of the interior progressively severed ties with Tripoli, asserting local independence through revolts in the second half of the century. The Libyan economy also declined after 1745, especially during periods of stagnation and crisis in the later 1770s and mid-1780s (Folayan 1979: 4–21).

In 1795, Yusuf Karamanli seized power and installed himself as pasha. In a throwback to the policies of Ahmad Pasha, he worked to tame the tribes of the interior while defying Ottoman and British naval power and supporting Napoleon Bonaparte during his 1798–9 Egyptian campaign. The Napoleonic conflict marked an early recognition by Europe of Libya's strategic position on the North African coast, a consideration that later led to Four Power rivalries in the run-up to Libyan independence in 1951 (St John 2008a: 35–6). Dependent for state revenues on external trade, the income from trans-Saharan caravans, and control of Mediterranean sea lanes, Yusuf Pasha put a premium on naval strength. Where the fleet in 1798 numbered no more than 11 ships, it had grown by 1805 to 24 armed vessels, together with several skiffs. As Libyan sea power increased, Yusuf Pasha asked European states active in the Mediterranean to establish formal treaty relationships, including the provision of consular gifts. Most states responded in the positive, and those that refused soon found their shipping set upon by Libyan corsairs (Folayan 1979: 25–31).

Barbary corsairs

Before independence was won, American ships engaged in the Mediterranean trade enjoyed the immunities from Barbary corsairs that the British bought by tribute payments to the rulers of Algiers, Morocco, Tripoli, and Tunis. With the conclusion of the Treaty of Paris in 1783, the United States was left to face alone the uncertainties of Mediterranean corsairing (Field 1969: 27–32). As part of a broader effort to negotiate treaties of amity and commerce with the principal states of Europe and the Mediterranean, including the Barbary states, John Adams and Thomas Jefferson opened talks in 1786 with Sidi Haji Abdul Rahman Adja, the Tripolitanian ambassador in London. At the opening session in which Adams met alone with Adja, the former was shocked to learn that the Regency of Tripoli considered itself at war with the United States. The talks soon broke down over the financial demands of the Libyan emissary, but they remained historically significant as they marked the first direct US diplomatic exchange with Libya as well as with the entire Muslim world (Parker 2004: 41–2; Irwin 1931: 20–8; Malone 1970: 27–32, 51–2).

Eventually, the United States, in November 1796, concluded a treaty of peace and friendship with the Regency of Tripoli, which promised protection and free passage for the naval vessels of both states and stated that no periodical tributes would be made by either party (St John 2002: 22–3). In 1801, Yusuf Pasha demanded better terms from the United States than he had received five years earlier, including an annual payment of $250,000. When Washington refused, he broke off diplomatic relations, ordering the flagstaff in front of the American consulate in Tripoli to be chopped down. Bolstered by growing American nationalism and a new fleet of warships, President Jefferson decided to pursue a more aggressive policy in the Mediterranean, beginning with the Regency of Tripoli (Malone 1970: 97–9, 262–3). The latter had a reputation as a nest of corsairs, but it was never a major corsairing port, with present-day studies confining Tripoli to a minor role (Pennell 1989: 215–16). The relative weakness of Tripoli vis-à-vis other corsairing ports was a major factor in Jefferson's decision to make Tripoli an example of his new policy (St John 2002: 25). A similar appreciation of relative power relationships heavily influenced the US government's decision some 185 years later to bomb targets in and around Benghazi and Tripoli in April 1986.

In 1801, the United States dispatched a naval squadron to the Mediterranean, where it imposed a blockade on the port of Tripoli. With the blockade only partially successful, Washington in May 1804 agreed to support an overland expedition by William Eaton, the newly appointed navy agent for the Several Barbary Regencies, to overthrow the Tripoli government. In what was the first time the United States attempted to unseat a head of state, Eaton's plan was to oust Yusuf Pasha and replace him with a pro-American regime headed by his brother, Ahmad, whom Yusuf had deposed in 1795. Eaton left Egypt in the spring of 1805, and as he slowly proceeded westward toward Tripoli, Yusuf Pasha made overtures for peace which the United States soon accepted (Field 1969: 52–4; Irwin 1931: 106–48). After hostilities ended in early June 1805, a final settlement provided for the release of all prisoners with the United States giving the Regency of Tripoli an ex gratia payment of $60,000 because the latter held considerably more prisoners than the former (St John 2002: 25–7). Ahmad Karamanli went into exile and Yusuf Pasha remained in power for another 27 years.

Repeated economic crises, growing socioeconomic problems, and deepening political malaise characterized the final decades of Karamanli rule. After the European powers united to end the corsair system, dealing a crippling blow to the Libyan economy, Yusuf Pasha mortgaged the regency's agricultural production and debased the local coinage in unsuccessful attempts to settle mounting debts. He also tried to expand the Saharan slave trade, but these efforts failed because he was not able to establish the necessary control of the interior. Unable to pay for basic imports or service its foreign debt, Tripoli increased customs duties and imposed new taxes, provoking fresh internal opposition which eventually degenerated into civil war (Folayan 1979: 106–68; Pennell 1989: 217–18).

Second Ottoman occupation (1835–1911)

Alarmed by Egypt's achievement of near-independence under Muhammad Ali and fearful the civil war would provide Europe with a rationale to occupy Tripoli as France had occupied Algiers in 1830, the Sublime Porte overthrew the

Karamanli dynasty in 1835. In what is known as the second Ottoman occupation (1835–1911), it established direct control over the formerly autonomous province of Tripoli, and, in so doing, the power of long influential Libyan groups was modified or destroyed as new relationships developed between rulers and ruled. Ottoman reformers attacked the entrenched power of Libyan tribes in the belief that the Ottoman Empire's traditional policy of decentralization, dependent in the past on local notables for provincial administration, was outmoded. They sought to replace it with a more efficient and effective administrative system which would be capable of reviving Ottoman power in the face of European expansion (Anderson 1986a: 87–92; Cachia 1945: 29–63).

By the mid-1850s, the Sublime Porte was caught up in the reform movement known as the *tanzimat*. Over the ensuing 25 years, Ottoman officials in Libya introduced policies that encouraged urbanization, administrative reorganization, the development of commerce, land reform, and the furtherance of education. Institutional changes included the creation of administrative and village councils, the establishment of civil and criminal courts, and the introduction of new methods of tax assessment and collection. Further modifications to the administrative system were implemented later in the century as the trend toward settlement and urbanization made municipal government increasingly possible. In the process, pastoralism gave way to settled agriculture, which moved from a subsistence to a revenue-generating activity, replacing the caravan trade as a source of income. Ottoman rule also became increasingly centralized and Libya more highly integrated within the authority of the Sublime Porte. In the wake of the Italian invasion in 1911, Italian historians later downplayed the importance of these reforms, but they marked an important beginning in the modernization of Libyan society (Anderson 1984: 325–6; Cachia 1945: 74–103, 109–76).

Long concerned with French activities in Algeria and Tunisia and British interests in Egypt, the Sublime Porte had concluded by the mid-1880s that Italy represented the most serious threat to Libya. Consequently, Ottoman officials pursued a policy intended to mollify the British and French to gain their support against Italian designs in the region. The failure of this appeasement policy was clear by the turn of the century, when Europe divided Africa into spheres of interest with little or no consideration for Ottoman claims. In 1902, France and Italy concluded an agreement recognizing the "special interests" of France in Morocco and Italy in Libya (Anderson 1984: 336–9; Simon 1987: 44–7).

Italian invasion and occupation

Well before it achieved national unity, Italy recognized the need to acquire colonies and to play an active role in European colonial expansion. Imperialistic ambitions had their roots in the later part of the nineteenth century; however, as the Italian city-states were not united until the second half of the century, Italy was a late participant in imperial expansion, unable to exploit early colonial opportunities. At the outset of the twentieth century, Libya remained one of the few African territories not occupied by Europeans, and its proximity to Italy made it very attractive to Rome. Consequently, a pacific penetration of the region, led by the Banco di Roma, began at the turn of the century, with a more forceful approach to follow at the end of the decade (Ahmida 1994: 40–1; Hesnawi 2003: 49–51; Childs 1990: 1–5; Wright 1982a: 25).

In seeking to colonize Libya, many Italians saw themselves as carrying on the traditions of the Roman Empire. Visionaries argued that the application of Italian sovereignty to regions once ruled by the Empire was not only an historic right but an obligation. Other Italians saw overseas expansion as a means to divert attention from the vexing internal problems left over from the recent unification of the country. It also offered the armed forces, an organization highly regarded at home but held in low esteem throughout Europe, an opportunity to develop their skills and test their weapons. Others argued that the colonization of Libya, a sparsely populated land widely believed to have a pleasant climate and a favorable coastal terrain, offered a means to settle Italy's emigration problem (Bosworth 2006: 43; Wright 1982b).

In need of overseas markets and cheap raw materials, many Italians assumed that the occupation of Libya would support these objectives as well as enable Rome to control profitable trade routes in Africa. Buoyed by extravagant hopes and falsely encouraged by official propaganda, few Italians realized that Libya's agricultural capacity was limited, its industry virtually nonexistent, and most of its territory empty (Hesnawi 2003: 51–62; Childs 1990: 29–48). It was not until the end of World War II that Europe recognized that the real value of the Ottoman Empire's last remaining African possessions was not as a colony for settlers or as a portal to the largely illusory riches of central Africa but as a strategic base on the central Mediterranean (Wright 1989b: 221).

First phase, 1911–22

The Young Turk Revolution of 1908 shook Libya, as it did the rest of the Ottoman Empire, dividing the Libyan elite and disrupting the local economy. Supporters of the new regime initiated a campaign to rid the provincial administration of old guard, reactionary elements, not a few of whom then offered their services to Italy. Seizing on the disorder, the Italian government used alleged Ottoman hostility to Italian enterprise in Libya as a *casus belli*, delivering an ultimatum to the sultan on 28 September 1911, which demanded that the Empire agree within 24 hours to an Italian occupation of Cyrenaica and Tripolitania. Determined to annex the entire territory, Italy declared war on 29 September 1911 and moved quickly to establish bridgeheads at Benghazi, Derna, Homs, Tobruk, and Tripoli. Enjoying early success, the Italians remained for several weeks in coastal towns within range of their naval guns, enabling the Libyan forces organized and trained by Ottoman officers to develop determined and effective opposition. Consequently, the war soon developed into a military stalemate, and by early 1912 the Italian invasion force was bogged down, heralding the outset of a prolonged and bloody conflict (Cumming 1968: 384; Anderson 1982: 44–5; Childs 1990: 49–91).

Although it had checked the advance of the Italian forces, the determination of the Ottoman Empire, isolated diplomatically and concerned with events in the Balkans, to resist quickly evaporated. In July 1912, the Sublime Porte opened negotiations with Italy, and in October 1912 the two parties concluded a peace treaty. Although the Ottomans did not cede sovereignty over their North African province, the sultan did issue a declaration to his Libyan subjects, granting them full and complete autonomy. He also agreed to withdraw Ottoman military and civilian personnel, reserving the right to appoint an agent to protect Ottoman interests in Libya. Following the agreement, most of the Ottomans in Libya departed, but a few officers and enlisted men, together with substantial quantities of military equipment, stayed behind, especially in Cyrenaica. The Italians reaffirmed their annexation of Cyrenaica and Tripolitania on 5 November 1911; however, it was not recognized by international law until after the Allied peace settlement with Turkey in 1924. With both Libyan autonomy and Italian sovereignty absent convincing validity, the status of Libya remained anomalous, and the 1912 peace treaty failed to end the fighting (Cumming 1968: 384; Simon 1987: 98, 150–4; Childs 1990: 174–230).

Libyan response

Few Libyans had love for the Ottomans as rulers, but the political consequences of the socioeconomic transformation that occurred during the second Ottoman occupation were later evidenced in the successful Ottoman mobilization of popular feeling in defense of the province against Italian encroachment. Forced to chose between Ottoman and European rule, most Libyans opted for the former (Wright 1982a: 20–3). The invading Italians preferred to interpret this opposition in fanatical religious terms; however, although the role of religion was not insignificant, it was not the only, or even the primary, motive for opposition to Italian rule. Whereas Islam provided legitimacy and a vocabulary for disaffection which encompassed virtually all of Libyan society, it often was not the principal impetus for resistance. On the contrary, most Libyans viewed the Ottomans as the lesser of two evils, with the common denominator, Islam, bridging the difference (Anderson 1986a: 112–13, 117–20; Simon 1987: 21, 185–6, 327–30).

In the wake of the 1912 peace treaty, a few Ottoman officers and troops stayed on and Ottoman aid continued to flow to Libya; nonetheless, Libyan notables and tribesmen were increasingly left to face the Italians alone (Simon 1987: 104–6, 111–33, 180–4; Del Boca 2003: 25). In the process, the differing responses to the invasion in Cyrenaica, Fezzan, and Tripolitania reflected the existence at the beginning of the twentieth century of three largely separate, well-defined political economies based on different ecologies and the failure of the central state to control them (Ahmida 2005: 2). Their differing responses also reflected the extent to which patron–client ties had begun to replace kinship as the central organizational structure of rural politics (Anderson 1986a: 130).

Early resistance proved strongest in Cyrenaica, where the forces of the Sanusi Order were the heart of military opposition. Sayyid Muhammad bin Ali al-Sanusi, a religious scholar from Algeria who established the Order in Cyrenaica in 1842, based it on trade, regional tribal structures, and revivalist Islam, an approach well suited to the Bedouins of the area (Evans-Pritchard 1949: 1–61; Ahmida 2005: 9). Granted considerable autonomy by the Ottoman government, the Sanusiyya promoted educational development and sedentary living, encouraging changes similar to those the Ottoman administration was advocating elsewhere in Libya (Peters 1990: 10–28; Vikor 1995: 181–240). Supplied with arms and other equipment by Ottoman forces before they departed in 1912, the leader of the Sanusiyya, Sayyid Ahmad al-Sharif, formed a Sanusi state and declared *jihad* (holy war) on the Italian invaders in 1913 (Evans-Pritchard 1949: 109–24; Anderson 1986a: 117–18).

In Tripolitania, two deputies who had represented the province in the 1908 Ottoman Parliament, Sulayman al-Baruni and Muhammad Farhat al-Zawi, immediately took up defense of the province against the invaders, traveling throughout their districts preaching resistance and recruiting volunteers. In the wake of the 1912 peace treaty, Baruni and Farhat organized a meeting of Tripolitanian chiefs and nobles to formulate a common response. Unable to reach a compromise, the attendees split into two camps, with one side favoring negotiation and the other favoring resistance. After forming an autonomous state in western Tripolitania in early 1913, Baruni was forced into exile. Later, he returned to Libya and was active in forming the short-lived Tripoli Republic, one of several local efforts to create independent states in the aftermath of World War I (Simon 1987: 42, 211–13; Anderson 1986a: 126–7, 130–1).

In Fezzan, the withdrawal of Ottoman forces in 1913 resulted in a power vacuum which France moved to fill, challenging Italian aims in the region. To counter French ambitions, Italy launched a campaign against the tribes in the region, which failed owing to local resistance and the subsequent Italian need to divert troops to World War I. By August 1914, the Italians appeared to have completed their occupation of Tripolitania and Fezzan; however, by the end of the year, tribal forces had pushed them north out of Fezzan. Over the next few months, the Italian position in Tripolitania also deteriorated, with Italian forces suffering a string of military defeats. For the duration of World War I, the Italians controlled little more than Tripoli and al-Khums in Tripolitania and Benghazi, Derna, and Tobruk, together with al-Marj and Benina, in Cyrenaica (Cumming 1968: 385–8; Anderson 1982: 45–9; Simon 1987: 196–7, 213–15).

While many Libyans resisted Italian colonization, other indigenous responses included emigration, negotiation, accommodation, and collaboration. In Tripolitania, large comprador merchants, such as Hassuna Karamanli, mayor of Tripoli; powerful Muslim merchant families, for example the Muntasir clan; and Jewish merchants, such as the Halfuns family, collaborated with Italian interests well before 1911 and later assisted Italian forces in occupying Tripoli. Political ambition motivated Hassuna Karamanli whereas the Muntasir clan collaborated with the Italians in order to retain fortune and influence in the region. Jewish merchants with ties to Italian interests also worked with the invaders before, during, and after the occupation. In a word, economic self-interest prompted many Libyan merchants in Tripoli and elsewhere in Tripolitania to accommodate or collaborate with the Italian occupation. In the interior, the loyalty of the tribal leaders of Tripolitania fluctuated between collaboration and resistance in an effort to retain status, power, and position in an uncertain, shifting political landscape (Ahmida 2005: 27–30; Anderson 1986a: 126, 189–90; De Felice 1985: 28–48).

In Cyrenaica, a smaller number of urban notables, mostly situated in coastal urban areas where ties to the Sanusi-dominated interior were weak, collaborated with the Italians. In the hinterland, education, socialization, and mobilization in the Sanusi-controlled areas, together with an anticolonialist mentality that fostered armed resistance by a volunteer army, resulted in a considerable cohesion among the tribes. Senior tribal leaders successfully conducted an aggressive campaign against the Italians which prevented the latter from expanding beyond coastal areas. Espousing a pan-Islamic anti-colonial ideology, some senior Sanusi leaders, notably Sidi Umar al-Mukhtar (c. 1862–1931), refused to give up their arms and, after a six-year truce broke down in 1922, turned again to armed resistance (Ahmida 2005: 30–1; Evans-Pritchard 1949: 112–30).

Under the leadership of Sayyid Muhammad Idris al-Mahdi al-Sanusi, grandson of Sayyid Muhammad bin Ali al-Sanusi, the Sanusi Order opened negotiations with Italy in 1916, leading to a final agreement in 1917. The so-called Akrama accords recognized Italian sovereignty on the coast and Sanusi sovereignty in the hinterland, permitted free trade, exempted the Sanusi from taxes, and, in effect, gave the people of Cyrenaica a degree of autonomy. In 1920, the Sanusi Order reached a new agreement with Italy, but a central element of the pact, the dismantling of Cyrenaican military units, was never accomplished. Related Italian attempts to bribe the Sanusi leadership into cooperation proved ineffective, and by 1922 Sayyid Idris had concluded that Italy and the Sanusi Order could not share Cyrenaica. Accordingly, he went into exile in Egypt, leaving the militant members of the Order to wage guerrilla war against the Italians.

In Fezzan, the response of the tribes and peasants was similar. Although most tribes opposed the Italians, viewing them as a threat to tribal autonomy, a few collaborated, mainly because of long-standing tribal feuds. As for Fezzani peasants, they were mostly too isolated and impoverished to engage in widespread political action (Simon 1987: 268–93; Ahmida 2005: 30–2).

Riconquista, 1923–32

With the Fascist takeover in October 1922, the Mussolini government decided to forgo negotiation and turned to military force to pacify the country, initiating in early 1923 the *riconquista* (reconquest) of Libya. By 1926, the Italian army had 20,000 men in the field compared with a Libyan force that seldom numbered more than 1,000 and was largely confined to Cyrenaica. The Italians also deployed the most modern weapons, including airplanes, artillery, and poison gas. In June 1925, Italy signed the Geneva Convention, prohibiting the use of bacteriological or chemical weapons, but as early as January 1928 it employed poison gas in Libya (Del Boca 2003: 25–6; Ahmida 2005: 41–2).

By 1924, Italian forces had subdued most of Tripolitania, and in early 1928 the acting head of the Sanusi Order submitted to the Italian commander in Cyrenaica. With the northern Fezzan already in Italian control, Italian officials in January 1929 united Tripolitania and Cyrenaica under a single governor, Marshal Pietro Badoglio, with the capital in Tripoli. In the spring of 1929, a brief truce was declared in Cyrenaica; nevertheless, resistance under the leadership of Umar al-Mukhtar soon resumed. In response, the Italian authorities sought to isolate the resistance fighters, denying them access to their people. Men, women, and children were corralled in large concentration camps, wells were blocked, and livestock slaughtered. Although exact figures are not available, most estimates agree that more than 110,000 people, two-thirds of the population of eastern Libya, were confined to concentration camps, and, based on Libyan archives and oral histories, as many as 70,000 of those confined later died from disease, maltreatment, or starvation. Eventually, the Italians constructed a tall barbed-wire fence, four meters thick, from the port of Bardia on the Mediterranean coast to the oasis of Jaghbub, to stop supplies from Egypt reaching the guerrillas in Cyrenaica (Bosworth 2006: 381; Ashiurakis 1976: 63–6; Ahmida 2005: 43–53).

Libyan resistance continued until the fall of 1931, when Mukhtar, the most effective guerrilla leader, was captured and hanged. The Italians collected 20,000 Libyans to witness his execution in a horrific spectacle staged to demonstrate that the days of compromise were over (Ashiurakis 1976: 67–71). An astute politician acutely aware of the power of imagery, Muammar al-Qaddafi would later promote the exploits of Mukhtar, including the provision of financial support for a feature film about his life, the *Lion of the Desert*, starring Anthony Quinn, to stress the ongoing struggle for national liberation (Nassar and Boggero 2008: 203–4). On 24 January 1932, Marshal Badoglio declared the rebellion in Cyrenaica finished, and the war begun in 1911 for the worst of reasons officially ended.

Italian colonial policy

One measure of the importance Fascist Italy attached to Libya is the high rank of men sent to govern it. Appointed governor of Tripolitania in August 1921, Count Giuseppe Volpi had been one of the first of the bankers and industrialists to join the Fascist Party. Following a two-part strategy in which economics and politics worked hand-in-hand, his decisive policies contrasted sharply with those of earlier liberal regimes. In the first of several decrees, Volpi announced in July 1922 that all uncultivated lands in Libya were presumed to belong to the public domain. He later decreed that uncultivated land would revert to the state after three years and that all land held by rebels or those who aided them would be confiscated by the state. The effect of these decrees was to increase by more than 10-fold the amount of land available to Italian colonists. Effective in creating a public domain for colonization, Volpi was less successful in attracting immigrants. Italian capital did not move quickly to buy newly available concessions, and immigration rates remained well below official expectations (Segrè 1974: 35–56; Anderson 1986a: 216–18).

Volpi's departure in 1925 and Mussolini's visit in 1926 marked important turning points in Italian plans for Libya. Where Volpi had insisted on subordinating political goals to economic means, the Fascist regime increasingly ignored the economic side of the equation. Marshal Emilio De Bono, successor to Volpi, was a staunch colonialist who steered a middle course between the conflicting doctrines, pleasing no one in the process. Under his successor, Marshal Pietro Badoglio, social goals and political aspirations, as opposed to cost accounting, increasingly dominated colonial policies in Libya (Segrè 1974: 56–81; Lombardi 1982: 101–6).

Air Marshal Italo Balbo, Italian governor from 1934 until his death in 1940, was an early supporter of Fascism. Assuming office after the Sanusiyya resistance had ended, Balbo became governor at an opportune moment for the development of the colony. For the first time in over two decades, Libya was at peace, and the Italians could concentrate on economic development. Socioeconomic conditions in Italy also favored Balbo as a strong lira and a negative balance of trade combined to aggravate the persistent unemployment problem, encouraging emigration to Libya. The Libyan example, especially its emphasis on large-scale public works and resettlement projects, also appeared to some to offer new answers to a world troubled by depression and unemployment (Segrè 1987: 291–307).

As a socialist agitator, Mussolini was imprisoned in 1911 for protesting the Italian invasion of Libya, but as a Fascist dictator he visited the colony three times, in 1926, 1937, and 1942. Of the visits, his 1937 tour was the most successful. The main purpose of the visit was to affirm Italy's increased prestige and to showcase its growing military might, as demonstrated by its conquest of Abyssinia (Ethiopia) in 1935–6. Mussolini's inspection of public works during his visit also constituted an endorsement of the three-year-old governorship of Italo Balbo, himself no particular friend of the Duce (Wright 1987: 29). In an act intended to appeal to a Muslim audience, Mussolini was presented with the "Sword of Islam" (fabricated in Florence for the occasion) while surrounded by 2,000 Libyan cavalrymen. With colonial policy in Libya increasingly influenced by racist discourse in Italy, he would later fail in his stated ambition to be recognized as the "Protector of Islam" (Wright 1987: 31–3; McLaren 2006: 81–2; Segrè 1987: 307–10).

Under Balbo, the Italian state extended across the Mediterranean, incorporating Cyrenaica and Tripolitania into metropolitan Italy proper with Fezzan accorded the status of a colonial province. Known as the *quarta sponda* (fourth shore), joining the peninsula's Tyrrhenian, Adriatic, and Ionian coasts, Libya became an integral part of Italy in January 1939, enclosing the Mediterranean and rendering it a genuine *mare nostrum*. In so doing, the Italian colony of *Libia*, for the first time, was defined and delineated in legalistic, European terms (McLaren 2006: 6–7, 17–41; Segrè 1987: 311–33).

With the outbreak of World War II, Balbo's blueprint for the future prosperity of Libya faded. Unsuccessful in developing much of the country, the Fascist regime proved equally incapable of defending it. Some two-thirds of the Italian troops transported to Libya were lost to the British between December 1940 and February 1941, when 130,000 Italians were taken prisoner. The North African campaign of 1940–3 ended in February 1943 after the British Eighth Army occupied Tripoli. With the end of fighting, Great Britain occupied Cyrenaica and Tripolitania, and France took control of the oases of Fezzan (Wright 1990: 32).

Conclusions

Three decades of Italian rule left Libya with an infrastructure of roads, agricultural villages, and other public works but a poor legacy in terms of a skilled, informed, and politically active citizenry. Italy failed to encourage political participation or to develop political institutions; on the contrary, it actively discouraged indigenous political activity. In Cyrenaica, Fascist policy aimed to destroy the power of the Sanusi Order, abolishing traditional tribal assemblies and weakening the authority of established leaders. In so doing, the Italians effectively disrupted the delicate balance that had emerged between enduring tribal alliances and emerging class and economic formations. Elsewhere, the Italians destroyed the local administration and the networks of patronage-based clientele that had grown up around it, replacing the precolonial administration with an exclusively Italian one in which the local population was not allowed to participate. The absence of local government, the revival of kinship, and the widespread distrust of bureaucracy left the country to be governed after independence in 1951 by leaders whose claims to legitimacy rested on external patronage or military might (Anderson 1986a: 9–11, 34–5).

Where the Ottoman administration encouraged education as a means to promote development, Italian colonial policy, embodied in a June 1928 decree, effectively sanctioned educational and economic apartheid, limiting educational opportunities for Libyans to the elementary level, along with the learning of traditional arts and crafts, in an effort to confine them to menial, labor-intensive jobs. As late as 1939, there were only 120 students in the one secondary school for Libyans in the entire country (Anderson 1986a: 220; Jerary 2003: 17, 21–35; Appleton 1979: 32–3).

After 1911, the Italian administration also stifled a promising cultural and literary revival which had begun in Libya in the second half of the nineteenth century. Italian officials quickly suppressed some 16 periodicals and journals that had appeared regularly in the years before the occupation. In the ensuing three decades, they conducted what one Libyan writer described as "a racist physical and cultural war of extermination" in which few Libyan newspapers or journals survived beyond the first issue (Fagih 2000e: 2). Libyans were viewed by their occupiers as a primitive, backward people, and Italian attempts to civilize them were normally ethnocentric, biased, and racist. With Libyan culture and values held in contempt, any discussion of civilizing Libyans was generally synonymous with Italianizing them (Jerary 2003: 18–21; McLaren 2006: 41).

Both resistance to and collaboration with the Italian occupation must be understood within the context of questions of political economy and state formation. The differing responses within Cyrenaica, Fezzan, and Tripolitania have to take into account differing class configurations and levels of socioeconomic development in order to account for the degree of resistance or collaboration found in different classes, tribes, and ethnic groups. In Tripolitania and Fezzan, a central leadership in opposition to the Italians was never formed because internal divisions deepened with the growth of the political and military might of several tribal leaders. In contrast, the Sanusi Order in Cyrenaica, with its extensive network of religious lodges and its close ties with the local population, including local notables, provided a centralized leadership which was able to exert a significant and sustained influence over the resistance to the invaders.

As for the Italians, their time in Libya lasted just over three decades, by far the shortest period of any of the many occupiers of the country; nevertheless, the practices they followed had an enormous impact on the future capabilities and policies of the state. By the mid-1930s, the Libyan population had been almost halved by famine, war, and emigration, and it would be 1950 before it returned to 1911 levels. The loss of virtually the entire educated elite and entrepreneurial merchant class was especially significant. The protracted warfare also forced large numbers of peasants and tribesmen into the hinterland, resulting in a rekindling of kinship ties and a retribalization of the population, particularly in Tripolitania. As for education, colonial authorities hoped, on the one hand, to eliminate illiteracy in order to prepare Libyans to work for Italians, and on the other, they intended to keep the Libyans as ignorant as possible by restricting their ability to acquire advanced education. Instead of developing political institutions and encouraging political participation, the Italians deliberately weakened or destroyed both local administrations and established indigenous leaders. The end product of such policies was that Libya in 1951 would find itself the poorest independent country in the world with an annual per capita income of around $50, a dearth of post-primary school graduates, and an illiteracy rate of around 90 percent.

2

STATE FORMATION

The United Kingdom of Libya proclaimed its independence on 24 December 1951. It was the first African state to achieve independence from European rule and the first and only state created by the UN General Assembly. The United Kingdom of Libya was influenced by early twentieth century efforts at state formation, including the Congress of Aziziyya (1912), the Tripoli Republic (1918), and the Sanusi Amirate (1920), and also by the activities and experiences of Libyan exiles in 1911–51. International forces, including Four Power talks during and after World War II and the belated role of the United Nations, later combined with domestic forces to shape a precarious statehood. Once independence was achieved, the United Kingdom of Libya faced a myriad of challenges and difficulties which eventually led to its demise in 1969.

Nascent political movements

The political turbulence that began in Libya shortly after the Young Turk Revolution in 1908 and accelerated with the Italian occupation in 1911 strongly influenced Libyan conceptions of their place in modern Arab and Islamic identities. Between the Young Turk Revolution and the end of World War I, Libyans generally remained loyal to pan-Islamic aspirations instead of turning to the Arab nationalism which had surfaced as an organized movement in the Arab revolt in the Hijaz in 1916–18. A segment of the Libyan elite attempted to develop a political organization in Tripolitania based on secular, republican grounds, but internecine disputes doomed their efforts to failure, and they were destined to turn to the religiously inspired leadership of the Sanusiyya in Cyrenaica to continue the fight against Italian rule. Throughout this period, the most widely embraced political identity in Libya, in terms of both a wider loyalty to the Ottoman Empire and a narrower form of provincial patriotism, was provided by Islamic as opposed to Arabic symbols and attachments. As a result, an important legacy of the Italian colonial era was the close association in Libya of nationalism, anti-imperialism, and pan-Islamic loyalties forged during this period (Anderson 1991a: 225–6, 234, 241; Khadduri 1963: 9–10; Baldinetti 2003: 73).

Italy's precipitant withdrawal to the coast, combined with its subsequent preoccupation with World War I, encouraged political activity in Tripolitania and Cyrenaica, and local chiefs or notables created a number of regional governments after 1912. Sulayman al-Baruni in western Tripolitania after 1912, Ramadan al-Suwayhli in Misurata and eastern Tripolitania after 1915, Sheik Suf al-Mahamudi in western Tripolitania after 1915, and Khalifa al-Zawi in Fezzan after 1916 were among the more important. Most of these regional governments were short-lived; nevertheless, they highlighted the inter-factional conflict that plagued Libya in 1910–20. Socioeconomic differences, magnified by struggles over power and revenues, led to frequent hostilities among notables and chiefs, undermining effective resistance to the Italians (Anderson 1991a: 231–3).

On the morrow of the signing of the 1912 peace treaty, Sulayman al-Baruni, a leader of the Ibadi Berbers of the Jabal al-Gharb in western Tripolitania and a member of the 1908 parliament, and Muhammad Farhat al-Zawi, a judge in his hometown of Zawilah and also a member of the 1908 parliament, organized a meeting of Tripolitanian notables and chiefs to discuss a common response (Anderson 1986a: 188–9; Simon 1987: 135). At the meeting, held in late October 1912 and known as the Congress of Aziziyya, the equivocal response of provincial leaders to the Italian occupation was readily apparent. In answer to Italy's declared occupation of the province, the participants split into two camps in an acrimonious meeting in which one group led by Farhat and other coastal notables favored cooperation with the Italians to preserve Tripolitanian independence while another group led by Baruni and other tribal chiefs favored resistance (Simon 1987: 199; Khadduri 1963: 13). The pro-negotiation faction later opened talks with Italian authorities outside Tripoli, but, when they realized that the Italians intended to occupy the entire country, they joined the resistance group. About the same time, Baruni, in early January 1913, announced the formation of an autonomous state in western Tripolitania. When Italian forces defeated the Tripolitanians on 23 March 1913 at the battle of Al-Asabah, Baruni and other provincial resistance leaders were forced into exile. Baruni later returned to Libya once Italy entered World War I, rejoining the resistance movement (Ahmida 1994: 118–22; Baldinetti 2003: 74–5).

Ramadan al-Suwayhli, another prominent nationalist leader, was active in Misurata in north central Tripolitania. Related to a family long competitive for regional influence with the Muntasir family, Ramadan took the field against the Italians at the outset of the occupation in 1911, but, after the conclusion of the 1912 peace treaty, he cooperated with them for a time. At the April 1915 battle of Qasr Bu Hadi, also known as Gardabiyya, Ramadan switched sides ordering the troops under his command and thought to be friendly to the Italians to join the attacking forces, inflicting a severe defeat on the invaders. As a result, Italy lost any semblance of control over the hinterland for the duration of World War I, and Ramadan, who took most of the battlefield spoils, earned the enmity of the Sanusiyya (Anderson 1986a: 192–3; Ahmida 1994: 121).

Like many Libyan notables, Ramadan was as interested in extending his own political influence as he was in serving the Ottoman cause, and for several years he strengthened Misurata, both as a safe haven for Ottoman forces and as a de facto autonomous political district (Anderson 1986a: 198). In early 1916, the Sanusiyya attempted to extend their influence, including their taxing power, into eastern Tripolitania. Opposed to the move, Ramadan engaged the Sanusiyya near Bani Walid in Sirte, defeating them and marking the end of any real Sanusi influence in Tripolitania (Khadduri 1963: 13–14; Simon 1987: 227–9). In itself, the incident was insignificant; however, it made future cooperation between political forces in Cyrenaica and Tripolitania impossible at a time when a joint response to Italian aggression was desperately needed. By the end of 1917, Ramadan's influence, along with his tax-collecting powers, encompassed most of eastern Tripolitania (Evans-Pritchard 1949: 123; Anderson 1982: 48; Simon 1987: 234–5).

In 1913, Sayyid Ahmad al-Sharif (the title "Sayyid" denoting a claim to descent from the Prophet Muhammad) declared the formation of a Sanusi state, calling on his followers to fight for *jihad* against the invading Italians. Pressured by his Ottoman allies, Ahmad later attacked British forces in Egypt in what proved to be a foolhardy enterprise (Evans-Pritchard 1949: 127–8; Simon 1987: 161–7; 259–78; Wright 2003: 63–75). The Sanusi–British war had far-reaching consequences for Cyrenaica and Tripolitania as it led to the replacement of Ahmad with his cousin, Sayyid Muhammad Idris al-Mahdi al-Sanusi, who rightly blamed the former for the tragic war against the British. With Sayyid Ahmad discredited militarily and politically, Sayyid Idris in July 1916 opened negotiations with Italian officials at Zuwaytina, using the British as intermediaries. Although a final agreement was not reached at this time, renewed talks at Akrama in April 1917 led to an accord in which the signatories agreed to a *modus vivendi* in Cyrenaica, calling for the Italians to recognize Sanusi autonomy in the hinterland and for the Sanusiyya to recognize Italian administration along the coast. In addition to ending hostilities, the truce provided for the resumption of Sanusi commerce with the coast (Evans-Pritchard 1949: 144–5; Khadduri 1963: 15–17; Ahmida 1994: 118, 122–3). The Akrama agreement gave the people of Cyrenaica a degree of autonomy at a time when the Italian government was responsive to the liberal principles advocated by the US president, Woodrow Wilson, but the Italians never recognized the practical autonomy of Tripolitania even though it was no less real (Anderson 1991a: 235).

Early efforts at state formation

Organized in November 1918, the Tripoli Republic was the first formal republican government created in the Arab world, and the first indigenous political entity to emerge in Libya since the overthrow of the Karamanli dynasty in 1835.

Its formation was influenced by the April 1917 agreement in which Italy granted the Sanusiyya local autonomy and by President Wilson's January 1918 declaration in support of national self-determination. A compromise necessitated by the Ottoman defeat in World War I, the Tripoli Republic also represented a triumph for those who stressed consolidation and reconstruction before provincial loyalties (Roumani 1983: 159). The name of the new body was chosen before the form of government was agreed and, along with republican sentiment, it reflected the inability of the founders to agree on a single individual to act as head of state. In the end, a Council of Four, supported by an advisory group composed of individuals representing most of the regions and interests of the province, was established to act as a ruling board. The Council of Four consisted of Ramadan al-Suwayhli, Sulayman al-Baruni, Ahmad al-Murayyid of Tarhuna, and Abd al-Nabi Bilkhayr of Warfalla. Enjoying widespread popular support in Tripolitania, the Tripoli Republic demanded that Italy open talks aimed at independence in the spirit of President Wilson's principles of self-determination (Anderson 1982: 51–2; Ahmida 1994: 124–5).

The creation of the Tripoli Republic and the declaration of independence for Tripolitania generated little support among the European powers who had promised Italy sovereignty over Libya in the Treaty of London (1915). Italy agreed to meet with agents of the new republic, but only because Rome hoped to negotiate an accord similar to its pact with the Sanusi Order. When negotiations opened in April 1919, the Tripolitanians viewed themselves as equals to the Italians, in the sense that two sovereign states might discuss a dispute, but the Italians viewed the talks as simply a prelude to a system of government in which Italy would rule Libya through local chiefs. The disagreement was never resolved, but the talks did lay the groundwork for the April 1919 Qalat al-Zaytuna Agreement between Italy and the Tripoli Republic and the promulgation of the *Legge Fondamentale* (*Fundamental Law*) in June 1919 (Anderson 1982: 52; Ahmida 1994: 125).

A liberal document for the time, the *Legge Fondamentale* provided for a special form of Italian–Libyan citizenship and accorded all such citizens the right to vote in elections for local parliaments. Exempted from military conscription, the taxing power of this new type of citizen rested with the locally elected parliament. The law also provided for the Italian governor to appoint local administrative positions based on nominations from a 10-man council, eight of whose members would be Libyans selected by the parliament. Initially confined to the Tripoli Republic, the *Legge Fondamentale* was extended in October 1919 to include Cyrenaica. British intervention forced the Italians to work with the Sanusiyya, and the parliament in Cyrenaica met five times before it was abolished in 1923. In contrast, the Italians in Tripolitania, who were not under pressure from external forces, made no effort to apply the *Legge Fondamentale*. Parliamentary elections were never held in Tripolitania, and Giuseppe Volpi scrapped the agreement soon after he was appointed governor in August 1921 (Anderson 1982: 53–4; Ahmida 1994: 125–6).

The membership of the council responsible for overseeing administrative appointments under the *Legge Fondamentale* was virtually identical to the original founders of the Tripoli Republic; nevertheless, Italian officials refused to recognize the Republic or acknowledge its authority to administer the hinterland. Competition among the notables and chiefs of Tripolitania due to personal rivalries and diverse socioeconomic forces also undermined the Tripoli Republic (Ahmida 1994: 126–8). For example, a fatal quarrel broke out in late 1919 between Ramadan al-Suwayhli and Abd al-Nabi Bilkhayr when the former refused to confirm several of the latter's family members in administrative positions in Warfalla. In addition, Abd al-Nabi disapproved of Ramadan's ongoing animosity toward the Sanusi Order, and the two sides traded accusations over accounting for sums of money sent from Istanbul during World War I. In mid-1920, Ramadan launched a military campaign against his opponents in which he was defeated and then killed in August 1920 (Anderson 1982: 54–7; Ahmida 1994: 128–30).

In the Accord of al-Rajma, dated 25 October 1920, Sayyid Idris reached a new agreement with Italy in which the latter granted him the honorific title of amir of Cyrenaica and permitted him to organize an autonomous administration in the interior of Cyrenaica, including the oases of Ajadabiyyah, Awjilah, Jaghbub, Jalu, and Kufrah. In return, Idris agreed to cooperate in applying the *Legge Fondamentale* to Cyrenaica, to dismantle Sanusi military units (which was never done), and to tax the local population only to the level of the religious tithe (Anderson 1991a: 237–8; Evans-Pritchard 1949: 148–9). As part of the accord creating the Sanusi Amirate, the Italians granted Idris a personal stipend of 63,000 lire a month, with monthly payments also made to other members of the Sanusi family. In addition, the Italians also agreed to cover the costs of administering and policing the areas under Sanusi control and to pay regular stipends to tribal sheiks and administrators of the Sanusi *zawaya* (religious lodges) (Khadduri 1963: 18–19). This blatant attempt to bribe the Sanusi leadership into cooperation proved ineffective, and by late 1922, the Fascist government in Rome had resolved to undertake the military conquest of Libya (Anderson 1982: 54; Ahmida 1994: 123, 136–40).

Shortly after the announcement of the Accord of al-Rajma, the leadership of the Tripoli Republic in November 1920 called a general meeting in Gharyan. Sulayman al-Baruni declined to attend, and with disorder in the Jabal al-Gharb tantamount to civil war he departed Libya in November 1921 (Ahmida 1994: 130–2). Recognizing that the *Legge Fondamentale* would never be implemented and with internal dissension destroying any possibility of a united front, the Gharyan Conference resolved that a government based on Islamic principles and headed by a Muslim leader should be formed (Anderson 1991a: 238). However, the conference failed to designate such a leader, and it remains unclear whether or not they had a particular person in mind. The Gharyan Conference also established a 14-member government, known as the Central Reform Board, and agreed to send a delegation to Rome to inform the Italian government of its creation. Among its stated aims, the new body hoped to safeguard Arab rights as expressed in the *Legge Fondamentale*, to increase understanding between Arabs and Italians, and to spread knowledge in order to bring Western civilization to a country that preserved the glorious traditions of Islam. A delegation later traveled to Rome but failed to meet with anyone in the Italian government, and the elections called for by the *Legge Fondamentale* were never held (Evans-Pritchard 1949: 147; Anderson 1982: 57–60; Ahmida 1994: 133).

With Ramadan al-Suwayhli dead and Sulayman al-Baruni in exile, the principal obstacles to cooperation with the Sanusiyya were gone, and representatives of the Gharyan Conference met with Sanusi delegates in Sirte at the end of 1921. At the meeting, they announced their intention to elect a Muslim amir to represent the entire country and, although no specific name was mentioned, it was commonly understood that Sayyid Idris would be the amir. When further attempts to negotiate with the Italians proved fruitless, the Central Reform Board sent a delegation to Cyrenaica to request that Sayyid Idris assume the amirate of all Libya. Refusing at first, he accepted in October 1922 after it became clear that conflict with Italy was unavoidable. Sayyid Idris then fled to Egypt, where he remained until 1943. In turn, the Fascists, having consolidated their position at home, abrogated all conventions and agreements with the various Libyan factions and began the *riconquista* (Khadduri 1963: 21–3; Anderson 1991a: 240).

Bereft of international support, early Libyan efforts at regional autonomy or countrywide independence were overwhelmed by the aggressive policies of the Italian government. By early 1923, the Sanusi leadership was in exile, the Tripoli Republic had ceased to exist, and the belated attempts at cooperation between Tripolitania and Cyrenaica had proved too little, too late. In hindsight, the pretensions of the Tripoli Republic were far too ambitious; nevertheless, its mere creation marked an important early step in the political development of the nation as a whole (Anderson 1982: 60–1; Ahmida 1994: 135–6).

Road to independence

In the interwar period, Libyan exiles in a variety of Middle Eastern locations conducted an active if generally ineffective war of words against the Italian occupation. For example, Bashir al-Sadawi, a member of the 1922 Tripolitanian delegation to Sayyid Idris, established the Tripolitanian–Cyrenaican Defense Committee in Damascus to oppose Italian rule. Other emigré groups formed similar organizations in Chad, Egypt, the Gulf, Niger, Saudi Arabia, Syria, and Tunisia, and Sayyid Idris, in exile in Cairo during the interwar period, enjoyed cordial relations with the British. Precise figures on the number of Libyan exiles fleeing Italian colonial rule after 1911 are not available; however, recent estimates suggest they probably numbered in the hundreds of thousands. Recognizing the need for a common front but divided by personal and regional differences, Cyrenaicans and Tripolitanians differed as to who their acknowledged leader should be, with a majority agreeing that Sayyid Idris was the most logical choice (Anderson 1986a: 251; Khadduri 1963: 28–9; Baldinetti 2003: 73–9).

At the outset of World War II, many Libyan nationalists, like their counterparts elsewhere in the Arab world, were convinced that the Axis powers would win the war; consequently, they were reluctant to support the Allied cause. The imperial role of Britain and France in their lands of exile reinforced this reluctance. Having established good relations with the British, Sayyid Idris did not share their concerns, and, when the British requested his assistance in forming a Sanusi force to accompany the British army into Libya, he agreed. Mustered as the Libyan Arab Force, British reference to the units as battalions of Sanusi tribes, together with their uniforms, which were emblazoned with the Sanusi emblem, angered Tripolitanian notables in Egypt, who volunteered to organize Tripolitanian units but refused to support the Cyrenaican war effort. The internecine disputes that had weakened Libyan resistance during World War I were thus revived during World War II, exacerbating tensions that would plague Libya in coming decades (Anderson 1986a: 252; Khadduri 1963: 29–33; Wright 1982a: 45–6; Baldinetti 2003: 80).

Unsure that the Allied powers could win the war, and resenting Sanusi pretensions to leadership, Tripolitanian notables strongly criticized the decision of Sayyid Idris to collaborate with the British before the latter had delivered sound guarantees of independence for all Libya. In response to mounting pressure from his own followers as well as the Tripolitanians, Idris in 1940–1 pushed the British on the question of independence, threatening to terminate active collaboration if they failed to give public assurances on the issue. Reluctant to provide definite promises before the war ended, the British foreign secretary, Anthony Eden, made a statement in the House of Commons on 8 January 1942 in which he promised that the Sanusi of Cyrenaica would under no circumstances again fall under Italian domination. The statement did not promise independence for Cyrenaica, and it did not even mention Tripolitania, an omission which Tripolitanian notables took as implicit British recognition of Sanusi leadership over all Libya. In addition, the full implication of the foreign secretary's remarks were unclear as they could be taken to suggest different arrangements for Cyrenaica, Fezzan, and Tripolitania in the postwar era. Although the Eden statement was far less than the guarantee of Libyan independence that Sayyid Idris had been demanding, he declared himself satisfied with the oral pledge, recognizing that the British were not prepared to provide written promises (Khadduri 1963: 33–7; Wright 1982a: 46–7).

Military administration of Libya

After a series of intense battles that effectively destroyed the Italian-built infrastructure in Cyrenaica and damaged parts of it in Tripolitania, the conclusion of the North African campaigns of World War II left Libya in the hands of the British and French. The British Eighth Army occupied Cyrenaica in November 1942 and Tripoli on 23 January 1943, completing the Allied conquest of Tripolitania by February 1943. As the British advanced on Tripoli, the main oases of Fezzan were occupied in January 1943 by Free French troops from their garrison on Lake Chad. From 1942–3 to 1951, the British Military Administration ruled Cyrenaica and Tripolitania and the French Military Administration governed Fezzan and parts of central Libya.

Both the British and the French ruled in accordance with the Hague Convention of 1907, which governed the conduct of war. Under its terms, Libya was considered occupied enemy territory, and its government was on a care and maintenance basis. In theory, this meant that the institutions and laws in effect at the time of occupation would remain intact with their permanent status to be resolved after the war. In practice, the British and French administrations went well beyond the strict terms of their mandates, fostering the development of social and other services. Nevertheless, the development of the country suffered greatly from the war and the prolonged period of uncertainty that followed it (Wright 1982a: 44–5, 47–8; Khadduri 1963: 37–51; Anderson 1986a: 253).

Demise of the Jewish community

For most of the Italian occupation, the small but highly patriotic Jewish community had enjoyed an anomalous position. On the one hand, Italo Balbo was pro-Jewish, viewing local Jews as natural allies in his plans to modernize Libya. On the other, the legislation that closed shops on Sunday but enforced their opening on Saturday ignored Jewish susceptibilities, and laws enacted later relegated Jews to a status inferior to their Muslim neighbors. Balbo did his best to temper the introduction in Libya of the most severe racial laws implemented in Fascist Italy, including a welcome delay in the implementation of the new racial laws passed in Italy in 1938. Up to the outbreak of World War II, the plight of Libyan Jews was relatively good and, despite the presence of large numbers of Germans in 1941–3, the harshest anti-Semitic restrictions were not applied in Libya until only a few weeks before Tripoli was occupied by the British Eighth Army (De Felice 1985: 117–84; Goldberg 1990: 97–110; Wright 1989b: 226).

In the immediate aftermath of World War II, a state of euphoria characterized Jewish–Muslim relations in Libya, particularly in smaller towns and rural areas, with the two groups evidencing a desire to work together in peace (De Felice 1985: 185–92). Given the appearance of positive relations, the widespread anti-Jewish riots that broke out in Tripoli on Sunday, 4 November 1945, were something of a surprise to both communities. The genesis of the riots has remained unclear, with official British inquiries citing a fight that took place between a Jew and a Muslim, along with sporadic brawling between the youth of the two communities. In contrast, a report authored by the Jewish community suggested that the rioting occurred almost simultaneously in widely disparate locations, indicating that prior planning and coordination were involved.

Although the whole truth is unknown and unknowable, it seems apparent that the riots, rooted in the specific political conditions of the time, also reflected a much longer-term cultural and religious rivalry between Jews and Muslims in Libya (De Felice 1985: 192–210; Goldberg 1990: 110–21).

The anti-Jewish riots of 1945 marked an important turning point in Jewish–Muslim relations as well as in the relationship of Jews to Libya itself. With the authorities slow to react, some 130 Jews but only one Muslim were killed, and there was also a substantial loss of Jewish property from looting and burning. In addition to dealing a severe blow to any Jewish sense of security, the pogrom challenged any illusions Jews held of taking future initiatives in Libya. The riots occurred almost three years before the state of Israel became a reality in May 1948, but they were an important motivation in bringing about a mass emigration of Jews to Israel after 1948. In the wake of the May 1948 proclamation of the state of Israel, fresh riots left 14 more Jews dead, hastening the departure for Israel of most of the Libyan Jewish community. Of the 36,000 Jews in Libya in 1947, only 6,000 remained at independence in December 1951, and most of those resided in Tripoli (De Felice 1985: 210–33; Goldberg 1990: 121–2; Wright 1989b: 226).

Cold War competition

With the disposition of the former Italian colonies the key to the preservation of Anglo-American interests in the central Mediterranean, strategic considerations were central to the question of Libyan independence well before World War II ended. As early as mid-1943, a memorandum prepared by the US Department of State for the First Quebec Conference (August 1943) explored the essence of the policy alternatives that France, the Soviet Union, Great Britain, and the United States, the so-called Four Powers, would wrestle with over the ensuing half-decade. For the United States, the preferred alternative at this time was the creation of an international trusteeship, with a governing council composed of Great Britain, France, and Egypt, to govern Libya as part of a wider North African region. In a variation of this proposal, the United States in September 1945 proposed a United Nations trusteeship over Libya (St John 2002: 40–1).

In examining this first alternative, the memorandum implied that the rapid development of air power made it unimportant who actually controlled Libya. Over the next two years, the American position on the strategic importance of Libya would change dramatically, with the United States in 1945 joining Great Britain in recognizing that the 1,770-kilometer (1,097-mile) Libyan coastline was essential to the control of the central Mediterranean. Over time the Soviet Union also recognized Libya's strategic position, suggesting a Soviet trusteeship over Tripolitania in December 1945 (Khadduri 1963: 114–5; Haines 1947: 422–3). At the time of the 1942 Eden statement to the House of Commons on the future of Cyrenaica, Sayyid Idris had made clear his opposition to either the Italians or the Soviets playing a postwar role in Cyrenaica, preferring independence in conjunction with a close alliance with Great Britain. The notables of Tripolitania, professing an equal concern for a return to Italian domination and an even greater fear of Soviet occupation, shared the sentiments of Sayyid Idris, if not all his plans (Haines 1947: 424). Great Britain and the United States later refused to consider the December 1945 Soviet proposal; however, their response was influenced more by Cold War strategic calculations than it was by Libyan interests and concerns.

The second alternative outlined by the United States in August 1943 was to divide Libya, with Cyrenaica going to Egypt and Tripolitania to Tunisia. The memorandum questioned this option on the grounds that the poor administration of Egypt should not be extended to Cyrenaica and combining the Italians in Tripolitania with those in Tunisia would disturb the delicate balance between the French and Italians in Tunisia. In the spring of 1944, the British advanced a variation of this alternative in which Cyrenaica would become an autonomous principality under Egyptian suzerainty with safeguards for UN military requirements, including air and naval facilities at Benghazi. In turn, Tripolitania would be restored to Italy, subject to a guarantee of demilitarization and British retention of the use of the Castel Benito Airfield at Tripoli (Rivlin 1949: 32; St John 2002: 41–2).

The third alternative considered in 1943 was the return of Libya to Italy. There was little support for this approach, but there was widespread agreement that any course of action adopted should not preclude Italian migration into Libya or the enjoyment of equal opportunities by Italians in Libya. Over the next two years, the Department of State was torn by divided counsel, with the Office of European Affairs urging that Cyrenaica and Tripolitania be returned to Italy as trusteeships and the Office of Near Eastern and African Affairs advocating a UN trusteeship. At the Potsdam Conference (July–August 1945), the Harry S. Truman administration, which took over on the death of President Franklin D. Roosevelt in April 1945, supported a return of Libya to Italian sovereignty; however, at the London Conference (September 1945), the United States reversed its position, again supporting an international trusteeship (Haines 1947: 421–2; Bills 1995: 38–40).

The fourth and final alternative considered by the United States in 1943 was the creation of a Jewish refuge in Libya. This proposal included the formation of a Jewish state in Cyrenaica and the settlement of Jewish refugees both on the villages and farms vacated by Italians and on additional land. An obstacle to this alternative noted at the time was the limited arable land available in Libya, a shortcoming recognized as early as 1908–9 by the International Territorial Organization, a group in search of a Jewish national home (Slouschz 2005). The 1943 memorandum also suggested that it would prove difficult to persuade Libyan Arabs to accept Jewish settlement. With Arab nationalism on the rise, it recognized that any attempt to promote Jewish settlement would extend the arena of Arab–Jewish conflict without offering substantial relief to the Jewish refugee problem (St John 2002: 38–9, 41). The Muslim attacks on the Jewish minority in late 1945 later dashed any hopes remaining for the creation of a Jewish refuge in Libya.

These four alternatives, and their derivatives, would constitute the core of Four Power discussions on the future of Libya in the postwar period. With the occasional exception of Sayyid Idris and Cyrenaica, none of the proposals made any real effort to solicit, recognize, or respond to the wishes of the Libyan people. With all proposals focused on the future of Cyrenaica and Tripolitania, this was especially true in the case of Fezzan, which was mostly ignored in the Four Power dialogue. From the beginning of their occupation in early 1943, the French had made clear their wish to retain permanent control of Fezzan, linking it to their colonies in North and Equatorial Africa to create a buffer zone to protect them from outside influence and infiltration (Haines 1947: 420–1: Rivlin 1949: 32; Wright 1982a: 49–50). Established at the 1945 Potsdam Conference, the Council of Foreign Ministers would continue until late 1948 to discuss the disposition of the Italian colonies in a series of spirited but mostly unproductive sessions that mirrored the bipolar nature of the postwar world order (Bills 1995: 29–33; Khadduri 1963: 126–7). Throughout the negotiations, strategic considerations remained center stage in Four Power attempts to deal with the future of Libya, and, in the end, they proved to be the major reason for the failure of the Four Powers to reach a consensus.

Three zones, one goal

With the end of World War II, Sayyid Idris elected to remain in Egypt in lieu of returning to a Cyrenaica under British Military Administration. When the military government was eventually withdrawn, he believed he would be entrusted with civil responsibility, but he did not want to assume that responsibility as long as foreign military authorities were governing. In June 1945, his supporters addressed a letter to the British Minister of State in Cairo, outlining a plan for an independent Cyrenaican government under the leadership of Idris. One year later, in July 1946, tribal chiefs issued a manifesto which demanded, among other things, British recognition of a Sanusi Amirate under Sayyid Idris and the formation of an independent, constitutional government in Cyrenaica. When Sayyid Idris took up permanent residence in Cyrenaica in November 1947, he was alarmed at the political factionalism that had developed, mainly between the younger, more progressive, members of the Umar al-Mukhtar group and the older, more conservative, notables and tribal leaders of the National Front. In response, he dissolved all political organizations on 7 December 1947 and established a new united front which took the form of the National Congress. Shortly thereafter, the National Congress issued a statement calling for the creation of an independent sovereign state under a Sanusi Amirate (Khadduri 1963: 53–80; Pelt 1970: 44; Baldinetti 2003: 80–1).

Reflecting its experience in 1918–22, Tripolitania remained largely republican in outlook, and the end of World War II led to renewed political activity. Following a period in which political associations had been prohibited, Tripolitanian leaders took advantage of new-found freedoms to organize a wide variety of political parties, including the Nationalist Party, United National Front, and Free National Bloc. In a province with a long history of factional differences and conflicted leadership, family and feudal loyalties played a major role in the creation of these new political groups. Nevertheless, apart from the Sanusi Amirate and selected constitutional issues, most of the newly created political parties in Tripolitania reflected the earlier republican experience in that they agreed on the fundamental principles of unity and independence. Specific demands included complete independence, a united Libya composed of Cyrenaica, Fezzan, and Tripolitania, and membership in the Arab League (Khadduri 1963: 81–8; Wright 1982a: 50–2).

In Fezzan, the French administration, continuing to hope that the province would be joined with other French colonies in Africa, limited political activity to a far greater extent than the British did in Cyrenaica and Tripolitania. The administration of the province was tied to southern Algeria, and French officials also diverted Fezzani trade to Algeria. When indigenous leaders expressed a desire to establish an autonomous regime, the French tightened their control over the territory, prompting local leaders in late 1946 to organize a secret opposition society. French authorities later discovered the existence of the society and arrested some of its members in 1947; nevertheless, the organization continued to oppose French governance (Khadduri 1963: 107–9; Wright 1982a: 54).

In short, Libya as late as 1947 remained divided into three zones, consisting of a nascent Sanusi Amirate in Cyrenaica, a volatile mix of ethnic groups together with a more urbanized culture in Tripolitania, and the French-controlled oases in Fezzan. Even though a variety of proposals were made to the Council of Foreign Ministers after 1945, there was little reason to believe that a unified Libya would emerge in the foreseeable future. Great Britain hoped to maintain its close ties with Cyrenaica, but it was not interested in overseeing Tripolitania, and it could see little chance of dislodging the French from Fezzan. Uninterested in assuming trusteeships in Africa, the United States promoted a collective trusteeship plan that had some ideological appeal but generated little real political support. France was determined to retain its control in Fezzan, and it hoped to see Italy restored in Tripolitania. In turn, the Soviet Union sponsored the restoration of Italian rule in Italy's former colonies in an effort both to court the Italian electorate and to improve its bargaining position in Europe (St John 2002: 49).

Well before the end of World War II, strategic considerations were central to the question of Libya; nevertheless, it was the crisis in Italy surrounding the 1948 general elections that galvanized Anglo-American defense plans. Once the Gasperi–Sforza regime demonstrated in the elections that it could withstand a Communist challenge, the State Department and the Foreign Office pledged to coordinate future public statements on the former Italian colonies. The State Department also agreed to coordinate its strategy with the French. Before the Italian elections, Sir Orme Sargent, British Permanent Under Secretary, described Cyrenaica as the best aircraft carrier in Africa, and the American air base at Mallaha in Tripolitania, generally known as Wheelus Field, also took on new life in this time frame. By mid-1948, the United States had committed itself fully to British interests in Cyrenaica and to the development of a major postwar base at Wheelus Field. With the European crisis of 1948 serving as a catalyst, Anglo-American strategic interests in the central Mediterranean in general and Libya in particular had become intertwined (Bills 1995: 133–7, 142; St John 2002: 48–9).

Commission of investigation

In accordance with the provisions of the Italian peace treaty, signed on 10 February 1947, the Council of Foreign Ministers sent a Commission of Investigation to Libya in early 1948 to report on internal conditions and to consider the welfare and learn the wishes of the inhabitants. Composed of a single representative from each of the Four Powers, the commission was charged with gathering facts but was instructed to refrain from making recommendations on the final disposition of the territories. Arriving in Tripoli on 6 March 1948, the commission spent 40 days in Tripolitania, 25 in Cyrenaica, and 10 in Fezzan. In Tripolitania, leaders of rival political parties temporarily set aside their differences to offer a united front. They presented the commission with a declaration incorporating three major points: immediate and complete independence, a united Libya, and Arab League membership. In addressing inhabitants outside the political parties, the commission found the call for independence to be virtually unanimous while the calls for unity and membership in the Arab League enjoyed widespread but not universal support (Khadduri 1963: 98–9, 120–2; Wright 1982a: 52–3; Bills 1995: 129–30).

In Cyrenaica, the inhabitants, especially the tribes of the interior, called for an independent Cyrenaica under Sayyid Idris with whatever form of government he chose. During the visit, the National Congress, which had superseded most if not all political parties, submitted to the commission a proposal that called for immediate independence and constitutional government under Sayyid Idris and his heirs. As for Tripolitania, the National Congress expressed an equivocal position in that it was willing to unite with Tripolitania, but only on Cyrenaican terms (Rivlin 1949: 39–40; Bills 1995: 130–1).

In the course of the commission's visit to Fezzan, the secret opposition society formed in 1946 openly denounced the French administration and demanded the union of Fezzan with Cyrenaica and Tripolitania under Sanusi leadership. After the commission departed, French authorities arrested and jailed at least one member of the society, Muhammad Bin Uthman al-Sayd, for a period of six months. Otherwise, the commission found it difficult to gauge public opinion in Fezzan, with most inhabitants expressing only vague political views and many seemingly content with or undecided about French administration (Khadduri 1963: 108, 122–3; Wright 1982a: 53; Bills 1995: 130).

Torn by conflicting interests, the members of the Commission of Investigation agreed on only the most fundamental issues, often pursuing lines of inquiry in accordance with the views of their governments as opposed to dispassionately soliciting the views of the Libyan people (Rivlin 1949: 33–4). On the one hand, they recognized that Libyans were virtually unanimous in their desire for freedom from foreign rule, and they also acknowledged a widespread lack of sentiment for a return to Italian rule. On the other, they reported that a mature understanding of the responsibilities of independence was clearly lacking among the people of Libya. After taking into account the low level of economic development in the country, the commission concluded that Libya was not self-supporting and thus not ready for independence, a decision that produced widespread surprise and resentment in Libya (Khadduri 1963: 71, 123–4; Anderson 1986a: 255–6; Bills 1995: 131–2).

Decision United Nations

The 1947 Italian peace treaty called for Italy to renounce all right and title to its former African possessions, leaving the British and French military administrations in power until their final disposition had been agreed. In addition, the treaty stipulated that future arrangements regarding the former Italian colonies would be determined by the Four Powers. They were obliged to arrive at a settlement within 12 months of the treaty coming into force, which occurred on 15 September 1947, and, if they were unable to do so, they were to submit the question to the UN General Assembly (Haines 1947: 417; Khadduri 1963: 115–7; Bills 1995: 148–54).

The transfer of the issue of the former Italian colonies from the Council of Foreign Ministers to the UN General Assembly was decisive in determining Libya's future. The change in venue did not necessarily make the issue easier to resolve, but it did guarantee that it would be addressed in a wider forum under very different rules. With the General Assembly composed of 58 members voting on the basis of equality and deciding important issues by a two-thirds majority, unanimity was no longer a prerequisite, and all debates were public, excepting those in subcommittee. Consequently, the transfer of proceedings to the General Assembly gave all involved parties, especially the weaker ones, a larger and more accessible forum in which to plead their case (Pelt 1970: 74–5).

From the outset, the American delegation took an equivocal position, arguing that any decision on the future of Libya should consider the interests of the inhabitants as paramount but also take into account concerns for international peace and security (Pelt 1970: 88, 105). In taking this position, the United States, less than a decade after the issuance of the Atlantic Charter (August 1941), compromised and very nearly abandoned its pledged respect for the self-determination of peoples, despite a clear understanding in Washington as to the wishes of the Libyan people. By this time, the United States was especially reluctant to see a UN trusteeship in the area because such a step threatened its plans to develop Wheelus Field into a strategic air base. Under the UN trustee system, the administrator of a trust territory could not establish military bases except in the case of a strategic trusteeship, such as that enjoyed by the United States in the former Japanese islands of the Pacific. With strategic trusteeships subject to veto in the UN Security Council, of which the Soviet Union was a member, any form of UN trusteeship would make it impossible for Libya to play a role in the defense of the Free World (Villard 1956: 33–4). In contrast to the US position, the Egyptian delegate took the view that Libya was ready for immediate independence, but other delegates questioned its preparedness for such a decisive step (St John 2002: 51). When a prolonged debate identified no consensus for action, a subcommittee was appointed to study and propose a resolution to the opposing viewpoints on Libya.

After the subcommittee had been formed, Great Britain and Italy proposed a compromise, the so-called Bevin–Sforza plan, which would have given 10-year trusteeships to Britain in Cyrenaica, Italy in Tripolitania, and France in Fezzan. When this period ended, Libya would be granted independence if the UN General Assembly decided such a step was appropriate. While it acknowledged Libyan aspirations for independence, the joint proposal also safeguarded tem-porarily American and British strategic interests in the region (Dearden 1950: 403–4). Less than six weeks after it had declared the interests of the Libyan people to be paramount, the American delegation justified its support for the Bevin–Sforza plan on the grounds that it offered a path to unity and independ-ence. Actually, US support for the plan was just another example of strategic concerns outweighing the articulated and recognized interests of the Libyan people (St John 2002: 52). The Bevin–Sforza plan generated widespread, intense protests in Tripoli and elsewhere in Libya before it was finally defeated by the UN General Assembly in May 1949 (Khadduri 1963: 101, 128–32; Wright 1982a: 54–5). In this sense, the conflicting interests of the Four Powers became Libya's strongest ally in achieving independence.

The defeat of the Bevin–Sforza plan marked a turning point in the debate over the future of Libya. Thereafter, all parties reluctantly and belatedly declared themselves in favor of independence (St John 2002: 52–3; Khadduri 1963: 133). When the UN General Assembly met in September 1949, it learned that Sayyid Idris had proclaimed the independence of Cyrenaica at a 1 June 1949 meeting of the National Congress and, in response, the British Chief Administrator had recognized the desire of Cyrenaicans for self-government with the amir as head of state. Recognizing that Tripolitanians might question this unilateral decision, Sayyid Idris directed the National Congress to send them a cable, assuring them that he continued to work for the unity of Cyrenaica and Tripolitania. The Tripolitanian National Front responded positively to his overture, sending a delegation to Cyrenaica to congratulate Sayyid Idris and to request his sup-port in achieving the unity of Tripolitania and Fezzan. The French government eventually followed suit in February 1950, establishing a transitional government and representative assembly in Fezzan (Dearden 1950: 397–9, 401–3; Wright 1982a: 55–8).

Concerned that Tripolitania and Fezzan might be separated from Cyrenaica and denied independence, the leadership of Tripolitania called for unified independence under Sayyid Idris even though many of them, perhaps a majority, viewed with trepidation his accession to power over a united Libya. Tripolitania had a population of 738,000 people compared with only 291,000 in Cyrenaica and 59,000 in Fezzan; moreover, the physical infrastructure of Tripolitania was more elaborate and less damaged than that of Cyrenaica. The recognized attachment of Sayyid Idris to Cyrenaica and his open dislike for Tripolitania added to the concern of the inhabitants of the latter (Anderson 1986a: 253–4; Rivlin 1949: 40–2).

Following an extended debate, the UN General Assembly, on 21 November 1949, called for Libya to become an independent and sovereign state no later than 1 January 1952. In December 1949, the General Assembly appointed Adrian Pelt, Assistant Secretary General of the United Nations, as the UN Commissioner for Libya with a charter to assist its inhabitants to draw up a constitution and to establish an independent state (Dearden 1950: 395–6; Khadduri 1963: 133–9). Over the next two years, one of the most difficult challenges facing Pelt was the constant need to reconcile the extremely tight timetable for independence given him by the General Assembly with the need for due diligence and sound democratic principles in the constitution-making process (Wright 1982a: 65).

When it appointed Pelt as the UN Commissioner for Libya, the General Assembly also approved the creation of a 10-member Advisory Council, consisting of representatives of Egypt, France, Italy, Pakistan, Great Britain, and the United States, together with four Libyan leaders appointed by Pelt, to assist the latter to accomplish his tasks. To represent the three provincial seats, Pelt chose a tribal chief from Murzuk for Fezzan, the Cyrenaican Minister of Public Works and Communications for Cyrenaica, and a vice president of the National Congress Party for Tripolitania. To represent the combined minorities of Tripolitania, he chose the Italian vice president of the Savings Bank of Libya. The Council of 10 had a pronounced Western bias, and the Egyptian and Pakistani members, in league with the Tripolitanian representative, soon constituted a minority anti-Western faction, opposing several administrative and constitutional decisions (Khadduri 1963: 139–40; Wright 1982a: 60–1, 64–5). The Egyptian delegate was especially forceful on the question of federalism versus unity, advocating a unified form of government. In turn, the US delegation argued that federation was the optimum form of unity for Libya (Dearden 1950: 405–8; Golino 1970: 339; Pelt 1970: 514–15).

On 25 July 1950, Commissioner Pelt invited 21 prominent Libyans, seven each from Cyrenaica and Fezzan and six from Tripolitania with a seventh individual to represent the country's minorities, most of whom resided in

Tripolitania, to form a preparatory committee to discuss the organization and selection of a provisional national assembly. This Committee of 21 decided that the assembly should consist of 20 members each from the three constituent provinces, to be appointed by province chiefs (Khadduri 1963: 144–50). The Tripolitanian representatives on the committee had argued unsuccessfully that a truly democratic assembly would be based on proportional representation, but with both Cyrenaica and Fezzan favoring a federal form of government this initial decision of the committee in effect determined the future form of the Libyan state. Once established, the National Assembly passed a resolution proposing the state of Libya be a federal monarchy, under the crown of Sayyid Idris of Cyrenaica. A law to that effect was unanimously adopted by the National Assembly on 2 December 1950 (Khadduri 1963: 164–71; Wright 1982a: 62–3, 66–7; Pelt 1970: 290).

On 7 October 1951, the National Assembly approved a constitution, consisting of 213 articles. It declared the United Kingdom of Libya to be a hereditary monarchy with a federal form of government. The parliament consisted of a senate of 24 members, eight from each province, with half chosen by the king and half by provincial legislative councils, and a house of representatives, based on proportional representation, with adult male voters electing deputies in a ratio of 1 per 20,000 inhabitants. On this basis, Tripolitania was allotted 35 deputies, Cyrenaica 15, and Fezzan five. The constitution declared Islam to be the religion of the new state. With Benghazi isolated and damaged during the war, Tripoli seemed the logical choice for a national capital; however, fearful that naming Tripoli the capital would hinder the rebuilding of Benghazi, the Cyrenaican delegates refused to compromise. Therefore, Tripoli and Benghazi were named joint capitals in an inconvenient, expensive, and inefficient arrangement in which the capital was to alternate year by year (later every two years) between the two (Khadduri 1963: 171–208; Wright 1982a: 68–9; Sury 2003: 186, 189). A little over two months later, King Idris I, on 24 December 1951, only one week before the United Nations deadline, proclaimed the United Kingdom of Libya as a sovereign and independent state.

The United Kingdom of Libya

The United Kingdom of Libya was the fragile product of multiple accords, deals, and compromises, driven by diverse pressures and interests, and most observers were surprised that it survived for more than 17 years. From 1951 to 1969, a total of 11 prime ministers, more than 40 cabinets, and 101 different ministers, many of whom were appointed more than once, displayed an unexpected resilience in dealing with successive internal and external crises (El Fathaly 1977: 26; Wright 1982a: 77; St John 2008a: 109–10). In the process, Libya experienced dramatic socioeconomic and political change even as it brought a measure of stability to the central Mediterranean.

Socioeconomic inheritance

The poorest independent country in the world, Libya in 1951 faced daunting challenges. Upward of 80 percent of the labor force was engaged in agriculture or animal husbandry, activities that yielded pitiful returns at the best of times owing to limited rainfall, tired soil, destructive winds, primitive farming methods, and occasional locust swarms. Moreover, the industrial sector offered even less potential than agriculture. The country lacked raw materials, capital, and skilled manpower, inputs required for a successful industrial base, together with a known power source. In addition to the economic aid provided by friendly countries and international organizations, the Libyan economy in the first decade of independence relied on the export of castor seeds, esparto grass, and the scrap metal salvaged from disabled World War II vehicles (Lewis and Gordon 1954: 43–4; El Fathaly 1977: 16; Ghanem 1982: 149–54).

Along with the widespread destruction of Benghazi and the lesser damage to Tripoli, World War II visited additional problems on the Libyan economy. With the closure of all Italian banks in 1942, Barclays was the only functioning bank during the period of British Military Administration, and it played a highly limited role, functioning largely as a central bank for the military administration. With the banking system shut down and credit nonexistent, commerce was paralyzed in the run-up to independence. The widespread use of land mines during the war – as many as 12,000,000 were planted – further hampered agriculture development as well as air, land, and sea transport. With the balance of trade in deficit in 1943–51, Libya began the independence era with no outstanding public debt only because Western largess covered the trade deficit in the years prior to independence (Lewis and Gordon 1954: 43; Ghanem 1982: 148–9, 154–6).

In turn, the human resources of Libya were handicapped by debilitating quantitative and qualitative restraints. A population of slightly more than 1,000,000 people enjoyed a relatively high birth rate, estimated at 4 percent a year, but primitive living conditions and poor health care facilities resulted in a similar death rate. Consequently, annual population growth did not exceed 1 percent. Qualitative shortcomings were mainly the result of limited educational and vocational training facilities which left 90 percent of the population illiterate at independence. The British Military Administration emphasized secular education, opening 81 primary schools and separating vocational schools from religious educational establishments, and by 1950 more than 200 primary schools with more than 30,000 students were in operation, mostly in Tripoli. Three secondary schools had also opened as well as two teacher training centers and a center for training government employees; nevertheless, only 537 students were attending secondary and technical schools. Despite some progress, the United Nations in 1950 estimated that only 20 percent of school-age children were attending classes. Under the monarchy, severe economic problems, policy disputes, and poor management combined to thwart fresh efforts to develop a high-quality educational system (El Fathaly 1977: 12–15; Monastiri 1982: 316–17; Wright 1985: 46–56).

Political environment

The 1951 constitution established a hereditary monarchy based on Sayyid Muhammad Idris al-Mahdi al-Sanusi and his male successors, descendants of a distinguished North African family which traced its ancestry from the Prophet Muhammad through the Prophet's daughter, Fatima. As head of the Sanusi movement, Sayyid Idris had a strong claim to religious legitimacy. To strengthen further the religious legitimacy of the regime, the political role of the *ulama* (religious scholars) was recognized from the outset in the parliament and in provincial governments. The secular strength of the Idris regime centered on a tribal constituency whose fortunes were tied to the monarchy. Political authority was exercised through local notables and tribal leaders, who served as the link between the head of the system and tribal clans (Sury 2003: 180–1).

In theory, the king was a constitutional monarch, enjoying broad powers as head of state and commander of the armed forces. Inviolable and exempt from all responsibility, his right to issue decrees with the force of law, appoint and remove senior officials, and exercise legislative power in conjunction with the parliament resulted in a system of government dominated by his nominees. The selection of prime ministers and cabinet members was generally based on family, tribal, religious, or regional interests. Of 11 prime ministers appointed, seven were from important tribes, three came from influential families, three were university graduates, two had some administrative experience, and all but one had demonstrated loyalty to the king or his family prior to their appointment (El Fathaly 1977: 26). In theory, the king was the supreme arbiter in national affairs, with no one in or out of government in a position to challenge his ultimate authority. In practice, he devoted much of his time and energy to religious and tribal affairs, made no important policy statements, and seldom commented on public affairs (Villard 1956: 42, 319; El Fathaly and Palmer 1980a: 17; St John 2008a: 114). The king preferred to reside outside Benghazi and Tripoli in Tobruk (later in al-Bayda), where he was removed from the pressures and machinations of the two capitals. Isolated from the daily workings of government, he remained above the political fray, employing a system of palace power and patronage to dissociate himself from direct decision-making. The royal household, concerned with the king's personal and family affairs, and the royal diwan, a palace cabinet through which the king handled the affairs of the kingdom, were key institutions in this system of government (El Fathaly 1977: 24–5; Sury 1982: 122–3).

The parliamentary elections held in February 1952 proved decisive for the monarchy and for democracy in Libya. To this day, the details of the elections remain unclear; however, the results were likely manipulated by the government to ensure the defeat of a National Congress Party favoring a unitary state.

The party's challenge to the federal system posed a direct threat to the Idris regime as it would have moved the center of power from Cyrenaica, the base of the Sanusi Order, the principal interest of the king, and the likely limits of his sense of political community, to Tripolitania, where two-thirds of the population resided. National Congress Party allegations of electoral fraud led to rioting in Tripolitania, and when their protests threatened to expand into a full-scale uprising the government arrested several party leaders and expelled the head of the party. The 1952 electoral crisis destroyed effective, legitimate political opposition just as a democratic, parliamentary system was emerging. Thereafter, the obsequious parliament was little more than a rubber stamp for what the king and the royal diwan decided (Khadduri 1963: 217–20; Vandewalle 1998: 47; Sury 2003: 187–8). The year 1952 also marked the last time multiparty elections were held in Libya.

With the dissolution of the National Congress Party, political parties were outlawed, demonstrations banned, newspapers censored, and organized opposition suppressed. Libyan politics morphed into a kind of benign despotism, a contest of family, tribal, and parochial interests in which networks of kinship and clan became the principal structure for political competition. Instead of relying on ideological loyalty and administrative competence, the monarchy delegated authority to an oligarchy of powerful families and commercial interests, who consolidated their economic and political positions through intermarriage. Most Libyans rightly concluded that only a few families controlled the country and determined its destiny; nonetheless, the government was mostly immune to challenge from the base because the widespread ignorance of the masses, coupled with their passivity, conformity, and pervasive sense of fatalism, made it difficult for them to question the traditional system (Alexander 1981a: 210; Anderson 1990: 293–6; Sury 2003: 182–4, 190).

During the first decade of independence, four governments sitting in two national and three provincial capitals ruled Libya. There were 15 federal ministries with an average of eight in each of the provinces, and both Cyrenaica and Tripolitania employed more civil servants than the federal government. By the end of the decade, the government had become the largest employer in the country, with a payroll estimated at 12 percent of gross national product (GNP). Under the federal formula, liaison between federal and provincial governments and among the three provincial governments was poor, resulting in contradictory policies and a duplication of services. Matters came to a head in the early 1960s, when expanding oil revenues began coursing through the state's weakly developed economic institutions, highlighting the conflicting levels of jurisdiction and decision-making that characterized the interplay between the federal and provincial governments. After a decade of study, the federal system was finally abandoned in 1962–3 in favor of a unitary state. In December 1962, provincial administrators were subordinated to the federal government, and in April 1963 federal and provincial administrations were abolished with their powers combined into one central government. At the lower level, 10 administrative units (*muhafadah*) replaced the three provinces of Cyrenaica, Fezzan, and Tripolitania. With the change to a unitary state, the United Kingdom of Libya was renamed The Kingdom of Libya (Wright 1982a: 97–8; Sury 2003: 189; Vandewalle 2006: 63–4).

The replacement of the federal formula with a unitary form of government was the single most important political event to occur in 1951–69 as it provided a test case for whether the country could become a unified economic and political community. In theory, the move to a unitary state promised to improve governance, streamline cumbersome systems, and cut administrative costs. In practice, the amended constitution centralized state authority at the expense of the provinces and municipalities, vastly increasing the power of the king and the royal diwan. After 1963, a small group of people, driven mostly by self-interest, made all important decisions, and advancement in the public arena depended largely on background and connections. Patronage and other distributive mechanisms, such as food program subsidies, interest-free loans, and educational allowances, were employed on a massive scale at all levels of government to channel wealth and maintain political quiescence (Vandewalle 2006: 65–7, 73–4). In the process, the number of people employed by the government increased to 12 percent of the labor force, the highest level in the world (El Fathaly 1977: 27). Yet, even as the bureaucracies mushroomed, a national political identity centered on them failed to emerge.

Ties to the West

Throughout the first decade of independence, Libya maintained a generally Western orientation, and the Idris regime was widely viewed as one of the most conservative governments in the Arab world. Thought to lack natural resources, Libya's diplomatic orientation rested heavily on the income and developmental assistance generated by the American and British bases in the country. The United Kingdom concluded a 20-year treaty of friendship and alliance with Libya on 29 July 1953, in which the former received extensive extraterritorial and jurisdictional rights in return for financial aid and military training (Khadduri 1963: 363–82; Deeb 1991: 30–1). A little more than a year later, the United States, on 9 September 1954, also concluded a treaty of friendship and mutual support with Libya, scheduled to last until 24 December 1970. Under the terms of this agreement, the United States secured military base rights at Wheelus Field and other designated facilities in return for economic, technical, and military assistance (Ben-Halim 1998: 122–5; St John 2002: 66–70). By the end of 1959, the United States had extended over $100 million in financial assistance, making Libya the largest per capita recipient of US aid in the world (Vandewalle 2006: 45).

France hoped to negotiate a base agreement with Libya similar to those negotiated by the United Kingdom and United States; however, events in Algeria frustrated its plans. In late 1954, Libya agreed to allow Egypt to ship supplies through its territory to Algeria, where the war of independence had just begun. At the same time, Libya began pressuring France to evacuate its garrisons in Fezzan, troops well placed to intercept the flow of men and material from Egypt to Algeria. Eventually, on 10 August 1955, Libya reached an agreement with France which provided for the evacuation of all French forces by November 1956. In the agreement, France promised substantial development aid to Libya in return for transit rights and the rectification of Libya's borders in favor of French territories in Africa (Khadduri 1963: 258–61; Ben-Halim 1998: 147–76).

In October 1956, Libya concluded an agreement with Italy that belatedly confirmed the earlier transfer of most Italian public property to Libya and brought $7.7 million in aid in return for Libyan recognition of certain Italian commercial rights. Italy also agreed to spend some $3.7 million to complete several colonization schemes in Tripolitania, with the understanding that Italian colonists would become the outright owners of the land and be free to sell it to Libyans and transfer the capital (Wright 1982a: 85). At the same time, Italy rejected Libyan claims for compensation for damages stemming from the colonial occupation and World War II, insisting that the agreed-upon payments be described in the accord as a contribution to the economic reconstruction of Libya. The ambiguous wording of the 1956 agreement, in particular its failure to tie the payments to indemnification, exposed Italy after 1969 to additional demands for reparations by the revolutionary government (Del Boca 2003: 26–7). By October 1961, around two-thirds of the Italians in the settlement projects had sold their land to Libyans, and by 1964 only 120 colonist families remained in Tripolitania (Wright 1982a: 85).

Diplomatic and commercial relations with the Soviet Union were minimal throughout the period of monarchical rule. The Soviets vetoed Libyan membership in the United Nations from 1951 to 1955, when Libya finally established diplomatic relations with the Soviet Union, paving the way for Libyan admission to the UN as part of a package deal that included 15 other states. Uncomfortable with a Communist presence in its midst, Libya refrained for the remainder of the decade from accepting economic aid from the Soviet Union (Ben-Halim 1998: 99–101, 128–32). In the 1960s, commercial and diplomatic links expanded, with the Soviets participating in the annual Tripoli Trade Fair and a bilateral trade pact being concluded in 1963. Libyan parliamentary delegations also visited the Soviet Union in 1961 and 1968, following the visit of a Supreme Soviet delegation to Libya in 1966 (Khadduri 1963: 261–4; St John 1982: 132; De Candole 1990: 124–5).

Development of the Libyan oil industry

Oil deposits in commercially viable quantities were first discovered in Libya in 1959, when American prospectors confirmed their location in two separate locations in the Sirte Basin. The following decade witnessed dramatic increases in both production and revenues, but not in the posted price of oil, the basis of taxable income for producing countries. Like most Arab oil-producing states, Libya considered the posted price to be undervalued and unjust, but it continued to accept a volume-oriented policy out of fear that a confrontation with the oil companies over posted price levels might slow the momentum of industry development. Libya joined the Organization of the Petroleum Exporting Countries (OPEC) in 1962, two years after the organization was founded to stabilize, if not increase, the posted price of oil. For the remainder of the decade, Libya supported select OPEC policies, but it refused to endorse any policy change that might jeopardize its relationship with the oil companies (Ghanem 1985a: 158–63; Gurney 1996: 49–52).

The exploitation of Libyan oil deposits by the monarchy proved paradoxical in that it freed Libya from one form of dependence, the income from military bases, only to replace it with another. In order to develop its hydrocarbon resources, Libya had to remain on friendly terms with the West to encourage exploration and investment as well as to gain access to the technicians and technology of Western oil companies. The downstream importance of the oil companies was obvious as early as 1957, two years before the discovery of commercially viable petroleum deposits, when foreign oil companies spent $43.4 million in Libya compared with foreign aid in fiscal year 1957–8 of only $38.32 million. The subsequent discovery of oil increased public interest in greater independence from the West, but, at the same time, it bound Libya more closely to the latter because it depended on the West to provide the financial and technical assistance necessary to develop its oil reserves (Waddams 1980: 73–82; Wright 1982a: 87).

In addition to enriching the government, mounting oil revenues awakened the political consciousness of the populace, sparking a revolution in rising expectations and drawing attention to the highly conservative nature of the Idris regime. Per capita income increased from around $35 in 1951 to some $2,000 in 1969, but the per capita figures were misleading, and the bulk of the population did not prosper. Whereas the populace expected oil wealth to result in vastly improved personal circumstances, expanding oil revenues led to rapidly growing economic disparities among individual Libyans and between the three provinces (El Mallakh 1969: 313–16; Ghanem 1987: 58–62; Vandewalle 2006: 63). In the process, the rise in oil revenues, accompanied by improving economic conditions and greater social mobility, increased demands for an ideology that would satisfy new, albeit vaguely understood, spiritual and political yearnings. The Idris regime sought to respond to these needs, but in the end it failed to understand and accommodate them. By the end of the decade, increasing numbers of Libyans, especially the younger, more articulate segments in the urban areas of Tripolitania, had concluded that the domestic and foreign policies of the monarchy were parochial, if not corrupt, and must be changed (Cecil 1965: 32–3; Wright 1982a: 100–2; Sury 2003: 184–5).

The rapid growth of oil revenues also increased opportunities for groups and individuals to use oil income for personal advancement and enrichment. In a centralized political system, influential tribal leaders, powerful families, the royal diwan, and Sanusi family members effectively controlled the economic bureaucracy. As opportunities for bribery, corruption, graft, and nepotism multiplied, they undermined the well-intentioned, if sometimes ill-advised, policies of the government to develop the economic and social infrastructure of Libya. With corruption rampant and the resultant economic differentiation plainly visible, the centralized political system reduced the bulk of the population to the role of impotent bystanders, intensifying feelings of frustration and alienation with the system (First 1974: 81–2; Wright 1982a: 89; Vandewalle 1998: 54–6).

Competing ideologies

As it struggled to address an increasing number of domestic crises, the monarchy was enmeshed in the growing politicization of the Arab world. Contemporary events, such as the Palestine conflict, colonial struggles in neighboring states, renewed Soviet interest in the region, the growth of pan-Arabism, and anti-royalist movements throughout the Middle East, were not propitious for the development of a traditional monarchy. With its dependence on income from foreign military bases fostering a policy of support for the West, the Idris regime quickly exhausted its limited anti-colonialist credits. At the same time, the highly limited legitimizing force of Libyan nationalism, stemming from the attainment of independence, was challenged internally by opposition groups and externally by pan-Arab movements. In the process, the related issues of foreign bases and external aid regularly exposed the most obvious weakness of the monarchy's foreign policy, its vulnerability to decisions taken by others (First 1974: 83–4; Alexander 1981b: 821–4; Vandewalle 2006: 69–70).

Although the existence of American and British bases and the substantial remuneration derived from them led many critics to conclude that the monarchy was pro-Western, it was never as pro-Western as its many detractors claimed. Out of necessity, the monarchy maintained a close relationship with the West, but its approach was based not on an ideological commitment to Western ideals, traditions, and policies, but on the belief that the Western powers could best guarantee Libyan security. Within Libya, the monarchy worked to minimize the impact of Western sociopolitical values and structures, and externally it emphasized nonalignment in regional and international bodies, such as the Organization of African Unity and the United Nations (St John 1987a: 15).

As oil revenues increased, many Libyans, especially younger ones, were eager for social and political change, seeking an inclusive ideology that would explain and satisfy their demands. For them, Arab nationalism appeared to supply answers to the political divisions bedeviling the region and also to the socio-economic issues tied to them (Roumani 1973: 350; St John 1987a: 17; Sury 1982: 128–30). Ironically, the expanding Libyan school system was an early source of Arab nationalist thinking. Short of trained Libyan teachers, the monarchy looked to Egypt to supply both teachers and textbooks, and the curriculum that the Egyptians brought to Libya amounted to a form of pedagogical imperialism. Libyan adoption of Egyptian administrative and judicial models, widespread access to Egyptian newspapers and Radio Cairo's *Voice of the Arabs*, and young Libyans studying in Egypt compounded the problem of Egyptian influence. In monarchical Libya, Nasser's portrait was almost as widely displayed as that of the king (Norman 1965: 66, 69–70; Wright 1982a: 94; Obeidi 2001: 37).

Student demonstrations broke out in Benghazi and Tripoli in January 1964 in support of an Arab summit in Cairo and to protest Israeli plans to divert water from the Jordan River to the Negev Desert. The demonstrations intensified the following month after Nasser called for the liquidation of the American and British bases in Libya on the grounds that they were a threat to the Arab cause and intended to support Israel. In support of these allegations, Radio Cairo repeated the false charge that the foreign bases had been used against Egypt in the 1956 Anglo-French invasion of the Suez Canal (Pargeter 2000: 41–58). In an effort to placate its critics, the monarchy asked the United Kingdom and the United States to reconsider their future status at those bases. In response, the United States accepted in principle a withdrawal from Wheelus Field. The British took more aggressive action, withdrawing most of their forces from Tripolitania by 1966 and completing their evacuation from Cyrenaica in March 1970 (Ben-Halim 1998: 87–9, 96–7; Sury 2003: 190). Fresh demonstrations occurred in 1965 over the issue of retaining diplomatic ties with West Germany after it established relations with Israel. Although Libya withdrew its ambassador to Germany in protest, it was one of the few Arab states not to break diplomatic relations (St John 1987a: 15; Ben-Halim 1998: 87–9, 96–7).

The year 1967 was a pivotal one for the monarchy as its weak response to the June 1967 War, following its falsely criticized reaction to the 1956 Suez Crisis, was the catalyst for the 1969 *coup d'état* that removed it from power. With Egypt blaming its sudden defeat on the United Kingdom and the United States, public reaction in Libya to the war was widespread, prolonged, and violent, especially in Benghazi and Tripoli (Lewis 1970: 36; Sury 2003: 192–3). The monarchy's response included a veiled threat to close Wheelus Field, and it also joined Saudi Arabia and the Gulf states in shutting down oil production for a brief period. In the wake of these tentative steps, the prime minister was forced to resign in the face of widespread criticism that Libya had not done enough to assist its Arab brethren in the Arab–Israeli conflict. Thereafter, the monarchy continued to portray itself as a strong supporter of Arab causes, but it did not take a more aggressive role in Arab politics in general or the Palestinian issue in particular (St John 1987a: 15–16; De Candole 1990: 141). In the interim, two distinct opposition groups had emerged in Libya by the end of the June 1967 War. The first was an Arab nationalist movement which, despite its secrecy, attracted a surprising number of followers, particularly among students and oil industry workers. The second group was Libyan nationalist in orientation and emphasized the need to develop and modernize the country (Djaziri 1995: 181).

Conclusions

The United Nations in 1951 created a Libyan state without a strong Libyan nationhood. Over a few short years, a system of democratic governance which had taken the West centuries to develop was created and imposed on a traditional, hierarchical, and authoritarian society. Ties between the government and the population were weak, and essential elements of this new system of government, such as the separation of powers, free elections, checks and balances, political parties, and freedom of assembly and speech, were neither understood nor realized by the Idris regime.

Given the fragile nature of the monarchy, its survival for almost 18 years was due in large part to the fragmented nature of Libyan society. The Libyan elite exhibited agreement, at least officially, on most public policy issues, but the general populace more often lacked consensus on the direction and content of policy. With the polity absent social as well as political cohesion, the masses not yet mobilized in support of the goals of socioeconomic modernization, political parties proscribed, and the threat of coercion lurking in the background, Libyans lacked the means necessary to express collective dissent.

The most notable feature of the absolutist political system in place in Libya was its isolation from society at large. The power elite consisted of King Idris, a small coterie of retainers in the court entourage, and a revolving door of ministers. Employing a system of divide and rule, the aged king and his aides skillfully played personalities and institutions off against each other, using various centers of power, such as the royal diwan, parliament, and provincial governments for this purpose. Another distinctive feature of the political system was the physical remoteness of the king, who preferred to stand apart from the day-to-day pressures of government. Bemused by religious and scholarly pursuits, he left the management of public policy to his ministers, an arrangement that led to frustration, corruption, and frequent crisis. The absolutist system also lacked viability as King Idris had no heirs; therefore, the question of succession was clouded. The heir apparent, Hassan al-Rida, a nephew of the king with a lackluster personality, was known as the man without a shadow. Of course, the actions of King Idris added to the air of instability as he offered his resignation on several occasions after 1951, enhancing his image as a detached, reluctant ruler.

As oil revenues expanded, the rapidly transforming economy produced a dramatic restructuring of Libyan society, which led to calls for change that proved well beyond the capacity of the monarchy to manage. From an immature ideology centered on unity and independence with the king as a national symbol, a degree of Libyan nationalism had begun to develop, but it was seldom vital enough to satisfy most Libyans, especially younger ones. As the economy improved, the monarchy concentrated on the provision of increased material benefits, misreading the depth of popular sentiment and underestimating the need of its citizens for ideological fulfillment. The cautious pace of the monarchy remained incongruous with mounting popular demand for rapid change, and the instruments in the power of the monarchy, including the repressive elements of the police and security forces, proved unable to bridge the distance between the polarized forces of the country. Lured from traditional agricultural and animal husbandry endeavors to a rapid urbanization plagued with corrupt bureaucratization, more and more Libyans found themselves disconnected from their past yet unprepared for any future other than Western-style consumerism. As a result, Libyan society as a whole was largely adrift by the end of the 1960s.

On 1 September 1969, a small group of Libyan army officers, known as the Free Unionist Officers, executed a successful *coup d'état* against the aging monarchy and initiated a radical reorientation of domestic and foreign policy. Led by a 12-man central committee that designated itself the Revolutionary Command Council (RCC), the composition and leadership of the movement was at first anonymous. This changed when the RCC issued a terse statement, announcing the promotion of Captain Muammar al-Qaddafi to the rank of colonel and his appointment as commander-in-chief of the armed forces. Abroad at the time for medical treatment, King Idris settled in Egypt, living in exile in Cairo until his death on 25 May 1983 at age 94.

3

POLITICS

The Revolutionary Command Council (RCC) in the early days of the revolution focused on two goals, consolidation of its revolutionary authority and the socioeconomic and political modernization of the country. To advance these objectives, the RCC moved to increase the mobilization and participation of the general populace as it worked to improve the technical capacities and responsiveness of governmental institutions. Like most revolutionary movements, the central problem it faced in achieving these objectives was the difficulty involved in creating an institutional framework that generated the desired levels of mobilization and participation but did so within the centralized political system deemed necessary to retain control of the revolution.

From *coup d'état* to revolution

The *coup d'état* on 1 September 1969 surprised few observers as the overthrow of the monarchy had been anticipated for months. The only surprise came in the executors of the coup, as no one anticipated a bold stroke by a group of junior army officers intent on conducting a broad socioeconomic and political revolution (Yergin 1991: 577; St John 2008a: 139–40). Although the leadership of the coup was kept secret for a time, it soon became apparent that most of the Free Unionist Officers, including the 12 members of the RCC, shared similar backgrounds, motivations, and worldviews. Only two of the RCC members came from major tribes, and only one came from a prominent, well-to-do coastal family. The remainder came from minor, less well-to-do tribes of the interior or the poorer social strata of coastal towns. For this reason, some observers characterized the overthrow of the monarchy as a revolution of the oases and the interior against the dominant tribes and more established families of the coast (First 1974: 115; Ahmida 2005: 79).

In many respects, Muammar al-Qaddafi and the other members of the RCC were an uncanny reflection of the people they claimed to represent. Born in 1942, Qaddafi at the time of the coup was 27 years of age in a youthful country in which half the population was under 15 and only 10 percent was over 50 years of age. The only surviving son of a poor nomadic family in Sirte, the border region between Cyrenaica and Tripolitania, Qaddafi attended primary and secondary schools in Sirte, Sebha, and Misurata before enrolling in the military academy in Benghazi (Bianco 1975: 3–32; Muscat 1980: 21–81). Like many Libyans, he combined rural origins with substantial urban residence in a country where one-third of the population resided in Tripoli alone by the 1970s. Enjoying regular access to Egyptian newspapers and radio broadcasts, especially the *Voice of the Arabs* news program, Qaddafi's interest in the Egyptian revolution was stimulated by his Egyptian teachers in Sebha. Reflecting this influence, a junior American diplomat, meeting Qaddafi for the first time only days after the coup, noted that he spoke excellent Arabic, just like a *Voice of the Arabs* announcer (St John 2008a: 135–9). What separated him from most of his generation was his determination to bring the Egyptian revolution to Libya. Qaddafi also shared with many Libyans an ambivalence regarding loyalties to his kin. On the one hand, he was extremely proud of his tribal heritage and background and, on the other, he initially rejected tribalism as a suitable political foundation for a modern state (Anderson 1986a: 260–1; El-Kikhia 1997: 41).

First steps

The One September Revolution was totally military in conception, planning, and execution. It was implemented without the support or knowledge of any civilian group, and for a time the RCC insisted on maintaining its military composition, direction, and leadership. The members of the RCC retained their military ranks, after promoting themselves one or more times, and they normally wore uniforms when appearing in public to stress military affiliation, support, and discipline. In Qaddafi's case, he promoted himself to the rank of colonel, the rank held by Gamal Abdel Nasser when he seized power in Egypt in 1952 (Ansell and al-Arif 1972: 63). From the outset, the RCC assumed all executive and legislative functions, promulgating new laws through decrees that became effective as soon as they were gazetted. Later, civilians were brought into the administration to assist in operating the government; however, the RCC continued to reserve for itself supreme authority in all aspects of governance (Qaddafi 1973a: 131–2).

The One September Revolution unleashed a wave of popular enthusiasm and support throughout Libya. The positive reaction to the coup reflected a widespread desire for change, albeit not necessarily support for the largely unknown Qaddafi group (Roumani 1983: 152). Like the monarchy, the RCC prohibited the formation of autonomous political parties or organizations. Qaddafi later condemned political parties as dictatorial instruments of governing which enabled a part of the population to rule over the whole (Qaddafi

1976: 23–35). The decision to maintain the ban on political parties highlighted an early contradiction of the revolution. The RCC portrayed itself as close to the people, mirroring their thoughts and wishes, but it clearly distrusted them and refused to allow them to share power. The first rule of the revolution was total dominance by the armed forces as confirmed by the leadership of the RCC (Qaddafi 1970: 204).

The Libyan *coup d'état* shared obvious similarities in planning and execution with Nasser's 1952 coup, and the dependence of the Free Unionist Officers on the Egyptian model was even more noticeable when they began to issue policy statements. The RCC declared the new republic to be opposed to any form of imperialism or colonialism and neutral in great power disputes. In addition, it stated its intention to become more active in promoting Arab nationalism and in supporting the Palestinian cause (Qaddafi 1970: 211–12, 218–19; First 1974: 116–17). The RCC also mirrored the Egyptian experience in that it created a new organization to convey its programs to the Libyan people. In so doing, Qaddafi repeatedly stressed that the creation of a new society would require the dismantling of existing administrative structures at all levels and their replacement by new institutions and administrators better suited to a modernizing society (Qaddafi 1970: 205–7). Relying on the loyalty of the officer corps, the efficiency of the security services, and a police force recruited from minor tribes, the RCC immediately began to implement the basic socioeconomic and political changes necessary to turn a *coup d'état* into a revolution (Roumani 1973: 352).

At the outset, the RCC was a relatively closed organization; however, it soon became apparent that Qaddafi was its chairman and the de facto head of state. The other members of the RCC were not named and pictured in the *Official Gazette* until 10 January 1970, more than four months after the coup (St John 2008a: 134). The RCC gave the appearance of a collegial decision-making body, but this appearance was deceptive as Qaddafi from the start was more than first among equals. Well before entering the military academy, he concluded that only the armed forces could oust the monarchy, and he began organizing the Free Unionist Officers in October 1959 (El Fathaly and Palmer 1980a: 38–9). Responsible for planning and executing the *coup d'état*, he was the dominant figure among the Free Unionist Officers and the chief ideological innovator on the RCC. Qaddafi soon became the public face of the revolution, and by 1975 he had taken total control of it (St John 1987a: 11–12).

Ideology of the revolution

Qaddafi delivered his first major address in mid-September 1969, attacking the old social order and calling for radical change in the socioeconomic and political system. He also introduced related ideological themes which he later expanded. He described the events of 1 September 1969 not as a *coup d'état*, but as the onset of a much broader revolution. Declaring imperialism and Zionism to be the enemies of the revolution, he warned Libyans that the struggle against them was just beginning. Throughout the speech, the revolutionary goals of freedom, socialism, and unity were used repeatedly to reference the direction domestic and foreign policies would take (Qaddafi 1973a).

Like President Nasser, Qaddafi based his brand of Arab nationalism on a glorification of Arab history and culture that viewed the Arabic-speaking world as the Arab nation. As the custodian of Arab nationalism, Libya was the heart, vanguard, and hope of the Arab nation (Libyan Arab Republic 1973a: 10–11). The backwardness of the Arab nation was the product of four centuries of stagnation under Ottoman rule, the exploitation of first colonialism and later imperialism, and the repressive corruption of reactionary monarchical rule (Ansell and al-Arif 1972: 79, 83). At the core of Qaddafi's Arab nationalism was the firm belief that Arabs were equal or superior to other peoples of the world and enjoyed the duty and the right to manage their own resources and shape their own destiny (Qaddafi 1973b: 27–32).

Initially, Qaddafi concentrated on symbolic acts of national independence, which were widely popular and increased the legitimacy of the regime. The RCC ordered that signs, cards, and tickets should be printed only in Arabic, and it decreed the mandatory translation into Arabic of foreign passports and initiated a campaign for the adoption of Arabic as an official international language. The RCC also banned the consumption of alcohol and any public entertainment that might be considered pornographic, obscene, or vulgar (Qaddafi 1973b: 28–9). Of little practical value, policies like these were of enormous symbolic importance because they highlighted the regime's support for indigenous values and helped to establish its religious credentials. Qaddafi's emphasis on freedom also reflected the experiences of his tribe, which originated near where the Italians had established concentration camps in the 1920s (Ahmida 2005: 43–54). Later, the regime supported the efforts of investigative units, such as the Libyan Studies Center, to write revisionist histories of Libya, depicting a cohesive and nationalist society loyal to Arab and Muslim culture and opposed to Western imperialism (Anderson 1991b: 84–7).

Qaddafi also pressed for the early termination of the military base agreements negotiated by the United Kingdom and the United States in 1953 and 1954 respectively and due to expire in the 1970s. Once this was achieved, March 28, the day the British evacuated Al-Adem Base, and June 11, the day the Americans evacuated Wheelus Field, became annual holidays, normally accompanied by a nationalistic address by Qaddafi. Similarly, October 7, the day Italian-owned assets were confiscated and Italian nationals expelled, was also declared a national holiday (Ashiurakis 1976: 82–7).

If Arab nationalism was the core element of Qaddafi's ideology, *jihad* was its action element. Believing *jihad* to be the optimum means to achieve social justice in and out of Libya, Qaddafi saw *jihad* to liberate the oppressed peoples of the world as a duty and Islamic *jihad* to recuperate Palestine as an obligation for every Muslim. Initially, he considered communism to be the most serious problem facing mankind, but, over time, he increasingly identified imperialism

J. had =
supp for
IRA

as the principal target of *jihad* (Qaddafi 1973b: 51–5). This concept of *jihad* led him to support a diverse range of so-called liberation movements, including the Somali National Salvation Front, the Irish Republican Army, and Muslim separatist groups in the Philippines (Libyan Arab Republic 1973a: 4, 19–22).

In January 1970, the RCC lent practical support to the emphasis on *jihad* with the creation of a Jihad Fund to support armed struggle for the liberation of usurped Arab lands from Zionist control (Ansell and al-Arif 1972: 115–17). The Jihad Fund reflected Qaddafi's view that the Palestinian issue was the primary threat to the integrity of Islam and the Arab world (Libyan Arab Republic 1973b: 220). Advocating direct military action against Israel, he provided fervent support for Palestinian groups long after the Palestinian Liberation Organization (PLO) had turned to less militant means (Qaddafi 1975: 48–9).

The positive neutrality often espoused by other Arab revolutionary movements was also an integral part of Qaddafi's ideology. Like Nasser, he proclaimed a policy of absolute neutrality between East and West and professed a belief in Third World causes (Qaddafi 1970: 211–12). Critical of both communism and capitalism, he dismissed them as two sides of the same coin, and for a time Libyan policy toward the two states followed a dichotomous pattern. Opposed to US foreign policy, Libya for years maintained close commercial ties with the West, selling most of its oil to Europe or the United States and using the proceeds to purchase Western technology. Qaddafi was also critical of the Soviet Union, especially the atheist aspect of communism and the policy of allowing Soviet Jews to immigrate to Israel; nevertheless, Libya purchased Soviet technology, especially military hardware, in massive amounts (Qaddafi 1973b: 9–14, 23–6).

In the twentieth century, socialism was a central element of most revolutionary ideologies, particularly in the Arab world, and Libya was no exception. Trumpeting socialism as the solution to the world's economic problems, Qaddafi often discussed socialism in terms of social justice to distinguish it from classical European socialism as well as from common Arab usage, which often has connoted little more than nonmonarchical government (Libyan Arab Republic 1973a: 3–9). In order to achieve socialism through social justice, the One September Revolution aimed to eliminate socioeconomic exploitation, provide equal access to law, ensure a more equitable distribution of wealth, and eliminate class differences. Like Nasser, Qaddafi also gave his brand of socialism a strong Islamic base, arguing that Islam was a socialist creed and that Libyan socialism was the socialism of Islam (Qaddafi 1973a: 132–3; Libyan Arab Republic 1974: 8–9). At the same time, Libyan socialism differed from most other Arab socialist movements in that it had great wealth behind it from the start.

Unity was both a national and an international goal. At the national level, the RCC viewed unity in the context of unifying society in purpose and effort through a centralized political authority. Internationally, the RCC denounced regionalism as an innovation imposed by imperialism and maintained by its agents, electing to pursue the elusive, shop-worn goal of Arab unity (Qaddafi 1973a: 133). In so doing, Qaddafi and his colleagues took their lead from the

Arab nationalist views of the fiery Egyptian school of the 1950s and 1960s, not the more moderate Nasser of the post-1967 War period. The members of the RCC believed that Arab unity was a practical, realistic, and achievable goal that should be pursued with messianic zeal (Qaddafi 1975: 67–90).

Like most revolutionaries, Qaddafi and his RCC colleagues professed to be fresh and innovative when in fact their early statements contained much that was old and little that was new. It has long been commonplace for revolutionary governments to attack the past to justify the present, and it is also quite ordinary to invoke traditional values and an historical heritage in support of a new regime. In a similar vein, past revolutionary governments have often overemphasized for political purposes the dependence and corruption of the monarchy they replaced. As for the revolutionary trinity of unity, freedom, and socialism, it was a theme of the Baath Party as early as 1946 and was later adopted, albeit in the revised order of freedom, socialism, and unity, by the Egyptian government after 1952. Moreover, the theme of pan-Arabism was constant in Baath Party literature by 1945 and a leitmotiv of the Nasser regime after 1952. Overall, most of Qaddafi's early pronouncements bore an uncanny resemblance to the ideologies of previous revolutionary governments. This championing of old and often tired ideas was doubly significant because Qaddafi was speaking decades after his predecessors had first articulated them, and in some areas, such as Arab unity, long after they had been widely discredited elsewhere in the Arab world (St John 1983a: 472–3).

Constitutional proclamation (1969)

On 11 December 1969, the RCC canceled the 7 October 1951 constitution, issuing a temporary constitutional proclamation that gave legal expression to central elements of Qaddafi's nascent ideology. The preamble summarized the revolution's goals as freedom, socialism, and unity, emphasizing the regime's intent to fight reactionary forces and colonialism and to eliminate all obstacles to Arab unity. Article 1 described the newly coined Libyan Arab Republic as an Arab, democratic, and free republic that was part of the Arab nation and committed to comprehensive Arab unity. It also described Libya as part of Africa, a concept which took on new meaning in the late 1970s when Qaddafi's practical efforts at Arab unity faltered, and he looked at pan-African or pan-Islamic unity as an option. Article 2 described Arabic as the official language and Islam as the religion of the state; however, it gave no real indication as to the strong emphasis on Islam which would characterize the Libyan revolution, differentiating it from those in Algeria, Egypt, Iraq, Syria, and Tunisia. In suggesting that the state would protect the freedom of religious ceremonies, this article also failed to suggest the full extent to which the revolutionary government would later employ Islam for political ends (Farley 1971: 313–14).

Eight of the remaining 15 articles in the first chapter of the constitutional proclamation dealt with aspects of socialism. Grounded in the principle of social justice, Article 6 gave socialism a practical application in the form of self-sufficiency in production and equity in distribution, goals the regime struggled to achieve. Articles 7 and 8 promised to free the economy from foreign influence, suggesting that public ownership was the optimum path to develop society and achieve self-sufficiency in production. At the same time, the regime guaranteed a place for what it termed "unexploiting" private ownership in the new economic system, a pledge it would later fail to keep. Article 12 declared homes to be inviolable, once again a pledge the regime did not keep. Articles 14 and 15 declared education and medical care to be rights of all citizens (Farley 1971: 314–16).

The 15 articles constituting the second chapter of the constitutional proclamation outlined the structure of the government. Assigned both executive and legislative functions, the RCC was the highest authority in the state, responsible for deciding general policies on behalf of the people. Article 19 provided for a cabinet, consisting of a prime minister and other ministers, appointed by the RCC and responsible to it. Other articles assigned to the RCC the key functions of government, such as ratification of the national budget and control of the armed forces. Article 28 described the judiciary as independent, but this was never the case. The third and final chapter nullified the 7 October 1951 constitution, indicating that the constitutional proclamation would be effective until a permanent constitution was adopted (Farley 1971: 317–20).

Mobilization versus control

After seizing power, the RCC moved to solidify its control of the revolution by reducing regional and tribal power and identification, increasing political mobilization, and implanting new local leadership supportive of revolutionary goals. Every effort was made to tie the traditional leadership to the former colonial powers and to the negative aspects of the former regime, especially its corrupt systems and practices (El Fathaly and Abusedra 1977: 39–41). In so doing, the RCC correctly assumed that traditional rural elites would not support its goal of rapid socioeconomic and political modernization, an assumption the RCC shared with modernizing leaders in other Arab states, such as Algeria, Egypt, Syria, and Tunisia. A regime-sponsored research product conducted in Zavia province in the summer and fall of 1973 found that the hostility of traditional elites to modernizing institutions was both direct and explicit, confirming the early assumptions of the RCC (El Fathaly and Palmer 1980b: 247–61).

To reduce the influence of traditional leaders and their families, the RCC changed the administrative and political boundaries of Libya and appointed a new type of local leadership. Ancient tribal areas were divided into new administrative zones, based largely on population and geography, which crossed old tribal boundaries and combined different tribes into one zone (Joffé 1995: 145). In terms of reducing regional identity and the social and political power that accompanied it, the creation of new administrative areas was particularly effective when it was accompanied by supportive actions, such as changing the title of sheik to zone administrator. As this process continued, the RCC decreed that activities in the social, economic, and religious spheres that were formerly the prerequisites of tribal sheiks were now functions of the new zone administrators. In making these changes, the RCC demonstrated an understanding of the impact that socioeconomic and political structures had on development and of the consequent need to change traditional structures to accomplish their development goals (El Fathaly and Abusedra 1977: 40–1; El Fathaly and Palmer 1980a: 75–90).

On the other hand, the RCC failed to recognize the negative impact that its preoccupation with controlling the revolution would have on the ability of the freshly minted modernizers to effect change in these areas. Generally lacking the backgrounds and attitudes required to generate mobilization and participation, the new administrators were perceived by the general public to be poor community leaders. The reluctance of the RCC to delegate authority, especially to civilians, contributed to the failure of the modernizing leaders. Recognizing that its new system of regional and local governments was not mobilizing the level of popular support necessary to transform traditional society into a modern socialist state, the RCC scrapped the policy of appointing modernizing administrators less than two years after its initiation (El Fathaly and Palmer 1977a: 58–9).

On 11 June 1971, Qaddafi announced the formation of the Arab Socialist Union (ASU), an official mass mobilization party patterned after the Egyptian body of the same name. Organized from village to national level, the RCC hoped that the ASU would become the primary link between the people and the central government, filling the void left by the abolition of the tribal system. In the ASU, the RCC sought to create an organization through which the general populace could be motivated, mobilized, and politicized at the same time. The ASU also promised a pervasive network of organizations capable of observing and reporting on citizens at all levels of Libyan society and providing a reliable source of organized support for the regime (El Fathaly and Abusedra 1977: 22; Djaziri 1995: 183).

Designed to meet Egyptian needs, the Libyan variant of the ASU was stillborn. Unable to resolve the inherent contradiction of being both a reflection of regime interests and sensitive to local demands, the rigid direction maintained by the RCC stifled local initiative and suffocated local leadership (First 1974: 131–2). Operating in parallel with bodies already established by the RCC, the ASU was undermined by existing state institutions, which viewed it as a competitor. Moreover, the ASU organizers failed to cooperate with the modernizing administrators appointed after October 1969, who also viewed the new body as a competitor. Related shortcomings included a failure to understand the traditionalism of the citizenry, negative preconceptions based on the performance of its Egyptian counterpart, and a structure too complex for a people unfamiliar with modern organizations (El Fathaly and Palmer 1980a: 99–103).

The Third Universal Theory

By late 1972, Qaddafi had begun to give the tenets of his revolutionary approach a theoretical underpinning in what came to be known as the Third Universal Theory (also found as Third International Theory). As the title suggests, the new theory sought to develop an alternative to capitalism and communism, competing doctrines that Qaddafi rejected as unsuitable to the Libyan milieu (Libyan Arab Republic 1974: 3–4). The Third Universal Theory condemned both communism and capitalism, the former as a monopoly of state ownership and the latter as a monopoly of individuals and companies. Grouping the Soviet Union and the United States together as two imperialist countries intent on developing spheres of interest in the Arab world, Qaddafi also denounced the atheist nature of the Soviet regime (Qaddafi 1973b: 8–17, 27–8, 53–5).

Qaddafi grounded the Third Universal Theory in nationalism and religion, the two forces which he recognized as the paramount drives moving history and humankind. He viewed nationalism as the natural product of the cultural and racial diversity of the world and thus both a necessary and productive force. He considered Arab nationalism in particular to have deep and glorious roots in the past. With the Arab nation the product of an age-old civilization based on the universal message of Islam, Qaddafi argued that it had the right and duty to be the bearer of the Third Universal Theory to the world (Qaddafi 1973b: 32–44). Often a prisoner of his own theories, he believed that Arab and Islamic identities were inextricably linked; therefore, the Arab revolution must also be an Islamic one. It followed that the leader of Arab nationalism and the leader of Arab Islam must be the same and must offer revolutionary programs for both (Mayer 1982: 210).

While Qaddafi never produced a coherent, in-depth analysis of his religious beliefs, his thoughts in various speeches, seminars, and statements centered on the centrality of Islam to religion and the Koran to Islam. Considering Islam to be the final word of God to humanity, he reasoned that there was nothing in life for which the principles could not be found in Islam (Libyan Arab Republic 1974: 19–21). Qaddafi believed that the essence of religion was the unity of God, arguing that there was no distinction between the followers of Jesus, Moses, and Muhammad. Therefore, since there was only one religion, Islam, he considered all monotheists to be Muslims (Libyan Arab Republic 1973c: 11–15). In the same vein, Qaddafi contended not only that Islam was addressed to the followers of the Prophet Muhammad but that Islam meant a belief in God as embodied in all religions. He referred to his argument that anyone who believed in God and his apostles was a Muslim as the "divine concept of Islam" (Qaddafi 1973b: 67–128).

Pressing for a revival of Islam based on the Koran, Qaddafi suggested that Muslims had moved away from God and the Koran and should return. In the process, he sought to correct Islamic practices which in his mind were contrary to the faith. In so doing, he took positions on major issues which were at variance with orthodox Sunni doctrine, such as the role of the *sunna* (reported deeds and sayings of the Prophet Muhammad) as a source of *sharia* law, the role of the *ulama* (learned men of religion) as interpreters of *sharia*, the scope and nature of *sharia*, and the relationship between *sharia* and the state (Mayer 1982: 202–10). For example, he rejected official interpretations of the Koran, arguing that it was written in Arabic so that any Arab could read and apply it without the help of others. He also criticized the *hadith* (statements attributed to the Prophet and used to amplify the teachings of the Koran) on the grounds that the Koran was the single source of God's word. Finally, Qaddafi criticized the various schools of Islamic jurisprudence, charging that they were largely the product of political struggles and thus not connected to Islam or the Koran (Ayoub 1987: 62–3, 78–82; Joffé 1995: 150–2).

Initially, Qaddafi's approach to Islam was rooted in a combination of traditional Islamic identity and belief inculcated during his formative years and the secular Arab nationalist identity imbibed from his study of the works of Arab nationalists. As the revolution matured, his approach to Islam became increasingly reformist, if not secular. The ease with which Qaddafi was able to transcend Sanusi tenets can be explained in part from the fact that he hailed from Sirte, on the periphery of Sanusi influence, and in part from the decline of the Sanusi Order as a religious movement after World War II. Until early 1978, Qaddafi agreed with the Sanusiyya that the Koran and *sunna* were the basis of Islam; thereafter, he began to downplay the importance of the *sunna* and especially the *hadith* (Deeb and Deeb 1982: 98–100; St John 1983a: 477; Burgat 1995: 49–50).

Over time, the Islamic character of Qaddafi's approach to Arab nationalism and the allegedly universal elements of the Third Universal Theory became increasingly paradoxical. Although he continued to emphasize the centrality of Islam to Arab nationalism, he deemphasized Islam's role in the Third Universal Theory. In the early 1970s, he argued that the Third Universal Theory was rooted in Islam; however, by the early 1980s, he was suggesting that the theory was unrelated to Islam and was certainly not Islamic in character. Qaddafi's thoughts on this complex relationship never clarified; nevertheless, his argument that the Third Universal Theory was the basis for a universal civilization centered on the Arab nation logically appeared to result in Islam continuing to have a central role. In this context, his revisionist views on the role of Islam were likely a tactical move intended to give the Third Universal Theory wider appeal outside the Islamic world (Deeb and Deeb 1982: 103–4).

People's committees and the General People's Congress

Dissatisfied with the performance of the ASU, Qaddafi on 15 April 1973 proclaimed a popular revolution and called for the people to seize power throughout the country through the election of people's committees (also found as popular committees) in towns, schools, and companies. Newly formed people's committees soon dismissed most of the modernizing administrators appointed by the RCC and replaced them with individuals less modern in outlook yet more receptive to change than the traditional elites. Initially, popular elections were mostly limited to organizations within zones with representatives of zone committees elected to municipal and provincial committees; however, elections were also held in most public corporations and select government bodies. To prevent anarchy, the popular revolution was not allowed to take over the revolutionary administration (Lenczowski 1974: 59; El Fathaly and Palmer 1982a: 239).

A complex web of strategic and tactical considerations motivated Qaddafi to launch the April 1973 popular revolution (Vandewalle 2006: 84–5). First and foremost, the fledgling ASU had failed to break the power of the traditional leadership, a failure exacerbated by ongoing competition between the bureaucracy and the ASU. By increasing public participation, the RCC sought to create the supportive roles and attitudes necessary for its modernization objectives to succeed (El Fathaly and Chackerian 1977: 95). Second, the people's committee system offered new opportunities to isolate and control opposition to the revolution, a constant concern for an RCC with a well-developed sense of paranoia. Concurrent with the election of people's committees, the regime conducted a wave of arrests of Baathists, Marxists, and others who had not identified themselves fully with its policies. Most of these arrests were instigated by the internal security services, but some of those detained were denounced by the newly formed people's committees, leading observers to conclude that the new bodies were as much about mobilization and intelligence gathering as they were about the exercise of popular power (First 1974: 26, 138–40, 253–4; Djaziri 1995: 183–4).

The creation of people's committees was a very important step in the evolution of the Libyan political system. The people's committees assumed local administrative functions, and their chairmen became the chief administrative officials for their bodies. For the first time in Libyan history, the people's committee system thus provided for widespread participation in the selection of local leadership and allowed popular involvement in the local policy-making process. In so doing, the RCC increased the political experience and commitment of the masses through active political participation focused on issues of most interest to local communities (El Fathaly and Chackerian 1977: 96–9).

Viewed in the context of the goals of the revolution, the impact of the popular revolution was largely positive. With most people's committee decisions, especially those related to personnel, subject to RCC confirmation, the system refined its control of the revolution. At the same time, the election of people's committees clearly reduced the influence of traditional leaders and also resulted in the dismissal or arrest of actual or potential critics of the regime (Lenczowski 1974: 59). The popular revolution also changed the character of local leadership. The newly elected committees were closer to the masses than the modernizers had been and, unlike the traditional leaders, they were sympathetic to political participation and closer to the public in their evaluation of policies and programs. Moreover, as the new group of leaders achieved increased political experience and participation, the local leadership, the Libyan people, and the revolutionary government forged closer links (El Fathaly and Chackerian 1977: 96–9). On the downside, the chaotic activities of the people's committees disrupted the functioning of some institutions, including public sector companies and agricultural development projects, and their actions also led occasionally to jurisdictional disputes with the ASU.

Still dissatisfied with the level of popular mobilization, Qaddafi in September 1975 announced a fourth major political reform designed to increase cooperation between the people's committees and the ASU. In the new organization, he delegated political authority to the ASU with the proviso that its membership be elected from the membership of the mid-level organization, the basic people's congresses. He further strengthened the position of the ASU by declaring that the chairman of each basic people's congress must be a representative from the ASU. Finally, workers were required to join a local union based on their occupations and to elect from their membership representatives to district-level unions. The use of occupational groups as a basis for participation was an important departure from the earlier system, in which workplaces had formed the basis for representation. Qaddafi also created a national-level body, the General People's Congress (GPC), with himself as secretary general and the other RCC members forming its general secretariat. Meeting annually, the GPC became the central arena in which the plans, policies, and programs of the RCC, together with those developed at lower levels of government, were discussed and ratified (Qaddafi 1976: 55–66; El Fathaly and Chackerian 1977: 100).

In support of the new national body, Qaddafi retained the zone organization, together with the election of people's committees at that level. Each zone was part of a district which was similar to a municipality or branch municipality in the case of larger municipalities. Although there were no people's congresses at the zone level, representatives from them were elected to a basic people's congress at the municipality or branch municipality level. In addition to electing a basic people's committee responsible for administrative functions, each basic people's congress was responsible for reviewing the agenda of the GPC at the national level. As the system evolved, the chairmen of the basic people's congresses at the municipality and branch municipalities level, together with the chairmen of the municipal or branch municipality people's committees, normally served as delegates to the GPC (Qaddafi 1976: 60–2; El Fathaly and Palmer 1980a: 52, 140–1).

In August 1975, Qaddafi discovered a conspiracy against the regime which was centered in the armed forces but reflected major ideological differences within the ruling elite. Neither the first nor the last attempt to overturn the regime, this abortive effort was significant because it revealed a major split within the RCC and resulted in the demise of the RCC's technocratic wing (Bleuchot 1982: 157–8; Djaziri 1995: 182–4). The crisis arose when several RCC members objected to Qaddafi's emphasis on military spending and foreign adventures to the detriment of local development, together with his repeated interference in the details of government. With the discovery of the intrigue, the RCC conspirators were placed under house arrest or fled into exile, and their supporters within the armed forces were arrested (Ahmida 2005: 80–1). By the end of 1975, the RCC was reduced from its original 12 members to five Qaddafi loyalists and, under his leadership, this group would act as a cohesive ruling elite for much of the next two decades (Davis 1987: 133; El-Kikhia 1997: 51–2).

The Green Book

Having discussed and refined for several years the core elements of the Third Universal Theory, Qaddafi published his philosophical musings in three slender volumes known collectively as *The Green Book*. In the first volume, *The Solution of the Problem of Democracy: "The Authority of the People,"* which was published in English in 1976, he explored the theoretical bases for the system of direct democracy implemented in Libya after April 1973. Describing the "instrument of governing" as the prime political problem facing human communities, he argued that the political systems prevailing in the world today were all dictatorial systems that falsified genuine democracy. Rejecting political parties, parliaments, and plebiscites, he concluded that a form of direct democracy, based on a nationwide system of congresses and committees, was the optimum form of government for the world. Qaddafi's cryptic analysis spawned catch phrases such as "representation is falsification" and "no representation in lieu of the people" which were repeated ad nauseam after 1976 (Qaddafi 1976: 7–53).

In the second half of the first volume of *The Green Book*, Qaddafi outlined the committee and congress system, concluding that there can be "no democracy without popular congresses and committees everywhere." Devoted in theory, if not in practice, to revolutionary concerns as opposed to political issues, Qaddafi's self-appointed role in this new political system was to be the "guide" of the revolution (Qaddafi 1976: 55–66). Qaddafi also devoted considerable space in the final section of the first volume to a discussion of the law of society, which he defined as either tradition (custom) or religion, criticizing constitutions in particular as man-made law (Qaddafi 1976: 67–84).

In Volume 2, entitled *The Solution of the Economic Problem: "Socialism"* and released in 1977, Qaddafi explored the economic dimensions of the Third Universal Theory. He began his discussion with a sharp critique of contemporary economic systems, concluding that socialism offers the ultimate solution to the world's economic problems. In so doing, he contended that an important economic problem, true human freedom, remained unresolved, an argument that spawned his famous catchphrase, "in need freedom is latent." Defining mankind's basic needs as a house, an income, and a vehicle, he declared renting houses and hiring cars to be forms of domination over the needs of others. He also decried the private ownership of land because land was the property of society and not of individuals. The generation of savings beyond a level necessary to satisfy individual needs was termed exploitative because societies suffered from a scarcity of resources, and to accumulate wealth beyond one's immediate needs was to do so at the expense of others (Qaddafi 1978: 7–20, 26).

In the second volume, Qaddafi also outlined a theory of natural socialism based on what he described as the three economic factors of production, namely, equality in raw materials, the means of production, and the producer. In his mind, each of these inputs was equally important in the production process; consequently, each was entitled to an equal share of what was produced. Suggesting that earlier approaches to socialism were wrong to focus on ownership, wages, or a single factor of production, he argued that production itself was the real economic problem. Expanding this logic, Qaddafi suggested that the wage system was the most salient characteristic of the modern economic structure because it deprived the worker of a fair share in production. Advocating the abolition of the wage system and the profit motive, he urged salaried employees (wage-workers) to rise up and become partners in production. As much a social reformer as a philosopher, Qaddafi concluded Volume 2 with a brief discussion of household servants, suggesting that they find new jobs outside the home, where they could become partners in production (Qaddafi 1978: 21–30).

In the third and final volume of *The Green Book*, entitled *The Social Basis of the Third Universal Theory* and published in 1979, Qaddafi explored selected aspects of social theory in a manner that illuminated some of the political and economic dimensions discussed in the first two volumes (Bleuchot 1982: 146–8; Ayoub 1987: 49). Despite his strong personal faith and stated commitment to the spread of Islam, Qaddafi did not speak of Islam or Islamic law anywhere in *The Green Book*, concluding in Volume 3 that everyone is entitled to their own religion (Qaddafi 1979: 8–9; Bleuchot 1982: 155–6). In downplaying the Islamic character of his theories, he hoped to make them more attractive to non-Muslims and thus widen his audience outside the Muslim world. After extolling the virtues of the family as a social unit, he described the tribe as one of the healthiest and most important units of any society. Given his attempts in the early 1970s to reduce the power and influence of tribes, his treatment of tribalism in *The Green Book* suggested a major rethink on the subject as well as a further effort to broaden the appeal of his philosophy (Anderson 1990: 297; Qaddafi 1979: 3–26).

After developing a general theoretical framework in Volume 3, Qaddafi addressed certain elements of society, including women, minorities, and black people, to illustrate his theory. In so doing, he articulated largely conservative, even reactionary, social values after advocating radical political and economic theories in the first two volumes. In an egalitarian society, he said there was no room for any form of discrimination, especially sexual discrimination; nevertheless, his rather traditional characterization of the roles and responsibilities of women was patronizing in tone if not sexist in approach (Qaddafi 1975: 135–6). Similarly, his description of black people as backward and sluggish, far from proclaiming a new social order, was reminiscent of Western views toward slavery in the nineteenth century (Qaddafi 1979: 27–64). Given its scope and content, the last volume of *The Green Book* understandably was by far the most controversial, remaining an endless source of comment and debate to the present time.

Consolidating the revolution

While *The Green Book* was being published, Qaddafi continued to tinker with what was becoming an increasingly novel form of political organization. On 7 October 1976, he expanded the authority of the GPC, giving it the power, in theory if not in practice, to appoint and dismiss cabinet ministers, issue laws, and determine foreign policy. In a major address on 2 March 1977, he further clarified the structure and authority of the wider organization in what came to be known as the "Declaration of the Establishment of the People's Authority." Direct popular authority was the basis for the new political system, and the people were to exercise this authority through approved, official organizations. At the same time, the GPC announced it was establishing a General People's Committee, a form of cabinet with secretaries for agriculture, health, housing, industry, and so forth. Reiterating the commitment of the revolution to freedom, socialism, and unity, the March 1977 declaration changed the official name of the country from the Libyan Arab Republic to the Socialist People's Libyan Arab Jamahiriya, *Jamahiriya* being a neologism widely interpreted to mean "state of the masses" (El Fathaly and Chackerian 1977: 117–18).

The refinements to the political structure introduced in 1975–7 increased mobilization, participation, and control. with the emphasis on the last. Levels of mobilization and participation increased with the creation of the GPC along with the reduction in competition between the people's committees, basic people's congresses, and the ASU. Revolutionary control was strengthened by requiring everyone in the country to participate in the political system but restricting that participation to official organizations controlled by the GPC. People's committees were reelected or disbanded whenever their activities were judged inconsistent with the policies of the revolution, and workers were required to join unions, where their activities were closely monitored (Alexander 1981a: 220; Mason 1982: 327–32).

Following the creation of the people's committee and congress system, Qaddafi called for the formation of revolutionary committees, an entirely new echelon of organization not mentioned in *The Green Book*. A response to the lethargy plaguing the people's committee system, the principal task of the revolutionary committees was to reduce the high levels of absenteeism at committee and congress meetings. In addition, they were a reaction to the pursuit by people's committees of local interests at the expense of wider national interests and to the use of the people's congresses by traditional leaders to promote sectional interests. Revolutionary committees were established within all people's committees, basic people's congresses, professional unions, and state institutions (Bleuchot 1982: 157; Mattes 1995: 89–93; Vandewalle 1998: 101).

After March 1979, the revolutionary committees transitioned from a motivational role to one of revolutionary enforcement, empowered to force their will upon people's committees and congresses. In so doing, the presence of the revolutionary committees expanded to encompass all segments of society, including three areas the regime considered to be of critical importance in consolidating the revolution: educational institutions, the mass media, and the internal security forces. By the early 1980s, the growing stature that Qaddafi had bestowed upon the revolutionary committees made them the regime's principal instrument for imposing its ideological and political goals on the people of Libya (Mattes 1995: 93–104; El Fathaly and Palmer 1995: 174).

As the foreign policy of the regime increased in scope and militancy, Qaddafi in March 1978 told the basic people's congresses that general military training was necessary to protect the country from internal and external threats. In response, the GPC in 1979 made conscription and military training compulsory for all young people, including university students. Later, compulsory military training was extended to include students in preparatory and secondary schools, and to facilitate the training of students the academic year was reduced to six months. All adults were also trained in the use of a variety of weapons. Ambivalent toward the armed forces, Qaddafi appreciated military power, but his near-contempt for military hierarchy and organization was less apparent (Bleuchot 1982: 157–8; El Fathaly and Palmer 1995: 170–3; Martinez 2007: 55, 95). With a goal to replace the conventional military establishment with a popular military force, Qaddafi in September 1989 announced the creation of a people's army, declaring that all institutions were now under the command of the masses and Libya had finally become the *Jamahiriya* called for in *The Green Book* (Vandewalle 1991: 217–18).

On 1 September 1978, Qaddafi called for a revitalization of the people's committee system in order to eliminate the bureaucracy of the public sector and the dictatorship of the private sector. In what came to be called the producers' revolution, people's committees were elected in several hundred companies, and by early 1979 private sector ownership had been largely eliminated from the productive sector of the economy (Bearman 1986: 191–6; Mattes 2008: 66). At the outset, foreign contractors, together with the banking, insurance, and oil and gas sectors, were outside the scope of the people's committees; however, in early February 1979, the takeover of a company associated with the hydrocarbon sector was first announced (Alexander 1981a: 221; Davis 1987: 137–78).

In a further effort to consolidate revolutionary control, a reshuffle of the General People's Committee was announced on 3 February 1979, with the existing 26 secretariats reduced to 19. The General Secretariat described the reorganization as a means to facilitate the people's control of state affairs, but in reality it constituted a further concentration of power and authority. On

2 March 1979, Qaddafi announced that he was stepping down from his position as secretary general of the GPC in order to concentrate on revolutionary activities with the masses. Retaining the title of commander-in-chief of the armed forces, he adopted a new title, Leader of the Revolution, and since that time he has preferred to be called simply the Leader. When Qaddafi stepped down, the remaining members of the RCC also resigned their GPC posts to focus on revolutionary activities (El Fathaly and Palmer 1980a: 150; Alexander 1981a: 221).

Termed the "separation of power and revolution," the changes implemented in early March 1979 effectively divided the Libyan state into two parallel components. Thereafter, the revolutionary sector consisted of Qaddafi, the remaining RCC members, the Free Unionist Officers, and the revolutionary committees. Directed and controlled by the Leader, the activities of the revolutionary sector were not in any way regulated by legal statutes. In contrast, the ruling sector consisted of the various bodies constituting the direct democracy system, especially the nationwide system of people's committees and congresses. Their functions and activities were regulated by law as promulgated by the GPC. After 1979, minor modifications were made to both the revolutionary and ruling sectors; however, the basic duality of the Libyan political system remained unchanged (Vandewalle 2006: 119; Mattes 2008: 57–8).

In March 1979, Qaddafi also launched a mass campaign to eliminate dissidents, calling for the liquidation of all opponents to the regime inside and outside Libya. In response, revolutionary zealots initiated a campaign of politically inspired murders, targeting anyone considered a regime opponent. Over the next few years, well over three dozen individuals were killed or wounded by revolutionary zealots inspired by the Leader (Harris 1986: 78–9; Anderson 1986b: 231–3). On 1 September 1979, Qaddafi called on Libyans abroad to seize control of all Libyan embassies because the latter represented governmental bodies when government had been abolished in Libya and replaced by people's power. Scores of embassies were turned into people's bureaus with the resident ambassador replaced by a people's committee. This projection of the Libyan revolution into an arena where traditions had developed over centuries caused considerable confusion (Alexander 1981a: 222).

Socioeconomic reforms

As Qaddafi continued to refine the political system, the regime introduced a series of increasingly radical socioeconomic reforms grounded in the theories found in *The Green Book*. In so doing, it effectively transformed the overthrow of the monarchy from a *coup d'état* into a wide-reaching social, economic, and political revolution that touched on all aspects of Libyan life. The management of the economy became socialist in intent and practice, and wealth, whether in capital, housing, or land, was redistributed or scheduled for redistribution (Allan 1981: 244).

Social services

Committed to an overhaul of education policy, the RCC immediately suspended all laws passed by the monarchy, and in October 1970 it promulgated a new education law that outlined a more activist role for the Ministry of Education and National Guidance, restructured the Higher Council of Education and Teaching, and reorganized the school curriculum. A second law promulgated in 1975 extended the period of obligatory education at the preparatory level to three years. When combined with the six years of mandatory primary schooling already in place under the monarchy, this law extended the period of obligatory schooling to nine years, a major step forward, especially for females. Previously, most young girls had dropped out of school after the compulsory six-year primary stage. Thereafter, an increasing number of female students attended primary and secondary school and a few moved on to university (Monastiri 1982: 317–18).

The monarchy had laid the foundation for a modern system of education, taking steps to build schools, train teachers, and educate children and adults, and the revolutionary government built on these efforts, launching initiatives to improve the quantity and quality of education within the dictates of the revolution (Libyan Arab Republic 1973b: 127–38). New laws stressed technical and vocational training, and in higher education the regime emphasized the applied sciences. Budget allocations for the construction of new educational facilities increased, and mobile classrooms were deployed in remote areas to increase learning opportunities for rural populations. Efforts were also made to merge secular and religious education, and, in a country plagued with illiteracy, the regime placed renewed emphasis on adult education (Deeb and Deeb 1982: 32).

As a result of regime policies, the number of primary, intermediate, and secondary schools increased after 1969, as did the percentage of eligible students enrolled in school. The number of teacher training schools also increased beginning in 1972, as did enrollment in vocational schools. With the growth of public schools, religious education declined in importance; however, religious instruction, together with Koranic schools and Islamic institutes, remained a presence in the overall educational system. As for higher education, the revolutionary government built on the universities established by the monarchy, expanding faculties and facilities. At the same time, it used the educational system to instill a sense of revolutionary vigor among students, insisting that the curriculum reflect the ideology of the revolution (Deeb and Deeb 1982: 35–48, 97; Monastiri 1995: 81–6).

The revolutionary government achieved considerable success in improving the quantity of education in Libya. Adult literacy levels, at 82 percent, are among the highest in the region, with youth literacy near 100 percent and female literacy higher than in most states in the region. Primary and secondary school enrollment levels are also high. On the other hand, the quality of education leaves much to be desired. According to the Global Competitiveness Report

(2005–6) and a Libya Business Executive Survey (2005), Libya ranks 110 out of 111 countries surveyed in terms of the overall quality of the education system. The quality of public schools ranked 84 and the quality of math and science education ranked 87 (Monitor Group and Cambridge Energy Research Associates 2006: 62). Anecdotal evidence supports these findings, as companies working in Libya complain that intermediate and tertiary school graduates typically require extensive training to make them productive. Inadequate vocational training and poor language skills are two common areas of complaint. Although the available data on the quality of education are inadequate, they suggest that the Libyan educational system has problems with the quality of inputs, including teachers and curriculum, as well as structural problems, such as the absence of reliable and objective standards, no central body to provide planning and monitoring, and the inefficient allocation of resources (Monitor Group and Cambridge Energy Research Associates 2006: 118–24).

In part to boost its legitimacy, the regime promoted a more open, expansive, and inclusive role for women, and this was especially noticeable in the field of education. In addition to providing nine years of compulsory schooling for all Libyans, women were also encouraged to take up administrative and clerical jobs and to engage in skilled professions such as health care and nursing. As a result, the number of women enrolled in teacher training increased almost sevenfold between 1969–70 and 1974–5 while female enrollment at university increased well over fourfold in the same period. By 1974–5, over 50 percent of the people enrolled in teacher training were female; however, female enrollment at university was only 12.8 percent of the total, reflecting an ongoing gender gap in higher education (Bearman 1986: 196–201; Obeidi 2001: 174).

Other positive steps taken by the regime to improve the status of women included legislation restricting polygamy and fixing for women the same minimum age for marriage as for men. Libyan women were among the first in the Arab world to attend a military academy with a special facility built for them on the outskirts of Tripoli. In addition, the government established the Department of Women's Affairs as part of the secretariat of the GPC and set up a center for women's studies. The government also established the General Union of Women's Associations as a network of organizations focused in part on employment opportunities for women. In 1998, the World Bank estimated that nearly 100 percent of all girls and boys were enrolled in primary education, and by 2002 adult female illiteracy had dropped to 29 percent. Although female illiteracy was still 10 percent higher than male illiteracy, these were impressive results which compared favorably with similar statistics in neighboring states (Dris-Aït-Hamadouche and Zoubir 2007: 274–8).

At the same time, a generational gap among women continued to exist in Libya. Women under 35 years of age were much more likely to have received a public education and to participate in the public sphere than older women, who were more apt to stay at home and to enjoy lower levels of education. Moreover, even though men and women in principle were guaranteed equality under Libyan law, a lack of application and control resulted in a notable level of inequality in practice. A survey of Gar Younis University students conducted in 1994 by Amal Obeidi, a prominent Libyan political scientist, found that female students generally subscribed to full gender equality whereas their male counterparts were more apt to support the principle but to express reservations about its practical application (Obeidi 2001: 175–8). The conflicted position of women in contemporary Libyan society has been a recurrent theme in modern Libyan fiction, including short stories by Najwa Ben Shetwan, Maryam Salama, and Lamia El-Makki, among others (Chorin 2008a: 69–75, 123–7, 177–80).

Guaranteed health care at little or no cost to the patient was regime policy from the start, and the government moved quickly to improve the quality of the health care delivery system. The strategy followed included both an expansion of the health care network and an enlargement of the medical workforce (Libyan Arab Republic 1973b: 139–57; Allan 1981: 225–7). In the first two decades of the revolution, annual per capita health care expenditure increased sixfold, and by 1988 Libya, among Arab states, was second only to Saudi Arabia in terms of public health expenditure as a percentage of GNP. Over the same period, the government established 103 hospitals, 40 polyclinics, and 248 health care centers, and the number of basic health care units increased from 414 in 1969 to 1,038 in 1988. Moreover, basic health care units were better equipped and more evenly distributed around the country. Although official targets were not always met, statistics for related areas, such as the number of physicians and the number of hospital beds per capita, showed similar levels of improvement (Salem 1996: 99–112, 120–2).

Even though headline health system indicators such as numbers of physicians and hospital beds have continued to suggest that human resources and service delivery levels are in line with neighboring states, other data indicate that the health system is delivering mixed results. Life expectancy and health-adjusted life expectancy levels are among the best in the region, but maternal, neonatal, and infant mortality rates are at best on a par with neighboring states and certainly well below the average in OECD member countries. Similarly, most births take place in health care facilities attended by skilled personnel, but the coverage of immunization programs has deteriorated in recent years. Some of the challenges faced by the health care system include poor service quality owing to low staff training and motivation and a lack of equipment. In addition, public resources are allocated inefficiently in terms of both the employment and training of health workers and the purchase of medical supplies. Finally, environmental and behavioral risk factors, such as poor road safety and diminishing water quality, increasingly threaten the health of Libyans (Monitor Group and Cambridge Energy Research Associates 2006: 109–18). To address these and other issues, the regime has continued to emphasize high-quality health care, concluding a series of agreements with British hospitals, institutions, and universities in 2009 aimed at further advancing the health sector (*JANA*: 10.10.09).

As for the provision of housing, the initial three-year development plan

(1973–5) targeted the construction of 80,000 housing units in an early effort both to replace substandard housing and to address the overall housing shortage (Libyan Arab Republic 1973b: 158–61; Bennett 1975: 112; Allan 1981: 223–5). Although these targets were not met, the ensuing five-year development plan (1976–80) set a more aggressive target for new housing, calling for the completion of upward of 200,000 new housing units by 1980. In conjunction with these efforts, the General Secretariat of the GPC, in March 1978, passed resolution four, which established new guidelines for home ownership. Codified in a law issued two months later, the guidelines stipulated that all families had the right to own one home, but with a few exceptions, such as widows whose only source of income was rent, no individual or company could own more than one housing unit. As a result, most tenants in rented housing became the instant owners of their homes. The new owners did have to make mortgage payments to the government based on the income of the family; however, the monthly payments typically amounted to one-third or less of the former rent. Moreover, former rental properties were deliberately undervalued by the government, often by as much as 30–40 percent, to facilitate their purchase (Deeb and Deeb 1982: 116).

The new housing policies affected many segments of Libyan society. Investment in real estate in 1973–5 had accounted for more than 40 percent of all private investment and, because it was profitable, it constituted the main instrument by which Libyans with wealth had buttressed their position in society. Understandably, dispossessed landlords, despite the promise of compensation, were distressed by the new policies as they closed a profitable area of investment. As for former tenants, some 30 percent of Libyan urbanites at the time were housed in privately owned accommodation, and the rents for these homes had become oppressively high in recent years. Therefore, the housing redistribution policy was a windfall for them, and they naturally welcomed the redistribution of ownership titles (*MEED*: 1.9.78; Burgat 1995: 52).

Radical reforms

Resolution four marked the onset of an increasingly radical socioeconomic revolution. In 1979, the regime initiated a widespread redistribution of agricultural land on Libya's coastal strip, in part to rectify the unfair acquisition of holdings by politically powerful people during the monarchical era. In addition, Qaddafi held the view that only farms of a size required to support a family without outside labor were ideologically acceptable; consequently, a related motivation for the policy was the desire to break up farms either made up of large holdings not fully used or utilizing hired labor. The redistribution policy, which generated determined opposition from those with substantial agricultural holdings, continued into 1980–1 (Allan 1981: 241–4).

In May 1980, the regime declared null and void all paper bills in denominations greater than one dinar (approximately $3.40 at the time), and people were given one week to exchange the money in their possession. A straightforward socialist measure, redistributive in intent and effect, the regime set the maximum exchange at 1,000 dinars, with deposits in excess of that amount frozen and depositors turned away with cash receipts (Allan 1981: 241). The devastating impact of the demonetization campaign on personal lives and savings was later captured by the Libyan author Hisham Matar, in his widely acclaimed novel *In the Country of Men* (Matar 2007: 235). In early 1981, the GPC announced the state takeover of all import, export, and distribution functions. With a series of state-run central and satellite supermarkets under construction, this policy signaled the end of a once large private sector, consisting of wholesale and retail merchants. The end result of the campaign against trade as a profitable enterprise was that scarce commodities became more difficult to obtain and the queues outside shops and cooperative societies became even longer (St John 1981: 429; Mason 1982: 332).

Impact of socioeconomic reforms

The regime's increasingly radical socioeconomic policies had a negative impact on its development goals. The progressive elimination of the private sector put an unreasonable burden on the understaffed and poorly trained public sector, a problem aggravated by the conscription of public servants into the military. The home redistribution policy brought private real estate development to a halt, and the currency reform prompted a liquidity crisis. With its development plans dependent on offshore participation, uncertainty as to regime policies also increased the reluctance of foreign companies to sign contracts and to station personnel in Libya (St John 1981: 429; Mason 1982: 335).

The growing radicalization of domestic policies also resulted in a marked increase in opposition to the regime, activating what had been only dormant opposition in some areas. Paradoxically, the members of the middle class who had benefited from early regime efforts to develop the housing and service sectors were among the hardest hit. Other disenchanted groups included the elite of the old regime, conservative nationalists, disaffected farmers, disillusioned technocrats, most of the educated elite, the orthodox religious establishment, and selected elements in the military. In August 1980, an air force unit in Tobruk mounted an abortive coup, and over the next four years at least eight additional mutinies or assassination attempts were reported in the media (Anderson 1986b: 225–31; Harris 1986: 76–8).

At the same time, Qaddafi continued to enjoy considerable support in certain sectors of Libyan society, especially among the younger, less well-to-do elements. In the 1980s, many Libyans enjoyed better housing and health care and more educational opportunities than they could have dreamed of before the onset of the revolution. Moreover, with an increasing proportion of the population 15 years of age or younger, a growing number of Libyans had known no other government. Qaddafi took extraordinary efforts in the early 1980s to stifle opposition and to protect himself and his regime, but his much publicized efforts to intimidate his critics were only a part of a much wider effort to maintain himself in power (St John 1981: 429; Anderson 1985a: 200).

Islamic reforms

Qaddafi's approach to Islam took a reformist turn in the mid-1970s when he began to articulate a de facto functional secularism, arguing that mundane matters should be separated from spiritual matters, an approach which challenged the role of the *ulama*. In May 1975, he addressed the *imams* (prayer leaders) in the country's mosques, telling them to separate mundane, daily affairs from otherworldly concerns in Friday prayers and to concentrate their sermons on the latter. Over the next three years, Qaddafi's ideas on the foundations of Islam, Islamic jurisprudence, and the role of Islamic jurists shifted in the direction of the transcendence of God and the elimination of intermediaries between man and God. By early 1978, he was arguing publicly that the Koran was written in the Arabic language so that all could understand it without the need for *ulamas* or others to interpret it for them. When members of the orthodox religious establishment challenged him, Qaddafi responded in May–June 1978, purging the religious leaders critical of him (Deeb and Deeb 1982: 101–3; Joffé 1995: 150–1).

One month later, Qaddafi took a decisive step when he questioned the very justification for a religious elite. In July 1978, after the religious leadership had declared *The Green Book* to be incompatible with Islam, he argued that the core components of Sunni Islam, the *sunna*, *hadith*, *qivas* (practice of reasoning by analogy to amplify the *hadith* and the Koran), *ijma* (use of consensus to establish agreed doctrine), and *sharia*, were not essential elements of true Islam, which should be based solely on the Koran. In adding that individuals had the right to apply independent reasoning to the interpretation of Islam, Qaddafi greatly weakened, if not effectively destroyed, the power base of a religious elite who had long considered the interpretation of Islam as their prerogative. While Qaddafi proposed other changes to the established Islamic order, such as changing the Muslim calendar to begin with the date of the Prophet's death instead of the date he moved from Mecca to Medina, the crucial element was the application of independent reasoning to the interpretation of Islam (Joffé 1988: 623–7; Joffé 1995: 151–2).

The meandering path to additional reforms

At the time of the One September Revolution, Libya had largely completed the transition from a *sharia*-based legal order to a European-style system. Like many Arab countries, the monarchy had elected to reform the legal system along Western lines, leaving selected pockets of *sharia* law in areas such as personal status under the jurisdiction of *sharia* courts. After 1969, legal policy followed what Ann Elizabeth Mayer, an expert on Islamic law, described as a "meandering path," with Qaddafi adjusting and readjusting the mix of code provisions, religious law, and custom to fit political events. In so doing, legal reforms passed through four broad stages from Islamization to revolutionary legalism to legality and human rights to a second period of Islamization (Mayer 1995: 113–14). In the first stage (1969 to 1973–4), the regime moved to revive Islamic law and abrogate laws contrary to Islamic principles as part of a broader campaign to eliminate Western influence in Libya. In this period, Qaddafi repeatedly proclaimed his commitment to *sharia* law; nevertheless, the legal system remained firmly anchored in the European civil law tradition (Mayer 1978, 1980, 1990).

With the proclamation of the popular revolution on 15 April 1973, Qaddafi's emphasis shifted to a revolutionary transformation of Libyan society. When he announced the creation of people's committees, he suspended all laws in force, signaling his intent to circumvent the rule of law and all legal institutions that might hinder an overhaul of society. At the same time, he attacked Islamic legal institutions and any residual loyalties to Islamic tradition that might impede his plans for a radical socioeconomic transformation. This second stage of legal reforms, termed revolutionary legalism, extended well into the 1980s, and throughout this period Qaddafi assumed stances that were decidedly at odds with the principles he espoused at the height of the earlier Islamization campaign (Mayer 1995: 114–18). To circumvent the powers of ordinary courts, the regime in 1980 established a parallel system of revolutionary courts not bound by the penal code and without the right of appeal. In May 1981, the regime also prohibited the private practice of law, removing the last vestiges of an independent bar by making all lawyers state employees. *In toto*, these developments marked the beginning of a seven-year period notable for an arbitrary and repressive justice system which contributed to mounting tension throughout the country (Vandewalle 1991: 223–4; Joffé 1995: 147–50).

In the second half of the 1980s, internal political developments, including renewed tensions between the regime and Islamist elements, and foreign adventures, especially the conflict in Chad, combined with tumbling oil revenues, reduced imports, and delayed development plans to force a retreat from revolutionary legalism. In so doing, Qaddafi initiated a third phase of legal policy marked by an official respect for legality and human rights (Mayer 1995: 118–23). In a remarkable volte-face, the Leader overnight became a public advocate of legality, freedom, and human rights, castigating the absence of the rule of law and noting that abuses had taken place (Vandewalle 1991: 223–4).

To separate himself from the excesses of the revolutionary justice system, Qaddafi described the security services, police, and revolutionary committees as overzealous and antithetical to popular rule. Public criticism of the revolutionary committees had been building for some time, and the US bombing of Benghazi and Tripoli in April 1986 was likely the event that prompted the Leader to rethink their usefulness. In the aftermath of the attack, it was the army which had to put down scattered unrest after the committees failed to mobilize public support for Qaddafi. Thereafter, the power of the revolutionary committees was progressively reduced, and although they enjoyed a modest rehabilitation in the mid-1990s they never regained the preeminent position they once enjoyed (Vandewalle 1998: 123; Mattes 2008: 68).

In early March 1988, Qaddafi participated in the destruction of the central prison in Tripoli, and he also supervised the destruction of police files collected by the security forces. Later in the month, he helped to destroy a customs post on the Tunisian border, declaring that all Libyans were now free to travel. He also encouraged exiled Libyans to return home, with promises of jobs and assurances that they would not be persecuted, but few dared to accept his offer. He created the Ministry of Mass Mobilization and Revolutionary Leadership to limit the power of the revolutionary committees, and, in May 1988, people's courts replaced the revolutionary courts except in cases involving treason. Finally, a new Ministry of Justice was created in March 1989 (Vandewalle 1991: 221, 223–4; Burgat 1995: 56–8; Mattes 1995: 105–7).

Qaddafi also offered Libyans a human rights charter, the Great Green Charter of Human Rights in the Jamahiriya Era, adopted by the GPC on 12 June 1988. With most of the document taken verbatim from earlier Qaddafi pronouncements, the principles outlined therein guaranteed some rights and freedoms that Libyans had not enjoyed in 1978–88; however, the charter did not protect civil and political rights as understood in international law. It did not guarantee freedom of conscience, freedom of worship, the right to peaceful assembly, protection against unreasonable searches, or a public trial. Moreover, it did not contain an equal protection clause or prohibit arbitrary arrest, detention, and torture. Although the charter provided some protection in terms of enhanced personal rights and freedoms, it provided no room for successful challenges to the authority of the regime. Consequently, it did little to improve the status of political, religious, or other dissidents (Mayer 1995: 123–31).

After 1990, Qaddafi initiated a second wave of reforms meant to reduce state control of the economy, increase private sector initiatives, and curtail state spending. Qaddafi also proposed a form of devolution in which the country would be divided into 1,500 self-governing communes, each of which would have its own executive and legislative powers and its own budget (Vandewalle 2006: 164–6). Unfortunately, the reality on the ground seldom matched the rhetoric of the Leader. New rules and regulations were implemented half-heartedly or not at all, and most Libyans proved unable or unwilling to take entrepreneurial risks in an uncertain economic and political climate. Considered by the regime to be a serious attempt at liberalization and reform, the corrective measures taken by Qaddafi in 1987–91 were in reality little more an effort to relieve popular grievances and safeguard the status quo (Deeb 1990: 149; Burgat 1995: 58–9;

Vandewalle 1995a). They did not reflect a new spirit of reform, and there was no significant change to the fundamental principles of the regime.

Evidence of the temporal nature of this so-called era of liberalization surfaced after 1993, when international sanctions were beginning to take their toll on the economy and domestic discontent was growing as Islamist fundamentalism surged in neighboring Algeria and Egypt (Ronen 2002: 4–5; Wharton 2003: 35, 42–3). In response, Qaddafi came full circle, initiating a second stage of Islamization. Borrowing elements from Islamist programs, he remained a determined foe of fundamentalism, recognizing that it posed a serious threat to his regime. In this fourth stage of legal development, which consisted of a quixotic synthesis of *sharia* law and *The Green Book*, there was little or no concern whether or not torture and executions violated the human rights of Libyans (Mayer 1995: 131–2; Deeb 1999).

Mounting opposition in the 1990s

Throughout much of the 1990s, the regime faced opposition from a number of different groups, including disaffected tribes, the armed forces, and militant Islamists. In the armed forces, unpaid wages and reduced perks, the Libyan defeat in Chad and its withdrawal from the Aouzou Strip, and cuts in arms spending combined to result in several abortive coup attempts. A failed military plot in October 1993, for example, led to the arrest of 1,500 people and the death of dozens, if not hundreds (Deeb 1999: 79–82). Tribal opposition was centered in Cyrenaica, a region loyal to the Sanusiyya movement, and, although opposition to the regime had long existed here, several tribal uprisings occurred during this time frame, with tribal and Islamist opposition occasionally overlapping. In addition, a number of opposition organizations, mostly divided against themselves, continued to be active outside Libya (Deeb 2000: 146–8; St John 2003a: 5–10).

By the middle of the decade, Qaddafi had largely quelled opposition within the armed forces and among dissident tribal groups; therefore, he was able to concentrate his efforts on the suppression of Islamic fundamentalist movements operating inside Libya. In addition to well-established groups such as Islamic Struggle (*Jihad al-Islami*), Islamic Group – Libya (*al-Jama'a al-Islamiyya Libya*), and Islamic Movement – Libya (*al-Haraka al-Islamiyya Libya*), the fundamentalist opposition included shadowy new groups such as Apostasy and Migration (*al-Takfir wal-Hijra*), the Warning (*al-Tabligh*), and the Libyan Islamic Fighting Group (*al-Jama'a al-Islamiyya al-Muqatila bi-Libya*) (Deeb 1999: 78–9; Takeyh 2000: 160–2). In 1994, the GPC extended the application of Islamic law and granted selected new powers to religious leaders, including the right to issue religious decrees. At the same time, the state sought to refute militant Islamist authority through an anti-Islamist campaign. In so doing, the regime steered a middle path between hardline religious opponents and the general population, which in Libya was largely opposed to militant Islam. Finally, the GPC in 1997 passed a series of measures authorizing collective punishment for individuals or groups who harbored Islamists, and in 2000 the regime executed three of eight Islamist militants extradited from Jordan (Ronen 2002: 7–13; Martinez 2007: 60–70; St John 2008b: 63).

The only constant is change

Since the Declaration of the Establishment of the People's Authority in March 1977 and the separation of power and revolution in March 1979, Libya has been ruled by two parallel power sectors. The people's sector is a form of direct democracy based on a system of congresses and committees. Over time, only minor modifications have been made to the structure and operation of this sector. The revolutionary sector originally consisted of Qaddafi, the remaining members of the RCC, the Free Unionist Officers, and the revolutionary committees, but in recent times new groups have been added. Qaddafi also relies on an informal network of advisors and trusted confidants, known variously as the Men of the Tent or the Forum of Companions, together with blood relatives and members of the Qaddafi and affiliated tribes, especially the Maghraha and Warfalla (El-Kikhia 1997: 89–92, 151–61; Vandewalle 2006: 150–2; Pargeter 2006: 227–9; Joffé 2009: 939–40). The duality of the operative political structure has not changed since 1979 even though the organization and operation of the revolutionary sector have evolved as the Leader explored new avenues to refine his control of the system.

The People's Guard and cleansing committees

In June 1990, Qaddafi created a new revolutionary organization made up of civilian volunteers and known as the People's Guard. Tied to the growing threat from militant Islamists, the main task of the People's Guard was to control the nation's mosques to prevent Islamist agitation. With the revolutionary committees under a cloud following the Leader's admonishments in 1987, the creation of the People's Guard appears in retrospect to have been an ad hoc solution to an immediate problem. Once the Islamist threat subsided, the activities of the people's guard passed from public view (Mattes 2004: 18).

On 1 September 1994, Qaddafi announced the formation of cleansing or purification committees. The members of the cleansing committees were called upon to reflect the personality and politics of the Leader, and their official duties included the identification and elimination of counterrevolutionaries. Thereafter, all Libyans were required to give the cleansing committee in their residential area a regular accounting of material wealth and their means of acquiring it. In the spring of 1996, the responsibilities of the cleansing committees expanded to include guarding against corruption, fraud, and breaches in exchange control. Since that time, the cleansing committees, like the People's

Guard, have maintained a low public profile (St John 2006a: 48–9; Mattes 2008: 63).

People's social leadership committees

In July 1994, Qaddafi announced the formation of yet another nationwide body, the people's social leadership committees (PSLCs), with the intent to incorporate tribal leadership into national decision-making (Obeidi 2008: 110). Over the next two years, PSLCs consisting of tribal leaders, heads of families, and other important local persons were formed throughout the country. Tasked with establishing social stability, maintaining control, and preventing opposition from family and tribal members, PSLCs were also given the responsibility for distributing state subsidies and later for issuing legal documents (Mattes 2008: 68). With the formation of the PSLCs, Qaddafi came full circle in his approach to tribes and tribalism. After challenging the power and authority of traditional tribal leaders in the early years of the revolution, he now turned to influential tribes, clans, and families to maintain the status quo (Martinez 2007: 73–4, 86–7). The rationale behind his decision was found in part in the aforementioned research conducted by Obeidi in 1994. In her survey of university students, she found that Libya, 35 years after the commencement of the One September Revolution, remained largely a tribal society in which the tribe remained one of the strongest social organizations and tribalism continued to play a significant social role (Obeidi 2001: 129–33).

In March 1996, Qaddafi brought the PSLCs together in a national organization, with each local committee sending a representative to the national PSLC. The national committee is directed by a general coordinator chosen by the coordinators at the municipal level for a six-month term. With only two exceptions, all PSLC general coordinators have been high-ranking members of the armed forces. After 1996, the general assemblies of the PSLCs became a favored venue for Qaddafi to debate domestic political problems. In addition, the regime has often turned to the PSLCs to mobilize support for regime policies. In March 2000, Qaddafi suggested that the general coordinator of the PSLC should be considered the formal head of state, in effect, his titular successor (Mattes 2008: 68–9, 71, 76–7; Obeidi 2008: 110).

At Qaddafi's urging, the national PSLC in October 2009 appointed Saif al-Islam al-Qaddafi, the Leader's first son by his second wife, the general coordinator with no term limit. In a surprise move, Saif later tied his acceptance of the new position to the implementation of additional political reforms, including transparent elections and a new constitution (*NYT*: 28.2.10). In the end, the general coordinator of the PSLC may not prove to be the eventual successor to Qaddafi; however, the tribal leadership around which the organization is built will almost surely play a central role in the deal-making involved in designating his successor.

Resurgence and reform

In August 1998, Libya accepted a joint American–British proposal to try two Libyan suspects in the December 1988 bombing of Pan Am flight 103 at The Hague in the Netherlands. Once the suspects had been remanded into custody, the United Nations suspended the multilateral sanctions regime in place since 1992, and Libya began to implement a variety of socioeconomic and political reforms. Some progress was made in reviving an ailing economy, but the social reforms put in place after 1998 were limited in scope and impact, and meaningful political reform did not occur.

In October 1998, the system of people's congresses and people's committees in place for two decades was modified with the creation of 26 regional units, known as *sha'abiyat*. The *sha'abiyat* succeeded the 42 municipalities created in 1975. Positioned between the basic and national levels of government, each of them has its own people's congress and people's committee. Their principal tasks are to improve the coordination of local interests and to decentralize authority (Mattes 2004: 23; Obeidi 2008: 108). The secretaries of the various basic people's congresses within the *sha'abiyat* constitute the people's congress of the *sha'abiyat*; however, the secretaries of the people's committee of the *sha'abiyat*, nominally elected by the members of the people's congress of the *sha'abiyat*, are nominated by the leadership of the revolution. With many of them high-ranking military officers, the structure of the *sha'abiyat* again exemplifies the extent to which the Leader insists on retaining control of the direct democracy system. The number of *sha'abiyat* increased to 32 in April 2001 (Mattes 2008: 59, 78).

In March 2000, Qaddafi abolished a number of central government functions, and the *sha'abiyat* assumed several responsibilities previously under the control of the GPC. Several ministries were eliminated, but central control continued in areas such as defense, education, health, and trade. Of particular significance, the Ministry of Energy was eliminated and control of hydrocarbons policy passed to the National Oil Corporation (NOC). The Leader again reshuffled ministerial responsibilities in January 2003, appointing Shokri Ghanem, a liberal technocrat and prominent advocate of a market economy, as the general secretary of the General People's Committee (prime minister) (Dris-Aït-Hamadouche and Zoubir 2007: 283; St John 2008b: 64).

Attempting too much, accomplishing too little

With Ghanem's appointment, the pace of change accelerated as his progressive administration moved to increase the breadth and depth of reform. Retail trade flourished, international banks established branches, and international travel became commonplace. In this period, Libya also took some steps to improve its human rights posture, including the abolition of the people's court, some of whose powers were transferred to other courts. At the same time, serious human rights issues remained, including the use of violence against detainees, restrictions on freedom of association and expression, and the incarceration of political prisoners. For many Libyans, the reforms implemented by the Ghanem administration were a welcome change after decades of isolation abroad and socialism at home. For others, including Libyans who had profited from the corruption and graft that developed during the embargo years and those who knew little beyond the years of Qaddafi rule, the change was unsettling if not deeply concerning (Pargeter 2006: 223–4, 231; Anderson 2006: 46–7). In a victory for hardline elements, Ghanem was replaced in March 2006 by Ali Baghdadi al-Mahmudi, his more conservative deputy, and demoted to the head of the National Oil Corporation (*FT*: 6.3.06).

Attempting too much, Ghanem accomplished too little, and, after more than three years as prime minister, there was scant evidence that far-reaching change had been implemented. Observers blamed the lack of progress on conservative, hardline elements; however, the disappointing performance of the Ghanem administration had deeper roots in the structure and operation of the *Jamahiriya* system. Resistant to change, the system is designed to perpetuate the rule of a small elite. As Mohamed Zahi Moghrebi, a respected political scientist teaching at Gar Younis University, noted, only 112 ministers served on the General People's Committee in the first three decades of the revolution, and this very small number becomes even more striking when one considers that some of them occupied their posts for no more than one or two years. Hamstrung by the limited authority of the office of the prime minister, frustrated by endless congress and committee meetings, and isolated by a cabinet not of his choosing, Ghanem's power to effect significant reform proved highly limited (Pargeter 2006: 224–6; Werenfels 2008: 11).

Frequent changes in governmental structures and ministerial responsibilities, a preferred tactic of the Leader since 1969, have proved highly effective in preventing potential political competitors from building a power base but have seldom heralded a meaningful shift in public policy. On the contrary, they tend to underscore the relative stability of the power balance and buttress Qaddafi's dominant power position. For similar reasons, the official media in Libya have long followed a practice of referring to important political players by position but not by name. With the exception of Qaddafi and his children, it is only in very recent times that the government-controlled media have begun printing the names of the current head of the GPC, the NOC and so forth. In part as a result of this long-time practice, the decision-making process in Libya has remained both impersonal and opaque, making it difficult if not impossible to identify how, where, and by whom, a decision is taken (Dris-Aït-Hamadouche and Zoubir 2007: 268). In this way, Qaddafi has been able to control important policy decisions from behind the scenes, blurring the lines of authority and responsibility crucial to a transparent government.

An attempt to coalesce the disparate groups opposed to the Qaddafi regime took place in London in June 2005, when the National Libyan Opposition held its first meeting. Stressing a return to constitutional legitimacy, the conference brought together a potpourri of largely moderate, mainstream opposition groups; however, others, such as the Muslim Brotherhood, rejected the narrow agenda insisted on by the organizers and failed to attend. At the end of the conference, the participants issued a "Declaration for National Consensus," which called for a return to constitutional legitimacy, creation of a transitional government, and the prosecution of all members of the Qaddafi regime guilty of crimes against humanity (St John 2008b: 63). While it called upon Qaddafi to resign, the conference rejected armed action and ruled out foreign interference, arguing that the United Nations was responsible for restoring Libya's constitution (*NYT*: 25.6.05).

There has been talk for many years of a new Libyan constitution. As early as 1998, 13 specialists drawn from the PSLC system were asked to prepare a draft constitution; however, nothing more was heard of their efforts. In 2004, Saif al-Islam al-Qaddafi created a committee to work with international experts to draft a charter. Their efforts resulted in a draft constitution of 152 articles, which was leaked to the press in the spring of 2008. It was then submitted to a legal committee for review under the following guidelines: (1) be sensitive to the spirit of *The Green Book*, (2) acknowledge the weakness of a formal system of governance and the strength of actors sitting outside the formal system, and (3) consider the need for stability in all existing bodies and units of governance. These guidelines, which appear to hamstring any effort at serious and comprehensive political reform, confirmed that there were certain red lines which could not be crossed in any new constitution, including the Leader's role and the socioeconomic and political thoughts collected in *The Green Book*. After review by the judicial committee, the draft constitution in the spring of 2010 was passed to the national PSLC for review.

Any constitution released in the future – if one is ever released – will almost surely be more of a social contract – à la Jean-Jacques Rousseau – as opposed to a practical document detailing a working system of representative democracy with separation of powers, checks and balances, political parties, and free elections. Selected elements of a Western-style, representative democracy are present in the Libyan model of direct democracy, but others, such as the rule of law, respect for human rights, and freedom to dissent, are not. Moreover, a thorough reform of the existing system of government, to include professionalization of the military, increased control of security institutions by civil society and the state, and strengthening the rule of law, is unlikely to happen as long as Qaddafi remains in power. Any such reform would destroy the system the Leader has spent 40 years constructing and destroy his power base in the process. In this context, the most enlightening section of *The Green Book* remains the final paragraph of the first volume, which reads: "Theoretically, this is the genuine democracy. But realistically, the strong always rule, i.e. the stronger part in the society is the one that rules."

Human rights in Libya

In February 2006, violent demonstrations outside the Italian consulate in Benghazi, sparked by an Italian politician who boasted on television that he was wearing a t-shirt emblazoned with caricatures of the Prophet Muhammad, left 10 Libyans dead and dozens injured. In response to the riots, which spread to other cities and degenerated into anti-regime demonstrations, the General People's Committee in March 2006 created a human rights office, and on the following day the regime pardoned 132 political prisoners, including 84 members of the banned Muslim Brotherhood. Although these were welcome signs of reform, the US Department of State in its 2007 report on human rights accurately described the Libyan political system as an authoritarian regime with a poor human rights record in which the Leader and his inner circle monopolize power, and it repeated those comments verbatim in its 2008 and 2009 reports (US Department of State 2010). Organizations such as Amnesty International and Human Rights Watch have also continued to chart the human rights violations committed by the regime (Human Rights Watch 2006a, b).

In mid-2009, the state nationalized the budding media empire of Saif al-Islam al-Qaddafi, including two newspapers (*Oea* and *Quryna*) mildly critical of the regime, dealing a fresh blow to the little free press that had begun to develop in the country. Although both newspapers later reappeared, the format was changed to topical, apolitical stories as opposed to daily news, analysis, and editorials. The regime also shut down *Al Libiya*, Saif's satellite television station, which later relocated to Jordan. In January 2010, the Leader told the GPC that a free press was one owned by the people, that is, the regime, as opposed to individuals or corporations. He also suggested that the real solution to a free press in Libya was a broadcast and print media operated by a committee consisting of representatives from all segments of society (*JANA*: 30.1.10). In the interim, the regime continued to block public access to a variety of internet websites.

In early May 2009, Ali Mohamed al Fakheri, better known by his terrorist *nom de guerre*, Ibn al-Sheikh al-Libi, died in the notorious Abu Salim prison. Captured by US forces in Afghanistan in 2001, he was turned over to Libyan authorities in late 2005 or early 2006. Although he reportedly committed suicide, the tight security commonplace in Libyan prisons made this highly unlikely (*Guardian*: 15.5.09). At the other end of the political spectrum, Fathi al-Jahmi, a prominent Libyan political dissident, human rights activist, and former provincial governor, slipped into a coma following a stroke on 4 May 2009 and later died. First jailed in 2002 after he called for free speech and political reforms in Libya, he was released in 2004 but rearrested after he labeled Qaddafi a dictator and again called for democratic reforms. Failing for years to provide adequate medical care, Libyan authorities, in an effort to escape responsibility for his death, transferred al-Jahmi to a hospital in Jordan after he had slipped into the coma. He died in the Arab Medical Center in Amman a few days later. A tale of two Libyans, both opponents to the Qaddafi regime, and both dead indirectly or directly as a result of regime policy (*NYT*: 22.5.09).

At the same time, there were small pockets of improvement in the human rights picture which offered some hope for additional reforms in the future. In January 2010, just as a committee appointed by Saif was about to propose laws setting out a new penal code and the formation of apolitical NGOs, the Leader surprised observers when he told the GPC that the concept of a civil society complete with NGOs had no place in Libya. In the interim, a foundation founded and chaired by Saif issued a report cataloging human rights abuses in Libya and calling for full liberalization of the media. Saif was also instrumental in assisting Human Rights Watch to conduct its first ever press conference inside Libya in late 2009. In March 2010, Saif announced the release of 214 Islamist prisoners, including 34 former members of the Libyan Islamic Fighting Group. Human Rights Watch supported their release but was quick to point out that several hundred more detainees remained in Libyan jails (*WP*: 26.11.09; *JANA*: 23.3.10).

Direct democracy in theory and practice

Over the last four decades, the Qaddafi regime has implemented a long series of political reforms in an effort to generate the levels of mobilization and participation required to achieve its goals but to do so within the centralized, authoritarian political system thought necessary to retain power. In so doing, a remarkable continuity has characterized the internal politics of the regime despite frequent changes in specific policies and structures. From the outset of the revolution, the dominant policy pattern had been the oscillation between the occasional emphasis on mobilization and participation and the constant refinement of socioeconomic and political structures believed necessary to ensure control of the political system. In this continuing tug of war, control has triumphed over mobilization and participation at every juncture.

In this regard, the most notable failure of the Qaddafi regime has been its inability to build an active, engaged, and participant citizenry. Inheriting a bland, nonparticipatory society, the regime devoted enormous time and resources after 1969 to creating units and institutions that would develop citizens aware of their role in the political system and actively participating in it. The reasons for its failure to do so are still not completely clear, but the regime has clearly been ineffective in preparing its citizens for a role in political participation. Moreover, most of the small minority of Libyans who do participate in the political process do not believe in its efficacy. Political participation is a minority endeavor in all societies; nevertheless, the widespread disbelief in Libya in the effectiveness of the current system suggests serious, deep-seated ideological and structural problems. Midway through the last decade, the Leader appeared to recognize that the One September Revolution as a mobilizing tool had run its course. In response, he declared victory had been won; however, in reality, it was more a case of snatching defeat from victory.

In the interim, Qaddafi continues to promote his system of direct democracy as the solution to the world's political ills, decrying multiparty democracy as a system in which people are ridden on like donkeys. In a speech to Libyan students in April 2009, Qaddafi concluded by proudly proclaiming that one day the world would implement *The Green Book*, the Third Universal Theory, and the *Jamahiriya* system. Eight months later, he told the GPC that there was no alternative to the authority of the people as expressed in the *Jamahiriya* system. Consequently, there seems little opportunity for meaningful change in the current political system as long as the Leader is alive and in power.

4

ECONOMICS

Following the discovery of oil, Libya developed into a classic example of a *rentier* state, one in which the economic rent derived from the sale of a single resource, often hydrocarbons, enables the state to act as the distributor of this rent in the form of education, housing, and other social services. In turn, this enables the state to command political allegiance and compliance from its citizens. Despite efforts by the revolutionary government to lessen the nation's reliance on the income from the sale of hydrocarbons, Libya after four decades of revolutionary experimentation remains a *rentier* state.

The analysis in this chapter centers on economic developments after 1969; however, to set the stage for this discussion, it is first necessary to review the oil and gas policies of the monarchy. It is only in this manner that the themes of continuity and change can be explored to their fullest extent. In so doing, the analysis pays special attention to hydrocarbons as the economic foundation of contemporary Libya. It also explores the interplay of the economic, social, and political forces which have impacted on the repeated economic crises suffered by Libya over the last four decades. A secondary theme is the ongoing conflict between political ideology and economic reality after 1969.

Setting the stage

As early as 1914, traces of petroleum were discovered in Tripolitania, and in the 1930s suggestions of oil deposits surfaced elsewhere in Libya. Field exploration began in 1940, when the Italian government instructed Azienda Generale Italiana Petroli (AGIP) to explore the Sirte Basin. World War II interrupted those early exploration efforts before significant hydrocarbon deposits were found. Consequently, American prospectors in 1959 became the first to announce the discovery of petroleum deposits in commercially viable quantities. From the beginning, geology and geography were enormous assets for the hydrocarbon industry. The Sirte Basin, site of most of the early oilfields, contains large deposits of oil and gas in sedimentary rock below an arid desert. Light in gravity, the oil deposits are a high-grade "sweet" (low in sulfur) crude, a quality much sought after by an environmentally conscious world. In addition, Libya is located closer to European markets than its African and Middle Eastern competitors, giving it an advantage in terms of transportation costs. Finally, it does not depend on pipelines, the Suez Canal, or transit around the Horn of Africa to reach its markets, making its oil supply less vulnerable to disruption (McLachlan 1989a: 243–4; Gurney 1996: 4–5, 11).

Production versus price

In August 1961, Standard Oil of New Jersey, through its Libyan affiliate, established a posted price of $2.21 per barrel for Libyan base crude of 39° API (American Petroleum Institute) gravity, with a ceiling of $2.23 for 40° API gravity and above. The prices for the remaining grades of crude oil were set by subtracting a few cents per barrel for each degree below the base grade (Barker and McLachlan 1982: 38). The posted price was based on an arithmetic average of already reduced prices for crude oil from Saudi Arabia, Iran, and Iraq with minor allowances made for the quality and proximity of Libyan crude. The decade of the 1960s saw dramatic increases in both production and revenues, but not in the posted price of oil, the basis of taxable income for producing countries. Concluding that the posted price had not been calculated fairly, the monarchy disputed it from the start, but, given the controlling position of the oil companies, it was powerless to do more than launch a formal protest each time it received a payment from them (Waddams 1980: 118).

Although the monarchy considered the posted price unjust, it pursued a volume-oriented instead of a price-oriented policy out of concern that a price dispute with the oil companies would slow industry development (Gurney 1996: 48–9). Inside Libya, the opposition to the monarchy increasingly challenged its approach to oil pricing, especially after the June 1967 Arab–Israeli War closed the Suez Canal. In response, the oil companies dramatically increased production in Libya to take advantage of the savings achieved from not having to ship oil to Europe via the Cape of Good Hope (Ghanem 1985a: 159–66).

The 1955 petroleum law

To provide a legal structure for the exploration and development of its hydrocarbon resources, Libya drafted a petroleum law in 1955. The law was amended in 1961 and 1965 to correct errors and anomalies; however, its basic structure did not change. The 1961 amendment altered both the procedure for granting concessions and the definition of taxable profits, and the 1965 amendment incorporated a royalty expensing agreement adopted by OPEC in the same year (Barker and McLachlan 1982: 38–9).

With no shortage of oil in the world, the monarchy's success in getting oil companies to begin exploration in Libya was largely due to the attractive terms of the new law. Any company that discovered oil could anticipate strong profits owing to Libya's favorable tax structure. The new law also provided oil companies with assurances that future decisions would be based on commercial as opposed to political considerations; consequently, the level of political risk in Libya was lower than elsewhere. The downside to the 1955 petroleum law was that it largely restricted the government to the role of tax collector, with the oil companies empowered to make key decisions. As a result, the oil companies were encouraged to produce too much, too fast, with negative consequences for the long-term health of the oilfields (Gurney 1996: 33–8).

At the same time, two features of the 1955 petroleum law gave Libya some leverage over the oil companies. Unlike the large concessions granted by the Gulf states, Libya divided its acreage into more than 80 separate concessions and restricted the number any one company could acquire so that no single company or consortium could lay claim to a large area (Epstein 1996: 217–18; Rogan 2009: 359). By requiring the oil companies to surrender a substantial part of an undeveloped concession in a relatively short period of time, they also were deterred from claiming acreage and not exploiting it. Owing to these features, a number of the concessions went to small, independent oil producers who did not have prospects elsewhere and thus had every reason to explore and produce as much oil as possible in Libya (Yergin 1991: 528). These smaller independents later proved vulnerable to manipulation by the revolutionary government (Gurney 1996: 38, 61–2).

With the 1955 petroleum law in place, the monarchy began to negotiate concessionary agreements with the oil companies. Under the concessionary system, the producing state typically entrusted the oil company with the right to explore, develop, extract, and export hydrocarbons from a large area over an extended period of time in exchange for financial payments. The monarchy awarded the first concessions in November 1955, and early awards went to British Petroleum (BP), Standard Oil of New Jersey (Esso), and Texaco, among others. Independent companies, including Amerada, Grace, and Nelson Bunker Hunt, also took acreage. By 1968, Libya had granted 137 concessions to 39 companies, either on their own or in partnership with others, and production had swelled to over 2.6 million barrels a day (b/d) (Gurney 1996: 38–9; Mahmud and Russell 1999: 216–17).

Under the terms of the concessionary agreements, the monarchy's share of net revenues was limited to 50 percent and the operating companies were granted a 25 percent depletion allowance (Gurney 1996: 35–9, 42–7, 52–3, 64–5). These terms generated considerable resentment in Libya because they were not as favorable as those negotiated by the Gulf states. On the other hand, when combined with a policy which invited many companies to bid on Libyan acreage, they made a major contribution to the growth in upstream (exploration and development) operations in the 1960s (St John 2007: 205).

End of the beginning

Libya joined OPEC in 1962, two years after it was formed. The monarchy generally supported OPEC policies but refused to endorse any policy that might threaten its relationship with the oil companies working in Libya (Gurney 1996: 49–52). In addition to concerns that it not antagonize the oil companies, the Ministry of Petroleum Affairs, which consisted of fewer than 10 people, none of whom was a college graduate, lacked the human and other resources necessary to develop and execute a more aggressive, forward-thinking policy. When several college graduates joined the ministry in 1962, their advice was largely ignored because their admiration for Egyptian President Nasser made them politically suspect and because they represented an administrative challenge to their conservative bosses (Ghanem 1985a: 158–9, 162).

In April 1968, Libya announced the creation of the Libyan General Petroleum Company (LIPETCO). The charter of the organization was to enter into more advantageous partnerships with the oil companies. LIPETCO also assumed the government's share in joint oil exploration and development ventures. Three months later, Libya announced that it would no longer agree to concessionary agreements; thereafter, new acreage would be awarded only within the framework of LIPETCO. In March 1970, the National Oil Company (NOC), now known as the National Oil Corporation, replaced LIPETCO. The domestic distribution of oil products was transferred to the NOC in 1970, and the Brega Petroleum Marketing Company was created shortly thereafter to conduct this activity (McLachlan 1989a: 244; St John 2006a: 176–7).

The volume-oriented policy followed by the monarchy produced sustained revenue growth at the expense of the rapid depletion of an exhaustible resource. From 1961 to 1969, government revenues from petroleum exports increased from $3 million to $1.175 billion (Table 4.1). Within eight years of its initial oil shipment, Libya was the world's fourth largest exporter of crude oil, a rate of growth previously unknown in the industry. In the process, Libya moved from a stagnant to an exploding economy, from a capital-deficit to a capital-surplus state, from an aid recipient to an aid extender (Ghanem 1987: 58; Mahmud and Russell 1999: 215–16, 221–7). By 1969, Libya's daily oil production was comparable to that of Saudi Arabia although its known reserves were far less (Yergin 1991: 529). Oil production peaked in April 1970 at 3.7 million b/d, over three times its level three decades later (Gurney 1996: 91–2).

The One September Revolution

The Revolutionary Command Council (RCC) implemented a series of economic measures to symbolize its determination to liberate the country from imperialist elements and foreign control. Within two weeks of the overthrow of

TABLE 4.1 Libyan crude oil production, exports, and revenues, 1961–70

	1961	1962	1963	1964	1965	1966	1967	1968	1969	1970
Production (million b/d)	0.018	0.182	0.442	0.862	1.219	1.501	1.741	2.602	3.109	3.318
Exports (million b/d)	0.014	0.180	0.460	0.856	1.213	1.500	1.717	2.582	3.070	3.312
Revenues ($ million)	3.0	40	108	211	351	523	625	1,002	1,175	1,351

Sources: OPEC 1980, Arab Petroleum Research Centre 1985, Mahmud and Russell 1999.

the monarchy, it issued a resolution requiring foreign banks to form Libyan joint stock companies with at least 51 percent of their shares owned by the government (Ansell and al-Arif 1972: 102–4). In September 1970, it negotiated major concessions from the oil companies operating in Libya, and in October 1970 it confiscated all Italian-owned property and expelled 20,000 Italian residents (Libyan Arab Republic 1973b: 226–8; Waddams 1980: 251–60).

Changing the rules of the hydrocarbon game

Focused on consolidating its power, the RCC first directed conciliatory statements toward the oil companies, promising to honor existing agreements; nevertheless, the ambiguity in its hydrocarbon policy was soon evident. On 18 September 1969, the prime minister spoke reassuringly, indicating that there would be no spectacular change in the nation's oil policy, but less than two weeks later he contradicted himself, suggesting that the posted price for Libyan crude oil was too low. On 6 October 1969, the petroleum minister hinted at a possible change in policy when he noted that the posted price of Libyan crude had been set long ago by one side in contravention of both the spirit and the letter of the 1955 petroleum law. He added in a threatening manner that his ministry would spare no pains to rectify the situation (St John 2007: 242). Ten days later, Qaddafi announced that the RCC had established a committee to study the question of a fair oil price, and when the results of its work were known Libya intended to get from the oil companies what it had coming to it (Ansell and al-Arif 1972: 95). Based on these statements and others, the RCC from the start appeared determined to reduce production to conserve supplies and to increase revenues by maximizing income per barrel.

For the oil companies, the honeymoon ended in December 1969, when the RCC moved to assert full Libyan sovereignty over its hydrocarbon resources and in the process to increase the posted price of oil. In so doing, the RCC focused on the independent oil companies, especially Occidental Petroleum, because they were the most vulnerable to a strategy of reduced production quotas on a company-by-company basis. Production cuts were also imposed on other oil producers, but they were not as adversely affected as Occidental, which had no source of oil outside Libya. When the RCC imposed large production cuts, Occidental scrambled to find alternate sources to supply its customers, but none of the larger oil companies extended a helping hand (McLachlan 1989a: 245; Yergin 1991: 578–9; Epstein 1996: 239–43).

After all the oil companies had rejected its initial demands, the RCC increased the pressure in the summer of 1970, cutting the companies' collective production by 800,000 b/d. In addition, Esso was told not to export liquefied natural gas (LNG), and, to add to the uncertainty, Libya nationalized the local distribution of petroleum products. The production cuts imposed in 1970 coincided with a break in Tapline, the Saudi Arabian pipeline through Syria, and the two events combined to produce a global oil shortage, especially in Europe. On 1 September

1970, Occidental Petroleum agreed to an increase of $0.30 per barrel in the posted price of crude oil, and it also agreed to give Libya control over future pricing (Ghanem 1975: 155). This was the first increase in the posted price since OPEC was formed in 1960, and it was quickly followed by additional price hikes as other OPEC members joined Libya in increasing prices. Occidental also agreed to concede a majority of profits to Libya, ending the traditional 50:50 split and introducing a new ratio of 55 percent for the producing state and 45 percent for the oil company (Epstein 1996: 244–5). The RCC immediately applied the Occidental model to all oil companies in Libya, and the other Arab oil-producing states soon followed suit. In short order, the hardline policy pursued by Libya succeeded in ending the myth that the oil producers alone could set the posted price of crude oil and, in so doing, the RCC changed forever the geopolitics of oil (Ghanem 1985a: 169; Rogan 2009: 360–1).

The Caracas Resolution and the Teheran and Tripoli Agreements

Following the One September Agreement, the OPEC member states met in Caracas in December 1970. The major resolution adopted at the meeting reflected Libyan leadership but went well beyond the new terms the Libyans had extracted from the oil companies. In the Caracas Resolution, OPEC called for an increase both in oil prices and in the rate of income tax, together with the elimination of marketing allowances and the adoption of a new system to adjust specific gravity (Ghanem 1985a: 170–4). In February 1971, the Gulf states concluded a pact with the oil companies, known as the Teheran Agreement, which incorporated many of the gains won by Libya in September 1970, including an immediate price increase, further price increases over five years, and a more favorable treatment of specific gravity. At the same time, the Gulf oil producers made two concessions to the oil companies. First, they rejected the principle of leapfrogging, agreeing not to negotiate individually for better terms, and, second, they agreed not to limit production in order to achieve improved financial terms (Waddams 1980: 236–40; St John 2006a: 151, 245–6).

The Teheran Agreement marked the end of Libya's short-lived OPEC leadership role, a role arising from its tough negotiating stance and its relatively large share (15 percent in 1970) of total OPEC crude oil output. The terms of the agreement infuriated the members of the RCC, who criticized the level of price increases, rejected the principle of collective bargaining, and denounced the prohibition on production restrictions. In response, the RCC opened fresh talks with the oil companies aimed at more favorable terms (Barker and McLachlan 1982: 39; Ghanem 1985a: 174–5). The structure of the resulting Tripoli Agreement, a series of separate pacts backdated to 20 March 1971, resembled the Teheran Agreement; however, the Libyans negotiated improved pricing, income tax, and specific gravity commitments from the oil companies. To compensate for underpricing in the 1960s, the oil companies also agreed to a supplemental payment on every barrel of oil exported for the duration of their concessions, and they committed to average at least one exploration rig in operation each year on all concessions (Ghanem 1975: 326–32). Exact figures were never released, but the combination of retroactive payments and price increases in the Tripoli Agreement brought Libya an estimated $1 billion in additional revenues in the first year alone (St John 2006a: 255–6; Waddams 1980: 240–5).

In December 1971, Libya nationalized the BP share of the BP–Nelson Bunker Hunt operation in the Sarir field, and in June 1973 it nationalized the Nelson Bunker Hunt share. For the most part, commercial considerations had dictated Libyan oil policy to this point; however, the action against BP was a political move in retaliation for the failure of the British government, which owned 48.6 percent of the company, to block Iran's seizure of three islands in the Persian Gulf (Waddams 1980: 251–3; Rogan 2009: 363). On 1 September 1973, Libya announced that it was nationalizing 51 percent of all foreign oil producer assets, and one month later, at the outset of the October 1973 Arab–Israeli War, it imposed a partial oil boycott which was supported by other Arab states, doubling the posted price of oil. OPEC ended the oil boycott in April 1974, but the higher prices stuck (Yergin 1991: 606–9, 613–32; Epstein 1996: 246). By the beginning of the next decade, the global price of oil had increased from a little over $2 a barrel in 1969 to as much as $41 a barrel in 1981 (Gurney 1996: 58–61).

In 1974, the revolutionary government converted all concessionary agreements to exploration and production-sharing agreements (EPSAs), the contemporary form of contractual agreement with the oil companies. In the first phase of EPSAs, the agreements provided for 35-year contracts with five years allotted for exploration and 30 years for production. To encourage timely exploration and development, all of the agreements expired at the end of five years if no discovery was made. Production was shared in a ratio of 85 to 15 percent onshore and 81 to 19 percent offshore, with the state taking the larger share in each case. Under the terms of the agreements, the oil companies were required to spend approximately $500 million on exploration activities, regardless of their success; however, their share of any crude oil found was exempt from fees, rents, royalties, and taxes (Waddams 1980: 260–3; Gurney 1996: 67–9).

Early natural gas policy

In contrast to its aggressive oil policies, the RCC failed to implement a clear strategy for the development of natural gas. The problems Libya faced in utilizing the gas produced in association with crude oil were similar to those faced by other oil producers in that most of the fields were located far from potential markets. Petroleum Regulation 8, adopted in late 1968, generally encouraged the exploitation of natural gas; unfortunately, the Ministry of Petroleum Affairs failed to publish the resolution in the *Official Gazette*, a step required to make it valid. The ministry also ignored the fact that any amendment to the petroleum regulations affecting concession holders required their consent. After the oil companies protested, the petroleum minister quietly let it be known that the regulation was a draft, subject to discussion and revision. While Regulation 8 gave the government the option to take, free of charge at the wellhead, natural gas not being used for "economically justified" purposes and imposed penalties for the excessive flaring of gas, all of the natural gas fields in Libya, with the exception of two owned by Esso, were abandoned with their wells plugged. The gas associated with oil production was flared with the exception of the relatively small amount used by the companies in their own operations (Waddams 1980: 180–2, 199; Barker and McLachlan 1982: 40).

In the second half of the 1960s, Esso built an LNG plant at Marsa al-Brega in Sirte. While the plant was under construction, Esso concluded contracts for the sale of the gas with Snamprogetti, a subsidiary of the ENI Group, for delivery at Genoa and with Catalaña de Gas for delivery at Barcelona. The initial supply of gas to the plant came from a pipeline originally laid to take sea water to the Zelten field for a reinjection project. A second supply came from a pipeline spur to the Raguba field with additional gas available from fields owned by the Oasis Group and American Overseas Petroleum (Amoseas). Over the next 25 years, production at Marsa al-Brega was limited to the gas transported from these fields. The RCC later attempted to carry over into the LNG area its tough negotiating position on oil prices, but the policy enjoyed limited success here as gas exports declined over the years owing to price disputes with Italy and Spain, the only two markets the Marsa al-Brega facility developed (Ghanem 1975: 151; Barker and McLachlan 1982: 45–6; Gurney 1996: 14, 56–7).

Socialism in theory and practice

Socialism, defined as a redistribution of wealth and resources, was implicit in Libya after 1969, but it did not take a concerted form before 1975. As early as 1973, the RCC began to take tentative steps to turn its socialist rhetoric into practice; however, it delayed implementation of the more radical elements of the program until the second half of the decade. The principal reason for the delay was the popular opposition a full-scale socialist program was expected to generate. Consequently, socioeconomic policy in the early years of the revolution concentrated on social welfare programs which enjoyed widespread popular support (Libyan Arab Republic 1973b: 127–33; Allan 1981: 221–34).

One aspect of the government's early economic policies, selective support for capitalism, was notable if for no other reason than the regime's efforts to disguise it. Even as the Third Universal Theory bemoaned the shortcomings of international capitalism, the RCC not only encouraged but actually subsidized indigenous capitalism from 1969 to around 1973 (Libyan Arab Republic 1973a: 6). Throughout this period, Qaddafi stressed his respect for private ownership and carefully differentiated between domestic and foreign capitalists. The latter were universally condemned and subject to severe regulation, but the former were characterized as bad only when they were exploitative (Qaddafi 1970: 207–9). As a result, domestic capitalism flourished and substantial private fortunes were accumulated in a period in which the regime officially advocated a socialist system (Bennett 1975: 103; Allan 1981: 223–4; St John 1983a: 482–3).

In common with other Arab revolutionary governments, central planning was a key ingredient in the RCC's approach to economic development. A three-year plan was announced in 1972 (1973–5), and it was followed by five-year plans in 1976–80 and 1981–5. The monarchy had also developed a five-year plan (1963–8, extended to 1969); however, the targets set by the revolutionary government called for an accelerated rate of development through higher levels of expenditure (El Fathaly 1977: 19–20; Birks and Sinclair 1979: 95–6; Allan 1981: 79–95). Developed in conjunction with revised oil production and pricing policies, the funds needed to achieve accelerated development came from the hardline approach the RCC took with the oil companies in Libya.

By the end of the 1970s, a socialist revolution had taken place in Libya, drastically modifying long-standing economic and social structures. The management of the economy was increasingly socialist in intent and effect, with wealth in housing, capital, and land significantly redistributed or in the process of redistribution (Allan 1981: 244). Private enterprise had been virtually eliminated, replaced by a centrally controlled economy. Moreover, progressive assaults on the individual accumulation of capital continued, with increasingly tight control of individual banking transactions. As the decade ended, agriculture was the only economic sector in which a significant share of production remained in private hands and, even here, the public share of production had increased threefold since 1969 as the result of government projects in coastal areas and in the south (Allan 1981: 244; Allan 1983: 380).

Agricultural and industrial development

At the outset of the revolution, the agricultural sector employed around 20 percent of the workforce and contributed less than 3 percent of GNP; moreover, its export value was negligible. In turn, the manufacturing sector represented less than 2 percent of GNP, employed less than 5 percent of the workforce, and produced an equally unimpressive output. With high expectations for the nation's resources, the development plans of the RCC called for the rapid creation of viable and productive agricultural and industrial sectors. The first five-year plan called for an annual increase of 10 percent in GNP, 25 percent in industrial output, and near-self-sufficiency in food output by 1980. More than one-sixth of the budget was allocated to agriculture, with industry receiving the second highest allocation (Allan 1981: 187–91; McLachlan 1982: 17–18).

Although it was clearly committed to agriculture, the regime failed to develop a coherent strategy and an integrated plan to achieve its goals. Misinterpreting its early success in the oil sector, it applied the same aggressive approach to agriculture with disastrous consequences (Allan 1981: 186–7). Large estates in private or corporate hands were sequestered, broken down into small farms, and allocated to individuals. A small farm policy made political sense, but the intensification of dryland farming on poor soils was not a sustainable policy. Moreover, the expansion of irrigated farming in other areas aggravated an already serious water shortage (McLachlan 1982: 18–20).

Major agricultural projects were undertaken in the arid or semi-arid regions of Fezzan, the Jefara Plain, the Jabal al Akhdar, Kufrah and Sarir, and Salul al-Khudor with little or no thought to the realities of water limitations, labor shortages, or the need to create an economically viable base in a post-hydro-carbon era. On the Jefara Plain, some 6,000 new farms were planned, while the Kufrah project expanded wheat cultivation, utilizing underground aquifers as the source of irrigation. In a country with no perennial water flows, limited rainfall, and only relatively small areas on the Jefara Plain and in the Jabal al Akhdar available for rainfed cultivation, the regime's goals for the agricultural sector were wildly optimistic from the start. Along the coast, intensified farm-ing efforts led to unsustainable water depletion rates and increased soil salinity. Inland, the use of underground water reservoirs to cultivate wheat and fodder crops at oases such as Kufrah and Sarir had no economic justification. Both sites were distant from target markets, and the problems of administering projects in remote locations proved formidable. With reliable economic data seldom avail-able, conservative estimates placed the cost of wheat grown at many of these large agricultural projects to be as much as 10–20 times the world market price (Birks and Sinclair 1984: 252–62; Latham 1985; Allan 1987: 127–8; Benkhial and Bukechiem 1989). As J. A. (Tony) Allan, a long-term observer of Libya, later emphasized, capital was no substitute for water in the Libyan case, a lesson the revolutionary leadership belatedly took to heart (Allan 1982).

Available manpower was a serious impediment to agricultural development in Libya. In a large country with a relatively small population, only a fraction of the citizenry was available for farming, and as oil revenues coursed through the economy, the number decreased each year as more and more Libyans moved to urban areas in search of an easier life. In response, the regime imported large numbers of expatriate workers, who brought with them indirect costs, such as increased imports of consumer goods, which put pressure on the balance of payments and drained foreign currency reserves. Labor sourced from a wide variety of countries also brought with it unfamiliar social problems for a largely insular society (Birks and Sinclair 1979: 97–102; Vandewalle 1998: 112).

The first five-year plan (1976–80) proved a watershed in the development of Libyan industry. The allocation of 19 percent of planned investment to the industrial sector signaled a major shift in investment priorities toward capital-intensive, heavy industry projects. By the end of the decade, more than 100 factories were being run by the public sector (Ghanem 1987: 64). A bold move symptomatic of many early RCC policies, the government's strong commit-ment to heavy industry proved premature as many of the projects proposed in the first five-year plan had to be rolled over to the second for completion or even commencement (Bennett 1975: 110–11).

In response to the failure of the agricultural sector to respond to the unrealistic demands placed on it, industry in the second five-year plan received a higher allocation than agriculture, and self-sufficiency in industrial production became a regime goal. With heavy industry exerting a natural appeal to most developing countries undergoing a socialist transformation, Libyan policy mirrored the experience of many other states. Over the years, petrochemical facilities and oil refineries were constructed, a steel mill and aluminum complex completed, food-processing plants built, and some consumer goods industries begun. With the regime committed to maximizing its return from hydrocarbon exports, special emphasis was placed on the development of oil refineries and petrochemical plants as they reduced the amount of crude oil exported, extending the life of the nation's reserves (Ghanem 1987: 68).

Available manpower was also a problem in the industrial sector. Both the monarchy and the revolutionary government invested heavily in educational facilities; nevertheless, the overall level of educational attainment remained low. With the system biased toward general education, the number of scientifically and technically qualified Libyans remained low. The persistent lack of capable administrators and technicians combined with an inadequate infrastructure to prevent the regime from spending the funds allocated in their development budgets. Another objective of the industrialization policy, the creation of job opportunities for auxiliary and service workers in what is by nature a capital intensive industry, also went largely unrealized. As a result, the goals of self-sufficiency in both agriculture and industrial production proved illusory, and, despite rhetoric to the contrary, the regime was not rewarded with viable accomplishment in either area (Allan 1981: 190–1, 211; Birks and Sinclair 1984: 262–72; Ghanem 1987: 66).

The Great Manmade River project

In 1983, Libya began a massive development scheme, the Great Manmade River (GMR), which involved the transfer of water from underground aquifers in the southern desert to the coast for agricultural, industrial, and household use. Initially, the project consisted of some 2,500 miles (4,000 kilometers) of pipeline designed to transport 5.6 million cubic meters of water daily (*MEED*: 20.7.85). The first phase of the project, completed in 1991, connected 108 wells in Tazerbo and 126 wells in Sarir to the coastal towns of Benghazi and Sirte. With the conclusion in 1996 of the first part of phase two, water flowed through the GMR pipeline to Tripoli (*FT*: 11.9.96). As the work progressed, the pumping of water proved more complicated than first thought and the demand for water proved far greater than expected; consequently, a project originally forecast to take five years was still a work in progress three decades later. The final cost of the GMR project is unknown; however, current government estimates, when capital investment and running costs over 50 years are included, exceed $33 billion (*JANA*: 20.3.09).

After the policies of self-sufficiency, import substitution, and job creation failed to produce the desired results, agriculture policy in the 1980s concentrated on the GMR project. The water supplied by the GMR was expected to provide irrigation for coastal grain cultivation on an additional 250,000 acres in summer and 450,000 acres in winter. The resultant increase in grain production, coupled with a planned increase in the national sheep herd to 3 million head, was forecast to transform Libya from a net importer of foodstuffs to a net exporter (Latham 1985; Benkhial and Bukechiem 1989). As it turned out, unforeseen events combined to prove the forecasters wrong in terms of both how much water was required and how it would be used. First, domestic and industrial demand on the coast increased at a faster rate than expected. Second, years of excess pumping from the aquifers around Tripoli and other coastal towns resulted in falling water tables, deteriorating water quality, and the intrusion of sea water into freshwater reservoirs. Finally, economics played a determinant role in how the water was used in that the revenue generated from urban and industrial uses covered the soaring costs of the GMR to a much greater extent than agriculture (Pim and Binsariti 1994; St John 2006a: 100).

A showcase of the regime, the GMR is not without its critics. Detractors argue that the project is too costly, will never ensure food security, and encourages agricultural development that will require government subsidies ad infinitum (Burgat 1987: 218–19; Allan 1988; *MEED*: 22.9.89). Once the project is completed, studies suggest an average cost of between $0.65 and $0.90 per cubic meter of water, a price point that makes the GMR cost-effective for municipal uses but not for agricultural applications (Monitor Group and Cambridge Energy Research Associates 2006: 95–6). On the other hand, a cost of $0.65–0.90 per cubic meter does make the project competitive with desalination plants. Critics have also charged that the GMR will quickly exhaust the underground aquifers in the southern desert, leaving giant sinkholes. In response, Libyan officials claim that the volume of recoverable water reserves in the aquifers is sufficient to supply the needs of Chad, Egypt, Libya, and Sudan for 4,860 years (*JANA*: 20.3.09).

From boom to bust, the 1980s

In 1980, Libya initiated EPSAs, phase two, a second round of exploration and production-sharing agreements, the terms of which reflected in part its growing concern for rapidly diminishing petroleum reserves. At the same time, political considerations once more encroached on hydrocarbon policy. Libya pursued an aggressive, often radical, foreign policy in the 1970s, and its diplomatic relations with the West, especially the United States, deteriorated as a result. In response, the regime decided to involve East European countries in the oil industry. Based on their limited financial capacity, NOC officials opposed this political decision; nevertheless, Rompetrol, the Romanian state oil company, and Geocom, the Bulgarian state oil company, were both assigned blocks in EPSAs, phase two (Allan 1983: 381–2; Gurney 1996: 69–70).

Otherwise, the second phase of the EPSAs resembled the first, with the significant exception that the production sharing pattern in the second phase varied for the first time in accordance with the assumed prospects of the acreage. For top category concessions, the split was 85 to 15 percent in Libya's favor, but the state reduced its share to 81 to 19 percent for medium category concessions and to 75 to 25 percent for less promising areas. Moreover, the oil companies concluding contracts under the EPSAs, phase two, were expected to spend around $1 billion in exploration activities in the first five years of the contract, double the requirement in phase one. Collectively, the agreements concluded in the EPSAs, phases one and two, resulted in 694 exploratory wells, 270 of which were successful, and the discovery of some 8 billion barrels of crude oil and 45 trillion cubic feet of natural gas. The new reserves added around 250,000 b/d to Libya's production capacity (Mahmud and Russell 1999: 218).

Despite the relative success of the early EPSA phases, the level of oil exploration and development in Libya declined appreciably in the 1970s and again after 1980. And the expectation of continuing high oil prices went unrealized as the underlying balance between supply and demand turned against OPEC. Consumers diversified their energy sources and developed energy-saving technologies, and the oil suppliers outside OPEC further reduced the organization's ability to influence a shrinking market. As both global oil prices and Libyan exports declined, Libya experienced a serious recession. Oil production averaged 1.8 million b/d in 1980, dropped to 1.2 million b/d in 1981, and then stabilized at around 1.0 million b/d for the next several years. Moreover, the combination of domestic consumption and the payment of offshore debts took about 40 percent of production each year, leaving only about 550,000 b/d for cash sales (Ghanem 1987: 67–8; Burgat 1987: 213–14; McLachlan 1989a: 247–8). Between 1982 and 1986, annual oil revenues dropped from $21 billion to $5.4 billion, forcing Libya to join other oil-producing states in reconsidering its strategies in pursuit of sustainable macroeconomic policies and in support of distributive largesse (Vandewalle 1998: 84).

In addition to the drop in oil prices and production, Libya had to adjust to the economic sanctions imposed by the United States in response to Qaddafi's alleged support for global terrorism. The United States began to impose trade restrictions in 1973, and a unilateral sanctions regime came into full force under the Reagan administration (1981–9). In 1982, the United States banned imports of Libyan oil and prohibited the export of oil and gas machinery to Libya, and three years later it ordered American oil companies out of Libya. Five American companies, Occidental Petroleum, W. R. Grace, and the three companies making up the Oasis Group (Amerada Hess, Conoco, and Marathon Oil), were affected by the withdrawal order. Between them, they accounted for almost half of Libya's oil output at the time. Exxon and Mobil had already pulled out of Libya in 1981 and 1982, respectively, claiming that their ventures were no longer profitable (Mahmud and Russell 1999: 219; St John 2002: 124–7, 131–5).

During the 1980s, Libya was forced to slow down or abandon a number of important development projects which would have led to a greater diversification of the economy because the regime refused to curtail military expenditures even as revenues dropped on account of declining oil prices. The deteriorating economy led some observers to conclude that the unilateral sanctions regime imposed by the United States was having the desired effect, but, in reality, its direct impact in 1986–92 was relatively small. The main effect of the ban on the US import of Libyan oil was to increase sales to European markets. Whereas Europe took 55 percent of Libyan crude oil exports in 1981, it took 68 percent four years later. The sanctions also prompted Libya to expand its downstream activities (production and distribution) in Europe. In 1985, Libya purchased a 70 percent holding in Tamoil, a company with a refinery in Italy and later ones in Germany and Switzerland, together with hundreds of retail outlets throughout much of Europe. The investment restrictions imposed by the United States in the 1996 Iran and Libya Sanctions Act (ILSA) also proved of minimal value as Libya seldom had need for investment that exceeded the $40 million limit imposed by ILSA. When it did, companies more often than not revised existing contracts as opposed to signing the new ones that would have triggered the ILSA regulations (St John 2002: 127–31, 190–1; O'Sullivan 2003: 186–95).

The third five-year plan (1981–5) was drafted on the basis of oil production at 1.4 million b/d and revenues of around $20 billion per annum. Instead, revenues over the period were barely $10 million per annum. In response, Libya implemented austerity measures which prolonged the deep recession plaguing the economy. It cut public sector spending, drew down foreign reserves, expelled foreign workers, and delayed payments to foreign contractors. While most Libyans were sheltered from the redundancies, their standard of living deteriorated, with chronic shortages of consumer goods aggravated by an inefficient distribution system. Industrial output, which accounted for little more than 3 percent of gross domestic product (GDP), experienced the effect of large cutbacks in investment, and agriculture, which still accounted for only 2–3 percent of GDP, continued to show little benefit from the massive outlays for large-scale projects. Grandiose schemes not immediately productive, such as the Sirte fertilizer complex, the Misurata steel works, and the Great Manmade River, were delayed, as were heavy commitments to petrochemical plants (Allan 1983: 377–9, 381–2).

Revolution within the revolution

Following almost two decades in which he was the foremost proponent of socialism, Qaddafi in the second half of the 1980s adopted a more moderate tone and signaled an interest in returning to a more open, free enterprise system in a package of reforms sometimes referred to as green *perestroika*. In February 1987, delegates to the General People's Congress (GPC) voiced open criticism of regime economic policies, the conflict in Chad, and the overzealousness of the revolutionary committees. In response, Qaddafi in March 1987 announced the first of a series of socioeconomic and political measures that rescinded earlier directives and led to a period of liberalization. Characterizing the changes as a "revolution within the revolution," the Leader envisioned a new role for the private sector, together with limited political liberalization. Later, he called for reforms in both the agricultural and the industrial sectors, including a reversal of import substitution policies and the adoption of modern management practices. He also embraced the concept of *tashrukiyya*, a form of self-management that allowed for the creation of cooperatives to which partners could contribute either capital or labor (Vandewalle 1991: 221, 226–7; Burgat 1995: 55; St John 2008c: 97).

In September 1988, the Leader called for an end to government control over trade, abolishing the state import and export monopoly. He also lifted some injunctions against retail trade, and *suqs* and small shops in urban areas began to reopen. The petroleum sector and heavy industry were exempt from the new privatization measures, but he called for greater efficiency in other state enterprises. After 1990, Qaddafi initiated a second set of economic reforms, intended to reinforce and extend those introduced in the first wave. The goals of the new initiatives were similar to the earlier ones and included less state control of the economy, added private sector initiatives, and reduced state spending. With most Libyans employed in the public sector, the Leader also called for the closure of unprofitable public enterprises, a reduction in the number of public employees, and higher fees for state-provided services, such as electricity and water. To facilitate change, commercial and state banks reopened, but it would be another 15 years before the banking sector was truly revived (Deeb 1990: 149; Vandewalle 2006: 164–5).

A combination of economic and political considerations prompted this moderation in the socialist policies of the regime. Economically, the state-run supermarket system, plagued with endemic shortages, was breaking down under the weight of corruption and a chaotic distribution system. Moreover, the unofficially tolerated black market, where everything was available at a price, provided little relief to the average Libyan. At the same time, the expulsion in 1985 of large numbers of expatriate workers, mainly Egyptians and Tunisians, a political decision with severe economic consequences, brought the agricultural and service sectors to a virtual standstill. Finally, as oil prices dropped in the first half of the 1980s, oil revenues plummeted, reducing the regime's ability to support extravagant socialist policies (Burgat 1987: 214, 217–18; Vandewalle 1991: 228–30).

Sensitive to political imperatives, Qaddafi realized that internal discontent was reaching an explosive level and responded with corrective measures. Ironically, his ability to execute a policy reversal at a vulnerable time was facilitated by the American bombing of Benghazi and Tripoli in April 1986. The United States had hoped to destabilize the Qaddafi regime, if not kill the Leader, but the attack had the opposite effect, solidifying his hold on power. Although the raid did little to rally the masses around him, it reaffirmed the preeminent position of the army, the single most powerful institution in the country, and it demoralized regime opponents inside and outside Libya (Vandewalle 1998: 123). Qaddafi seized on the moment to consolidate his domestic political position even as he maintained his opposition to the global status quo (St John 2002: 144–5).

About the time Qaddafi launched the revolution within the revolution, Libya announced EPSAs, phase three. The terms of the agreements again varied according to the prospects of the acreage, but the oil company share improved with a 70 to 30 split in the state's favor for first-class prospects and a 65 to 35 split for second-class prospects. Once more, the upfront cost of exploration was to be recovered from production; however, the NOC did agree in phase three to share development costs equally with the oil companies. The more lenient terms of the phase three EPSAs were driven by the regime's cash flow problems, resulting from lower oil prices, decreasing production, and the mounting cost of large development projects. With 25 foreign oil companies exploring in Libya by 1995, phase three EPSAs clearly succeeded in attracting new exploration; unfortunately, most of it was not productive. As a result, Libyan oil production was stagnant into the new millennium (Ghanem 1987: 67–8; Gurney 1996: 13–14, 72–3; St John 2002: 135–46) (Table 4.2).

Multilateral sanctions

In December 1988, Pan Am flight 103 exploded over Lockerbie, Scotland, killing 259 passengers, together with 11 people on the ground, and nine months later UTA flight 772 exploded over Niger, killing 179 passengers. When Libya failed to cooperate fully with American, British, and French officials investigating the attacks, the United Nations, on 15 April 1992, imposed mandatory sanctions, including a ban on air links with Libya, an embargo on the sale of aircraft, aircraft parts, and military equipment, and a reduction in personnel at Libyan embassies. In November 1993, the United Nations tightened the embargo, freezing Libyan assets overseas, banning some sales of petroleum equipment, and tightening the ban on air travel to Libya. Thereafter, the United States continued to press for additional sanctions, including a boycott of Libyan oil; however, its European allies, together a variety of other states, successfully opposed the move on the grounds it would damage their economic interests (Niblock 2001: 35–43; O'Sullivan 2003: 181–2).

From 1992 through 1997, Libyan policies were dominated by issues related to the UN sanctions regime, blocking progress on the economic reforms introduced after 1988. The regime went to enormous lengths to minimize the impact of the multilateral sanctions; nevertheless, they had a greater effect than the

TABLE 4.2 Libyan crude oil production and exports, 1990–2000

	1990	1992	1994	1996	1997	1998	1999	2000
Production (million b/d)	1.389	1.433	1.390	1.394	1.396	1.449	1.287	1.347
Exports (million b/d)	1.090	1.180	1.125	1.123	1.116	1.161	0.992	1.005

Source: OPEC 2008.

unilateral sanctions of the United States. Economically, the trade restrictions impacted negatively on downstream oil operations in particular because the ongoing need to maintain the country's refineries forced it to use substandard parts purchased at exorbitant prices. Oil production was also affected by Libya's inability to access state-of-the-art technology for exploration and development and to limit the natural decline in production from aging fields. The commercial aviation industry was especially hard hit by the loss of passenger traffic, a shortage of spare parts, and a reduced technical capability (Vandewalle 2006: 156–7). Throughout the period, the economy grew only 0.8 percent annually and, with oil prices down to as low as $10 a barrel, Libya's export income dropped to $5.7 billion in 1998. Socially, the most damaging effect of the UN sanctions came from the sharp increase in inflation rates. In a country in which salaries and wages had been static since 1981–2, the rate of inflation averaged around 35 percent per annum in 1993–7. Politically, the sanctions proved something of a boon for the regime as they partly absolved it of its mismanagement as it was able to blame the deteriorating economic conditions on the sanctions regime (Niblock 2001: 60–94; O'Sullivan 2003: 195–202; Martinez 2007: 13–14, 34–5, 39–41).

Challenging the ban on flights, Libya flew pilgrims to Mecca in 1995, and in mid-1996 the Leader flew to an Arab summit meeting in Cairo. In response to the earlier action, the Security Council, in April 1995, eased the ban on air travel to permit Libyan pilgrims to make the haj to Mecca. In an attempt to attract foreign investment, Libya in 1997 enacted a new foreign investment law, an imperfect code but certainly the most liberal legal framework adopted to date by the regime. By the end of 1997, the multilateral sanctions regime was beginning to collapse, with African states and regional bodies leading the opposition. In August 1998, Libya accepted an Anglo-American proposal to try the two Libyan suspects in the Lockerbie case at The Hague under Scottish law, and in April 1999 it remanded them into UN custody. In response, the United Nations suspended its sanctions regime, and with the conclusion of the trial and Libyan compliance with all applicable Security Council resolutions the multilateral sanctions were lifted permanently in September 2003 (Niblock 2001: 44–59; O'Sullivan 2003: 184–5).

New reform efforts

In the second half of 1999, Libya launched fresh initiatives in Africa and Europe aimed at ending its commercial and diplomatic isolation, and by 2000–1 it had reestablished ties with a large number of states. At the same time, the stronger economy dampened popular dissent. Domestic opposition remained a concern, but the regime used its enhanced global status to co-opt the opposition in and out of Libya. At home and abroad, Libyan officials aggressively marketed investment opportunities, emphasizing agriculture, tourism, and trade. Free trade zones promoted exports and technology transfer agreements, and offshore interest in hotel and tourism projects increased. In November 2000, the prime minister

called on investors to play a larger role in its $35 billion, five-year develop-
ment plan to liberalize the economy, and one week later the Leader chimed in,
describing Libya as the best place in the world to invest (St John 2003b: 465–72).

Competing views of liberalization

Around the same time, a mid-September 2000 report in *Al-Zahf al-Akhdar* (*The
Green March*), a publication of the revolutionary committees, strongly criticized
foreign companies operating in Libya, labeling them a threat to society. Although
such attacks were not new, this report provided a window into the growing
divide between progressive and conservative elements over the direction and
pace of economic reforms (*Reuters*: 15.11.00). When it appeared, most observers
dismissed the report as an anomaly, but in retrospect it proved an early indication that influential segments of official Libya were uncomfortable with the turn
toward economic liberalization (St John 2004a: B633).

In 2001, the Leader launched an attack against corruption, calling for a halt in
public expenditures until the problem was addressed. The rationale behind the
timing was unclear, but the remarks were significant for several reasons. First,
they added to growing uncertainty as to the depth and breadth of the liberalization process, with some observers seeing them as a harbinger of a crackdown
on private sector activity. Second, they opened the way for Qaddafi to repeat
earlier calls for a reduction in the number of public sector employees. Finally,
they again demonstrated his ability to read public opinion and to dissociate himself from the discontent generated by corruption and the inefficient use of oil
resources (St John 2008d: 81).

In 2001–3, Libyan officials continued to promote economic liberalization, but
real performance seldom approached official rhetoric. Hydrocarbons continued
to account for approximately 95 percent of exports and some 70–80 percent
of government revenues. Moreover, most of the new economic reforms were
implemented in an ad hoc and nontransparent manner (Otman and Karlberg
2007: 22). Consequently, potential investors continued to face many obstacles,
including inadequate legal protection, ambivalent attitudes toward foreign
workers, and a dearth of Libyan private sector business partners, all of which
were largely the product of the prolonged socialist experiment. Risk-adverse
officials understandably remained hesitant to repeat earlier attempts at diversification, which had failed miserably, when oil prices were at relatively high levels
and oil and gas production was expected to increase (St John 2006b: B644–5).

Piecemeal economic reforms

In June 2003, the Leader initiated a major shift in economic policy when he
told the GPC that the public sector had failed and should be abolished. He
called for a wholesale privatization of the hydrocarbon industry, together with
other sectors of the economy, and pledged to bring Libya into the World Trade

Organization (WTO). In the speech, Qaddafi envisioned an oil and gas sector owned by the people in partnership with international firms and managed by private enterprise. Four months later, Libya published a list of 360 state-owned enterprises targeted for privatization or liquidation (St John 2008d: 81–2). In conjunction with Qaddafi's call for economic reform, Shokri Ghanem, a former minister of economy and foreign trade and a strong proponent of privatization, was appointed prime minister (Pargeter 2006: 223).

In December 2004, Prime Minister Ghanem, speaking at the Arab Strategy Forum in Dubai, outlined an updated development strategy centered on economic diversification. Recognizing that hydrocarbon revenues would remain the engine of economic growth for the foreseeable future, he stressed the need for new industries and alternate sources of income so that oil and gas revenues eventually could become a reserve for the nation (Ghanem 2004). In May 2005, Libya temporarily dropped a decades-long requirement for visitor travel documents to be translated into Arabic, and in July 2005 it lifted customs tariffs on 3,500 imported commodities. In June 2006, after the International Monetary Fund (IMF) reported that only 66 of the 360 state enterprises slated for privatization or liquidation had been sold, Libya announced the creation of a stock market to support privatization efforts (IMF 2006: 9). In January 2007, Libya reversed a policy in effect since the early days of the revolution when it accepted the use of foreign languages on roadside billboards, commercial notice boards, and tourist forms, and in March 2007 it inaugurated the new stock market.

Despite the efforts of the Ghanem administration to set Libya on a firm course of economic liberalization, concrete progress outside the hydrocarbon sector remained tentative. In addition to the determined opposition of hardline elements opposed to any change that might move Libya away from its centralized political system, the reform movement was frustrated by the very nature of the system itself. Based on a large number of congresses and committees, together with scores of supervisory and regulatory bodies, the plethora of operative institutions made it very difficult to implement any kind of meaningful change. Moreover, Ghanem was unable to choose his own cabinet, which left him surrounded by individuals who often did not share his reformist vision. Isolated from both the formal and informal power networks, the prime minister's role was generally confined to the economic and administrative spheres (Pargeter 2006: 224–6).

Public criticism of liberalization policies increased markedly after May 2005, when the government imposed a 30 percent hike in fuel prices and doubled the price of electricity for consumers of more than 500 kilowatts a month. The related decision to lift customs duties on more than 3,500 imported commodities also raised concerns for job security in factories poorly equipped to meet foreign competition. Moreover, central elements of the reform process were implemented in an ad hoc, opaque manner, and they were frequently compromised by human capacity constraints. Qaddafi responded in early March 2006, replacing Ghanem with his more malleable deputy, Ali Baghdadi al-Mahmudi.

As part of the cabinet shake-up, Ghanem was appointed chairman of the NOC (*FT*: 6.3.06). With the cabinet reshuffle widely seen as a victory for conservative hard-liners, the much-trumpeted privatization program, which in the non-hydrocarbon sectors had gained little traction, slowed to a crawl (St John 2008d: 82).

In the aftermath of the cabinet reorganization, public statements by the Leader added to the uncertainty surrounding the speed and direction of reform policy. After Libya's planning minister in June 2006 encouraged international companies to look beyond the oil and gas sector and think of investing in construction, health, or tourism, Qaddafi in a July speech articulated a policy position reminiscent of the mid-September 2000 report in *Al-Zahf al-Akhdar* in that he said he wanted to curb the role of foreigners in the economy to ensure that Libya's wealth remained at home (*JANA*: 23.7.06). One month later, he scolded the nation for its over-reliance on hydrocarbons, foreigners, and imports, telling Libyans to manufacture the things they needed, and in September he surprised everyone when he encouraged unemployed Libyans to emigrate to Africa (*Reuters*: 28.8.06). Throughout the year, his comments totally ignored the obvious ties between regime socioeconomic policies and the high rates of unemployment and underemployment in Libya.

Hydrocarbons, the exception

In May 2000, the NOC announced a new bid round, offering 40 new oil blocks in addition to almost 100 offered in November 1999. By 2003, a total of 18 of these blocks had been awarded, with Spanish Repsol YPF participating alone or in conjunction with others in a dozen of them. With the unilateral sanctions still blocking American companies from investing in Libya, other European operators, including Royal Dutch Shell, Total of France, and Lasmo of the United Kingdom, also expressed interest in acquiring new acreage in Libya. Widespread European interest in Libyan hydrocarbons demonstrated once again that the country remained an attractive source for oil and gas because of its high-quality crude, low cost of recovery, proximity to European markets, and well-developed infrastructure (Energy Information Administration 2005).

After crude oil production peaked at 3.7 million b/d in April 1970, it declined to less than 1.0 million b/d in the mid-1980s. With proven reserves at the time estimated to be 39.1 billion barrels, the largest in Africa, a core objective of the Ghanem administration was to return to a level of 3.0 million b/d no later than 2015 (World Bank 2006: 1–2, 13). This was to be accomplished in two stages with the first stage an increase to 2.0 million b/d by 2010. Oil production in 2006 approached 1.8 million b/d so 2.0 million b/d by 2010 looked possible (OPEC 2008). On the other hand, the target of 3.0 million b/d no later than 2015 was problematic from the start. Moreover, the target year for reaching 3.0 million b/d moved around, depending on which official was talking, from 2010 to 2012 to 2015, with 2015 remaining the most realistic date (St John 2007: 210).

Eventually, the NOC in June 2009 was forced to lower its 2013 production forecast by nearly 25 percent to 2.3 million b/d, and in December 2009 it extended the much ballyhooed target of 3 million b/d out to 2017 (*AFP*: 5.12.09).

The Ghanem administration also assigned a high priority to the expansion of natural gas production, a relatively new objective for Libya. Proven natural gas reserves in 2006 were estimated to be 1.42 billion cubic meters (bcm), the third largest in Africa, and some experts suggested unexplored reserves could double that figure (World Bank 2006: 13). Further exploitation of this resource, including greater domestic use, promised to free up oil for export as well as to increase gas exports. The Western Libya Gas Project (WLGP), designed to move natural gas from the offshore Bahr Essalam field in the Mediterranean and the onshore Wafa field near the Algerian border to a new coastal processing plant at Melitah, was the showpiece for Libyan plans to exploit natural gas reserves. In full operation, the WLGP was expected to provide some 30 percent of Italy's energy needs (*MEED*: 17.8.01). Central to the project, the Green Stream pipeline, a 322-mile (520-km) pipeline connecting Libya and Sicily, came online in October 2004, and trial production from the Bahr Essalam field began in August 2005.

When Libya announced in December 2003 that it was abandoning its unconventional weapons programs and related delivery systems, the path was cleared for the return of American oil companies to Libya. In April 2004, the US government lifted some trade sanctions, and in June it restored diplomatic relations. Most of the remaining sanctions, with the exception of the export restrictions related to Libya's retention on the US list of state sponsors of terrorism, were removed in September 2004. In response to the relaxed trade restrictions, foreign direct investment (FDI) in Libya topped $4 billion in 2004, up sixfold from the previous year (*Reuters*: 12.1.05). FDI increased another $8 billion in 2005–8, confirming the Libyan argument that its decision to compensate the families of the victims of the Pan Am flight 103 bombing was a sound investment decision if not an admission of guilt. The United States lifted its remaining trade restrictions in May 2006 after Libya was removed from the terrorism list (St John 2006c: 4–5).

Prior to Libya's renunciation of unconventional weapons, the Oasis Group and Occidental Petroleum received permission from the George W. Bush administration to open talks with Libya. Initially, they hoped for a speedy return to acreage held in trust by Libya since 1986 in standstill agreements; however, this proved impossible. The NOC insisted that the Americans return on the same terms as when they left, but the latter pushed for better terms, including an increase in profit share and an extension of the 10-year leases agreed to under the standstill agreements. The oil companies argued, with good reason, that the productive acreage held in trust by Libya since 1986 had become by 2003 enhanced oil recovery projects, and the terms for their return should reflect the productivity decline. In the oil industry, enhanced oil recovery techniques are employed to soften the natural decline in maturing fields, which can be as much as 7–8 percent a year. Using the Oasis Group's Waha concession in Sirte as an example, production in 2003 was estimated to be no more than 375,000 b/d compared with a peak of 1 million b/d in the 1970s. Following prolonged talks, Occidental Petroleum returned to Libya in July 2005, and the Oasis Group followed at the end of the year, agreeing to pay the NOC $1.83 billion to resume production (*Houston Chronicle*: 29.12.05).

EPSAs, phase four

In August 2004, Libya announced a new round of EPSAs, phase four, which offered enhanced incentives for oil and gas exploration in an open, competitive bidding environment. In response to its offer of 15 onshore and offshore exploration areas covering 58 blocks in the six major oil and gas basins (Sirte, Ghadames, Murzuq, Cyrenaica-Batnan, Kufra, and offshore), the NOC received applications from 122 oil companies. The high level of interest in Libyan oil development was due in part to the fact that only 25 percent of the country had been explored to this point, making the discovery of new deposits highly likely, and in part to the absence of attractive prospects elsewhere in the world.

When bid results were announced on 29 January 2005, three American companies, Amerada Hess, ChevronTexaco, and Occidental Petroleum, alone or in partnership with others, were awarded 11 of the 15 contract areas. The NOC later announced that the successful bidders had agreed to pay a total of $132.9 million in signing bonuses. In terms of production share, the successful bids ranged from a ratio of 89.2 percent to 10.8 percent on the high end to 61.1 percent to 38.9 percent on the low end, with the larger share of production in each case going to the state (NOC: 29.1.05; *FT*: 31.1.05). The first round of EPSAs, phase four, marked an important change in the way Libya did business, validating Prime Minister Ghanem's promise that the NOC was committed to a more open business environment with streamlined approval procedures. For the first time since the EPSAs were introduced in 1974, the main consideration in choosing successful bidders was the percentage of oil and gas production that they were willing to share with the state. A secondary factor was the bonuses that the companies agreed to pay when the contracts were signed. The new process, which incorporated a public opening of bids with automatic awards based on pre-set criteria, was a welcome change from earlier times when the NOC negotiated in parallel with competing bidders, a process that lacked transparency and often produced delays in concluding agreements (NOC: 17.6.07; St John 2007: 211–12).

In the second round of EPSAs, phase four, the NOC in May 2005 offered a further 44 blocks in 26 areas. A revised framework adopted in this round boosted incentives for oil companies that employed Libyan nationals and linked upstream and downstream activities (NOC: 12.5.05). About the same time, NOC officials announced that Libya planned to sell a 60 percent stake in Tamoil, and they also stressed their interest in offshore investment in Libyan refining operations (*Forbes*: 7.9.05). Some 120 companies expressed interest in bidding in round two, and, with 23 successful, the second round marked a wider diversity of winners than the first. Successful bids ranged from a production ratio of 93 percent to 7 percent to one of 71.5 percent to 28.5 percent. Signing bonuses in the second round totaled $103.4 million, and four blocks in three areas received no bids (*Forbes*: 2.10.05; *FT*: 3.10.05; St John 2007: 212).

In May 2006, the newly appointed NOC chairman stressed that the next licensing round would be based on full transparency and open competition. At the same time, Ghanem indicated that his organization was negotiating with select oil companies to develop a variety of upstream and downstream projects, including the modernization and expansion of refinery operations. Confirming that Tamoil would be sold, interested parties were asked to submit offers for either 60 or 100 percent of the company (NOC: 18.9.06). Two years later, a sale to Los Angeles-based Colony Capital fell through amid speculation that Tamoil needed restructuring before it could be sold (*WSJ*: 20.3.08).

In mid-August 2006, the NOC announced the third round of EPSAs, phase four, covering 41 blocks in 14 areas. In promoting the third round, officials emphasized that only 30 percent of the country had been explored for hydro-carbons. After receiving 70 applications, the NOC pre-qualified 60 firms, and, in the end, 23 companies from 15 countries bid for contracts. Signing bonuses totaled $58.1 million, and four areas failed to receive a bid (NOC: 20.12.06; *NYT*: 24.12.06).

Shortly after the announcement of the third round, the General People's Committee in September 2006 created the Oil and Gas Affairs Council (later the Higher Council for Oil and Gas) to oversee investment strategies, produc-tion, pricing, and foreign contracts. The membership of the body included the prime minister, other cabinet ministers, the NOC chairman, and the central bank governor. Chairman Ghanem moved quickly to reassure investors that the new council would not change oil and gas policy; nevertheless, its creation represented a clear dilution of NOC powers, suggesting that the Leader was dissatisfied with hydrocarbon policy. The timing of the council's creation, only weeks after the Leader had called for increased Libyan involvement in the oil and gas sector, strengthened the impression of high-level discontent (*JANA*: 4.9.06; *Reuters*: 10.9.06).

Although the EPSAs were the preferred Libyan approach to the hydrocarbon industry after 1974, a bilateral model was also used to attract foreign investment. Royal Dutch Shell in May 2005 announced a strategic agreement with Libya covering an upgrade of the LNG plant at Marsa al-Brega, together with the exploration and development of five blocks in the Sirte Basin (*Reuters*: 6.1.06). After winning acreage in 9 of 15 exploration areas in round one of EPSAs, phase four, Occidental Petroleum in July 2005 announced the resumption of opera-tions in its historical contract areas. In December 2006, Italy announced that the ENI Group was set to renew its long-term partnership with Libya in a deal which included construction of an LNG plant (*Reuters*: 7.12.06). In June 2007,

BP announced the conclusion of a deal with the NOC in which BP would spend as much as $25 billion developing oil and gas fields in Libya (*Times*: 3.6.07).

Launched in July 2007, the fourth round of EPSAs, phase four, focused on natural gas deposits. With the completion of the Green Stream pipeline linking Libya to Italy through Sicily, Libya was keen to attract offshore investment from larger operators who could bring experience and integrated technology to their development (*FT*: 16.8.07). Thirteen companies from 11 countries bid for 12 development areas, and Gazprom of Russia, Polskie of Poland, Shell of the Netherlands, and Sonatrach of Algeria (in conjunction with Indian Oil and Oil India) were eventually successful. Two areas received a single bid and were later awarded to Occidental Petroleum and RWE of Germany (*IHT*: 9.12.07; NOC: 11.12.07). Following the four rounds of phase four EPSAs, some oil companies complained about their failure to find new oil and gas deposits; nevertheless, Libya's proven crude oil reserves increased from 36 billion barrels in 2000 to 44.3 billion barrels in 2008 while proven natural gas reserves increased from 1.31 billion standard cubic meters to 1.54 billion standard cubic meters (Table 4.3).

Backwards to the future

On 1 September 2008, the Leader again charged that government ministries were centers of mismanagement, graft, and corruption, arguing they should be eliminated, with their budgeted funds distributed directly to the people (*BBC News*: 1.9.08). In March 2009, the GPC announced that only 64 of the 468 basic people's congresses (BPCs) had approved the Leader's proposal whereas 153 had opposed it and 251 had endorsed it but only after "appropriate measures" had been put in place. In response, the GPC decided that wealth distribution would not begin until socioeconomic studies had been completed and a database of families established (IMF 2009: 4). As a part of this process, it called for each citizen to be issued a national number. Even though his plan was accepted in principle, the decision to delay its implementation constituted a not so subtle rejection of Qaddafi's attempt to shift blame for the country's economic problems from himself and the ideology outlined in *The Green Book* to a regime he

TABLE 4.3 Libyan proven crude oil and natural gas reserves, 1990–2008

	1990	1995	2000	2005	2006	2007	2008
Crude oil (billion barrels)	22.8	29.5	36.0	41.5	41.5	43.7	44.3
Natural gas (billion standard cubic meters)	1.208	1.313	1.314	1.491	1.420	1.540	1.540

Source: OPEC 2008.

had long dominated but belatedly recognized as inefficient and corrupt (*JANA*: 4.3.09).

In the interim, charges of inconsistency, lack of transparency, and favoritism dogged the reform process, with most observers in agreement that a strong investment code, contract sanctity, and the rule of law were among the things required to improve the business climate (*AFP*: 30.8.09). Exemplifying the unpredictability of the commercial milieu, Libya suspended the issuance of visas to most Europeans in mid-February 2010, following a spat with Switzerland, lifting the ban only in late March (*FT*: 6.4.10). As the drama played out, Libyan officials announced new plans to privatize half the economy in 10 years, claiming that investment laws had been revised to put foreigners on an equal footing with local investors (*Guardian*: 31.3.10). At the same time, Libyan officials continued to promote "people's capitalism," a halfway house between socialism and capitalism, described by them as looking like capitalism but acting like socialism (*FT*: 28.4.09). In reality, people's capitalism is nothing more than a transparent effort to mask the obvious differences between the anachronistic socialist ideology in *The Green Book* and current economic reality. Official attempts to rationalize privatization, clearly outlawed in *The Green Book*, as the "extension of popular ownership" fall in the same category.

Early in the new millennium, the hydrocarbon sector was the one exception to halting reform efforts elsewhere in the economy. Widely considered a success in terms of efficiency and transparency, reforms to the oil and gas industry stalled at the end of the decade. As oil prices declined, Qaddafi threatened to nationalize the industry, arguing that the oil-producing states should maximize revenues from their key resource (*WP*: 22.1.09). Although nationalization was never expected to take place, the NOC did renegotiate existing contracts. Beginning in 2007–8, it revised contracts with ENI, Occidental, Total, and Repsol, to name a few, reducing their oil take from as much as 49 percent to less than half that amount (NOC: 30.11.07; *Reuters*: 14.1.09).

Thereafter, the business climate for companies working in Libya steadily worsened. In August 2009, Libya issued a directive that all foreign companies must appoint a Libyan citizen to head up operations in the country. A few weeks later, Ghanem resigned from his position as head of the NOC in a surprise move that signaled a serious policy rift (*Guardian*: 15.9.09; *FT*: 5.10.09). Before he was reinstated, the body which became the Higher Council for Oil and Gas was created to oversee the NOC and to regulate the industry. Fresh evidence of the tug-of-war over hydrocarbon policy came in March 2010 when Ghanem announced that Libya was drafting a new law to replace the 1955 petroleum law, stressing the "need to create a new organizational framework for the industry and on the issue of governance" (*Guardian* 26.10.09; *FT*: 30.3.10).

With hydrocarbon policy in flux, the pending sale of Verenex Energy, a relatively small Canadian oil exploration company operating in the Ghadames Basin, to the state-owned China National Petroleum Company (CNPC) caused heartburn for other oil companies operating in Libya, especially the smaller ones. The sale required NOC approval, and the latter blocked it for months on the grounds that the NOC enjoyed the right of first refusal and could decide to match the bid. With other holdings in Libya, the Chinese government was not willing to challenge the regime over the sale and withdrew its offer in September 2009. In the interim, Verenex's share price slumped over uncertainty whether a sale would occur and, if so, when and at what price (*Reuters*: 8.9.09). Compared with giants such as BP and Exxon Mobil, Verenex was a small player in Libya, but it was the only one to have made a large find in the acreage opened to tender in EPSAs, phase four. Libya's treatment of Verenex thus caused other oil companies operating in the country to worry that in the event of a significant discovery Libya would also seek to revise their contracts to recover more revenues (*FT*: 21.9.09). It was especially concerning for the smaller oil companies because the Libyan strategy in 2009 mirrored its approach in the early 1970s when it initiated new production and pricing policies, beginning with the smaller, more vulnerable, independents. With no other option, Verenex at the end of 2009 sold its holdings to Libya at the discounted price.

Regional investment

As Libya struggled to update its hydrocarbon sector, it expanded its investment portfolio in related industries throughout the region. The principal vehicle to achieve this result was the Libyan Investment Authority (LIA), established in March 2007 and charged with investing the financial assets of six extrabudgetary funds, including the Oil Reserve Fund, the Long-Term Investment Portfolio, the Libya Africa Investment Fund, the Social and Economic Development Fund, Libya Financial Investment Company, and Oil Investment Company (IMF 2008a: 6, 8). In June 2008, a unit of the LIA acquired Mobil Oil Maroc, a wholly owned subsidiary of Exxon Mobil operating service stations in Morocco, and later in the year it purchased a 50 percent share in Kenya's only oil refinery (*All Africa*: 19.2.08). In August 2008, a unit of LIA announced the acquisition from Royal Dutch Shell of service stations in Djibouti, Ethiopia, and Sudan, together with an agreement with the Democratic Republic of Congo to build an 87-mile pipeline in the western part of the country (*Middle East Online*: 12.8.08). In September 2008, it became a major investor in Circle Oil, an international oil and gas exploration company with operations in Egypt, Morocco, and Tunisia, and in January 2009 it formed a joint venture with Egypt to collaborate on several projects, including a refinery west of Alexandria and 500 service stations (Martinez 2007: 127–8; *Bloomberg*: 13.1.09).

Libya in the post-hydrocarbon era

Based on the current state of the economy, it is difficult to be optimistic about the economic health of Libya in the post-hydrocarbon era. The dogged pursuit of socialist policies for most of the last 40 years has set the stage for severe economic challenges once oil and gas deposits are exhausted. Progress in developing a market economy has been slow and erratic, with the future pace and direction of economic reform a subject of continuing debate at the highest levels of government. A thorough discussion of the steps needed to prepare for a post-hydrocarbon future is beyond the scope of this chapter; however, policy areas in need of overhaul include diversification, education and training, the commercial environment, infrastructure, and political constraints.

Diversification

More than 50 years after the discovery of oil deposits in commercially viable quantities, Libya remains one of the least diversified countries in the Maghreb and among oil-producing states (IMF 2007: 4). On account of the socialist state and command economy that dominated Libya for almost four decades, private investment is dormant at around 2 percent of GNP, and, until recently, some 75 percent of employment remained in the public sector (World Bank 2006; IMF 2007: 10). Ironically, diversification of the nonhydrocarbon sector, a difficult challenge which Libya has had little success in meeting to date, is contingent on an increase in the productivity and competitiveness of the energy sector, the engine of economic growth, coupled with the prioritization and sequencing of diversification in other economic sectors. In an examination of prioritized development in Libya, the "National Economic Strategy," a report commissioned and funded by the Libyan government, suggested a concentration on five clusters, agriculture, construction, energy, tourism, and transit trade, to promote socioeconomic growth. In so doing, the study rightly noted that all of these clusters – with the exception of energy – were in an early stage of competitiveness and development (Monitor Group and Cambridge Energy Research Associates 2006: 75–107). To achieve the requisite level of diversification, reforms must also be put in place to facilitate private sector development which continues to be hindered by a complex regulatory regime, restrictive labor practices, and a legacy of policy uncertainty (St John 2008d: 87).

Education and training

Throughout the region, demographics have become a motor for change, and Libya is no exception. When the highest rate of population growth in the Maghreb is combined with an extremely youthful population, of whom one-third are 14 years or younger, the failure to create new jobs through a well-thought-out, long-term policy is a recipe for disaster. At least 30 percent of the Libya population is now thought to be unemployed or underemployed, a labor pool that represents both a huge, untapped potential for the country as well as a steadily growing liability.

A rapid improvement in the development of human resources through a strengthened education system and targeted job training is required to grow productivity, accelerate diversification, and ensure competitiveness in a global economy. In spite of high literacy and enrollment levels, the education system is not providing the skills necessary for graduates to be productive and competitive. The scarcity of technically skilled managers and workers remains a core human resource issue, with productivity outside the hydrocarbon sector extremely low (St John 2008d: 88–9). Employment regulations which are intended to provide private sector job opportunities through a policy of Libyanization have been of minimal assistance in this regard. In practice, they constitute a continuation of the policy of dependence on state largess in place since the early days of the revolution with foreign firms substituting for the state as the provider of that largess. Instead, what is needed is a thoroughly revamped education system which responds to the needs of the job market and develops the skills and attitudes required to create new products and services. In addition, the regime should formulate a program to attract Libyans abroad to return home in order to leverage their experience and expertise.

Commercial environment

Issues related to the commercial environment are manifold and begin with a lack of transparency, widespread corruption, limited institutional coordination, and the relative absence of a comprehensive plan. Broad policy areas in need of additional reform include incentive and regulatory regimes, exchange rates, trade practices, fiscal and monetary policies, and continuing improvements in the reliability of economic data. To promote private sector development, priorities include simplifying the approval process, reforming the labor code, and replacing the progressive corporate tax rate with a low flat rate competitive with other states. To encourage foreign investment, the legal framework must be modified, including the regulation of foreign direct investment, capital markets, intellectual property rights, insurance, and property rights (IMF 2009: 13, 16, 27–9). As for the privatization of the state-owned sector, the current process moves too slowly and is often compromised by the inability or unwillingness of public officials to recognize and evaluate the real value of public sector companies.

At the same time, economic reforms in themselves offer only a partial solution to the problems facing the Libyan economy. The radical changes required to ensure effective economic growth in the post-hydrocarbon era are not compatible with the retreat of the state called for by the Leader in recent years. On the contrary, the state will need to be more intensively involved in the economic life of Libya for a substantial period of time if meaningful and sustained economic reforms are to be implemented.

Infrastructure

Libya's physical infrastructure is in poor shape with much room for improvement. With the exception of electricity and water, Libya ranks low regionally and internationally in all metrics related to the quality of infrastructure, especially in the areas of transportation and communication. These weaknesses in infrastructure development reflect a low level of public investment and a lack of private investment for many years. Although the regime is taking steps to improve the situation, the underdeveloped state of the telecommunications network, which has suffered from a lack of expertise and competition, is particularly significant. An efficient telecommunications system is central to state-of-the-art information and communication technology, which in turn is a significant factor condition for business and entrepreneurship. Therefore, rapid improvements in the physical infrastructure, especially in information and communication technology, remain a priority area (Monitor Group and Cambridge Energy Research Associates 2006: 50–4).

Political constraints

There is also the related and more fundamental question of how far and how fast economic reform can progress in Libya under the *Jamahiriya* system. The state-sponsored "National Economic Strategy" argued that the system of direct democracy requires only minor tweaking to encourage and support desired socioeconomic reforms. It recommended leveraging information and communications technology, which it referred to as e-democracy, and redesigning processes to reduce inefficiencies and to perfect Libyan democracy (Monitor Group and Cambridge Energy Research Associates 2006: 140). On the contrary, the available evidence suggests that a wide variety of broader governance issues also must be addressed before economic reforms can prosper and Libya can prepare for the post-hydrocarbon era. The overall lack of transparency, a weak rule of law, an immature legal and court system, and recurrent conflict between local and central governments are among the issues that require attention. In so doing, the question of sequence remains at the heart of the issue. Sustained economic reform requires substantial legal reform to stimulate political reform followed by economic reform. Unfortunately, the Leader in recent years has shown little inclination for political reform, repeatedly supporting the direct democracy system in the strongest possible terms.

5

INTERNATIONAL RELATIONS

The revolutionary government first pursued a complex, aggressive, and often violent foreign policy, notable for the wide-ranging scope of its activities and interests. This continued into the early 1980s, when a series of setbacks caused the regime to rethink many of its failed initiatives. The following decade was a very difficult period in which Libyan foreign policy was hamstrung by the sanctions imposed by the United Nations. After 1999, Libya sought to return to full participation in the international community.

Ideology drives early foreign policy

Libya is positioned on the periphery of three worlds: African, Arab, and Mediterranean. Its location gives it flexibility as to how, when, and where it will play a regional role, but it also leads to uncertainty as to where it belongs. Before independence, the position of Libya in a strategically important part of the world contributed to its visibility on the world stage, and after independence it imbued its foreign policy with an extra-regional importance that it otherwise would not have enjoyed. Demography added to the parameters imposed by political geography on Libya. For a large country with an ambitious leadership, a population of only a few million people, most of whom live along the coast, was debilitating (St John 1983a: 96–7). In search of a stage larger than the Libyan playhouse, Qaddafi has long rued the demographic limitations imposed upon him, referring to himself on more than one occasion as a leader without a country. When compared with neighboring Egypt, Libya has 75 percent more territory, but its population numbers only 8 percent as many people. Libya's scarce demographic resources have impacted on a number of foreign and security policies, including universal military conscription, the recruitment of migrant workers, the enlistment of mercenaries, and its role as a transit point for immigrants bound for Europe (St John 1987a: 12–13).

Freedom and unity

From the beginning, Qaddafi employed the revolutionary trinity (freedom, socialism, and unity) to signal the direction foreign and domestic policy would take, with the freedom and unity legs central to the early foreign policy of the regime. Approaching freedom in a generic sense, he argued that everyone had the right to economic, social, and political freedom. In this context, the declared that enemies of the revolution were the forces of backwardness and evil, together with colonialism, imperialism, and Zionism (Qaddafi 1970: 204). Reflecting his strong commitment to freedom, Qaddafi pressured the United Kingdom and the United States for an early termination of the base agreements they had negotiated with the monarchy (Ansell and Al-Arif 1972: 90–1; Ashiurakis 1976: 82–7). Once their forces departed, the day the British evacuated Al-Adem Base and the day the Americans departed Wheelus Field became official national holidays (*JANA*: 12.6.10).

For Qaddafi, Arab nationalism and Arab unity were two sides of the same coin. Arab nationalism focused on opposition to the Jewish state, with Arab unity the solution to this most difficult Arab problem. The consummate Arab nationalist as well as an Arab unionist par excellence, Qaddafi approached both ideals with unbridled enthusiasm, refusing to acknowledge the practical obstacles in their path (Qaddafi 1973a: 133). At his first press conference in February 1970, he produced a formula for Arab unity which focused eastward on the Arab core. With the liberation of Palestine the focus of Arab interest, he considered Egypt the essential nucleus of an Arab union. He condemned the monarchy's equivocal stand on Maghrib unity but argued that North Africa was too remote from the Arab heartland to be a priority. He also minimized the role of the Arab League, considering it a platform for demonstrating support for Arab unity but not an effective means to achieve it (Ansell and Al-Arif 1972: 74–5).

In Qaddafi's view, the obstacles to Arab unity included monarchical governments, such as those in Jordan and Morocco, which maintained close relations with the United States and were a painful reminder of the Libyan experience. Qaddafi supported an abortive assassination attempt on King Hassan of Morocco in July 1971 and was implicated in a plot to kill King Hussein of Jordan in November 1972 (Carvely 1973: 714–15). In the process, Qaddafi's approach to Arab unity weakened any distinction between foreign and domestic politics, encouraging the involvement of one Arab state in the internal politics of another (St John 1987a: 50–1).

Over the next decade, Qaddafi doggedly pursued practical attempts at Arab unity long after the myth of pan-Arabism had been widely discredited throughout the Arab world. If the Libyan approach differed from that of its predecessors, it was in its union of oil and pan-Arabism, two forces generally at odds in recent

Arab history (Ajami 1978/79: 355–73). In 1969–74, Libya engaged in union discussions with Egypt (twice), Syria, Sudan, and Tunisia (twice). Frustrated with
the failure of earlier attempts to unite with Egypt, Qaddafi in 1973 organized
a motorcade of 20,000 vehicles to drive from the Libyan–Tunisian border to
the Libyan–Egyptian border in support of immediate union (El Saadany 1994:
112–17). Dubbed the Green March, the motorcade was the first public mani-
festation of the new concept of the masses, and when the Egyptians stopped
it at the border, it also marked the last official attempt to export the Libyan
revolution to Egypt. After 1974, Qaddafi continued to promote Arab unity, but
more as a long-term goal as opposed to an immediately recognizable objective.
By the late 1970s, he appeared to see more clearly the divisions and rivalries in
the path of Arab unity even though he refused to accept them (Alexander 1981b:
837; St John 1987a: 51–60).

Holy war

Arab nationalism and the quest for Arab unity were intertwined with the
Palestinian issue and thus an integral part of Qaddafi's call for *jihad*. He accepted
the common Arab nationalist viewpoint, centered on the notion of a conspiracy
against the Arab world, that Palestine was a part of the Arab nation and must be
liberated. The enemy was Zionism, a European movement, and not the Jews as
such, together with the colonial powers responsible for inflicting this indignity
upon the Arab people. Arguing that the Holy Land was lost because the Arab
world was divided, Qaddafi believed that Arab unity not only must precede
the liberation of Palestine, but was a prerequisite for its liberation. Adopting
the shop-worn slogan that Arab unity was the road to Palestine, Libya pledged
its moral and material capabilities to the Palestinian cause, emphasizing that
its relations with other states would be heavily influenced by their position on
Palestine (Qaddafi 1973a: 134).

For Qaddafi, *jihad* was the action element of Arab nationalism, the necessary tool to achieve social justice inside and outside Libya. At the outset, both
imperialism and communism were considered equal threats; however, imperialism soon became the principal target for *jihad*. In January 1970, the ideological
emphasis on *jihad* assumed a practical form with the creation of a Jihad Fund,
and an Association for the Propagation of Islam was created later in the year
(Ansell and Al-Arif 1972: 115; Libyan Arab Republic 1973a: 219–20). As early
as 1973, Qaddafi was stressing that "any contribution to liberate the world from
imperialism should be considered as an integral part of *jihad*" (Qaddafi 1973b:
53). At an Islamic conference in Morocco in 1979, Libya supported the creation of a pan-Islamic military force and, later in the year, the Islamic Legion,
largely composed of mercenaries from the Sahara and Sahel, appeared in public
for the first time. The declared aim of the Islamic Legion was to support the
Palestinian cause as well as any Islamic movement struggling against oppression
(Pipes 1981: 21).

The concept of *jihad* found its most practical expression in Libyan support for Palestinian groups, especially the mainstream Fatah wing of the PLO. Qaddafi eagerly embraced a war of liberation as the ideal approach to combat Israel, advocating direct military action long after the October 1973 war strengthened the PLO and the oil weapon proved the more effective instrument to support its goals (Fallaci 1979: 124–5). As the PLO modified its strategy and tactics in the second half of the 1970s, Qaddafi remained the unregenerate rejectionist, leading to a public feud and an eventual break with Fatah at the end of 1979 (*IHT*: 7.1.80). Elsewhere, Qaddafi extended assistance to a wide variety of so-called national liberation movements. Libyan support for such groups centered on Africa and the Middle East, but it also encompassed diverse groups in Central and South America, Southeast Asia, and Western Europe (Libyan Arab Republic 1973a: 4, 20–1). In the face of global condemnation, Libya later toned down its public support for such groups; nevertheless, evidence of ongoing material assistance for guerrilla-cum-terrorist groups mounted over the years. In a period in which state-sponsored terrorism was a form of surrogate warfare between states, Libya played an active role, in part because support for such organizations enhanced the international status of an otherwise not very important state. In the process, Libyan support highlighted the befuddled thinking found in the Third Universal Theory and later in *The Green Book*. Convinced of the universality of his theories, Qaddafi mistakenly thought he could parlay financial and other support for such groups into their adoption of his theoretical formulations (St John 1987a: 38).

Positive neutrality

During the first decade of the revolution, Libyan relations with the East, especially the Soviet Union, and the West, particularly the United States, underwent a major shift. Qaddafi's initial approach to positive neutrality was in line with that taken by Nasser in the mid-1950s. Qaddafi professed a belief in Third World causes and proclaimed a policy of absolute neutrality between East and West (Qaddafi 1970: 211–12). He considered positive neutrality, nonalignment, and peaceful coexistence as core elements of his Third Universal Theory, arguing that his theory was necessary to defend Third World states against the superpowers (Libyan Arab Republic 1974: 5–6). That said, Qaddafi's approach to positive neutrality was never uniformly neutral. Invoking the freedom leg of the revolutionary trinity, he rejected all foreign influence from the start, defining imperialism in terms of Western colonialism and political intervention (Qaddafi 1975: 47).

As for the superpowers, Libyan foreign policy followed a dichotomous pattern. Even as its criticism of US foreign policy intensified, Libya maintained close commercial ties with the West, exporting the bulk of its crude oil to the United States and Western Europe and importing large amounts of Western technology. Libya was also critical of selected aspects of Soviet foreign policy, especially the emigration of Soviet Jews to Israel, but events inside and outside the region combined to foster a deepening bilateral relationship, especially in the area of arms transfers (Qaddafi 1973b: 9–14, 23–6; Qaddafi 1975: 25–9, 87). Busy consolidating the revolution, Qaddafi welcomed early Soviet support, but at the same time, he harbored suspicion of the Soviet regime. Anti-communist, Qaddafi decried what he viewed as the perfidious, godless character of Soviet policy (Qaddafi 1975: 22–5, 53–4). As a result, the Libyan–Soviet relationship from the beginning was largely based on commercial and strategic considerations, including a common interest in preventing the spread of US influence in the region, as opposed to ideological affinity or shared ideological conviction (St John 1982: 134–5). As Qaddafi emphasized: "We deal with the Soviet Union on a commercial and not an ideological basis" (*WP*: 16.7.75).

The first delivery of Soviet military equipment was made in July 1970 and was exhibited at the parade commemorating the first anniversary of the revolution. Arms purchases continued throughout the 1970s, including a major purchase in 1974–5, and by the end of the decade Libya enjoyed the highest per capita ratio of military equipment in the Third World. As its appetite for modern armaments increased, Libya tried to diversify its suppliers, as exemplified by the purchase in the early 1970s of 110 Mirage fighters together with Crotale anti-aircraft missiles from France; however, its policy of arms diversification increasingly conflicted with Western concern for maintaining a military balance in the region. Soviet arms were accompanied by Soviet advisors, but, to keep their numbers as small as possible, Libya also employed other foreign advisors, including Americans, Cubans, and Pakistanis (Pajak 1976; Hersh 1981).

Qaddafi made state visits to the Soviet Union in 1977 and 1981, and in 1978–9 he first threatened to join the Warsaw Pact, a Communist bloc defense alliance (Fallaci 1979: 120). Although his threats received no support from Moscow, there were reports in the second half of the 1970s that Libya would conclude a 20-year Treaty of Friendship and Cooperation with the Soviet Union; however, the pact was never consummated. In 1975, the Soviet Union announced that it would provide Libya with its first nuclear reactor, and three years later it agreed to construct a nuclear research center and power plant. Libya ratified the Treaty on the Non-Proliferation of Nuclear Weapons in 1973, and Soviet policy at the time was to sell nuclear power plants to any state that had ratified the treaty (Pajak 1980–1; Anderson 1985b: 32–7). Qaddafi claimed to be interested solely in developing a nuclear energy program, denying any interest in the manufacture of nuclear weapons, but Western policy-makers remained unconvinced.

Diplomatic relations between Libya and the United States were not positive at any time after 1969; nevertheless, there were individuals in the Department of State, as well as in the Foreign Office in London, who believed that they could build on the anti-communism of the regime to protect American and British interests in Libya (Cricco 2002). Both the United Kingdom and the United

States quickly extended diplomatic recognition, and within days of the coup the British rejected an appeal from supporters of King Idris I to intervene militarily on his behalf to restore him to power (*NYT*: 2.1.00). The United Kingdom and the United States later agreed to evacuate their military facilities in the mistaken belief that this would open a new era of economic cooperation, but Qaddafi viewed their closure as simply the first step in the complete withdrawal of Western interests from the country. In its attempts to build a sound working relationship with the new government, the United States on one occasion, and probably on at least two more, provided Libya with information on potential counter-coup attempts (Seale and McConville 1974: 144–5, 152, 170–3; Cooley 1982: 80–100; St John 2008a: 140–1).

In retrospect, American attempts to cultivate positive diplomatic relations with the revolutionary government were doomed to failure from the start. With the two states holding diametrically opposed views on world issues in general and regional issues in particular, there was little opportunity for rapprochement. Qaddafi adamantly opposed the international status quo while the United States remained its strongest supporter. The revolutionary government increasingly tied its relations with other states to their position on Palestine even as the United States continued to be the main backer of Israel. Libya provided what it considered to be legitimate support for national liberation movements, but the United States viewed its actions as blatant interference in the domestic affairs of other states, if not active support for terrorism (ElWarfally 1988: 32–9).

At the same time, Libya and the United States were bound by a web of common economic interests that both sides were reluctant to forgo. The dominant position of American oil companies in Libya was an important component of a broader US policy to protect the flow of Middle Eastern oil to the United States on terms that maximized volume, minimized price, and avoided supply interruptions. In conjunction with this policy, Washington sought to recycle as many petrodollars as possible through the US economy, mainly in the form of US exports to the region. Given the large presence of US oil companies in Libya, a secondary objective was to safeguard the American community of several thousand people living and working in the country. In turn, Libya respected American expertise and desired continued access to American technology. Libyan cooperation with the US private sector remained at a high level, and several thousand Libyans continued to study at American colleges and universities. Owing to the importance of this commercial relationship, the United States initially pursued a policy of conciliation in Libya that emphasized the long-term compatibility of American–Libyan interests (Wright 1982a: 215; ElWarfally 1988: 85–93).

After 1972, the US policy of conciliation gradually became a policy of constraint. When the US ambassador returned to Washington in 1972, he was not replaced, ending official representation at the ambassadorial level until the end of 2008. For the remainder of the decade, US policy in the region tried to ignore Libya whenever possible, with successive administrations paying it as little attention as possible. The consensus in Washington was that provoking Qaddafi or precipitating any kind of showdown with his regime would run counter to the step-by-step peace process which the United States pursued in 1973–5 as well as the Camp David diplomacy of the Carter administration (St John 2002: 106–15).

The US policy of constraint proved ineffective because it was impossible to ignore the Qaddafi regime. Libya challenged US policies throughout the Arab world because they were antithetical to its own, adamantly opposing every Arab–Israeli peace initiative proposed by Washington. As Qaddafi's personal relationship with Egyptian President Anwar al-Sadat deteriorated, Libya also became a strong critic of Egyptian peace initiatives (El Saadany 1994: 99–106, 118–46). After Egypt attacked Libya in a brief, inconclusive war in July 1977, Libya became a founding member of the Steadfastness and Confrontation Front, formed in December 1977 to protest Sadat's visit to Israel and the talks leading to the Camp David Accords. Libya subsidized Palestinian factions opposed to a peace settlement, and in periods of regional tension it could also be counted on to urge Arab oil producers to use the oil weapon against the United States (*NYT*: 14.10.79). In response, the United States included Libya on the State Department's list of state sponsors of terrorism when the list was created in December 1979.

During the Jimmy Carter administration, bilateral relations were strained, especially after Libyan authorities stood by as demonstrators, in support of Iranian militants holding American hostages in Teheran, sacked the US embassy in Tripoli in December 1979. As demonstrated by a guerrilla attack at Gafsa in southern Tunisia in early 1980, the threat of Libyan intervention in the domestic affairs of neighboring states continued, particularly in countries with close ties to Washington (Damis 1983: 38). France along with the United States provided military assistance to Tunisia in the wake of the Gafsa attack and, in response, Libya allowed mobs to ransack and burn the French embassy in Tripoli and the French consulate in Benghazi in February 1980 (Alexander 1981b: 836). Later in the year, Libya denounced a military cooperation agreement negotiated by the United States with Egypt, Somalia, and Oman under the guise of the Carter Doctrine. As reports increased that Libya planned to assassinate dissidents living abroad, including some resident in the United States, the United States in May 1980 recalled all diplomatic personnel from Libya, and in May 1981 it closed the Libyan People's Bureau (embassy) in Washington (Wright 1982a: 215–16; Haley 1984: 6–7).

The third circle

Egyptian foreign policy under Nasser centered on the Arab, African, and Islamic worlds in what the Egyptian president referred to as the three circles strategy. Qaddafi did not adopt the three circles motif; however, Africa in effect became the third circle of Libyan foreign policy (Mertz and Mertz 1983: 88; Mattes

1987: 90–5). With early initiatives centered on the Mashriq and the Palestinian issue, the primary goal in sub-Saharan Africa was a reduction of Israeli influence (Libyan Arab Republic 1973b: 262–3). Qaddafi viewed the Israeli presence on the continent as a fifth column behind the front lines, sapping Arab strength at the back door (First 1974: 222). Opposed to Western interests and influence, related objectives included the elimination of foreign military bases, opposition to apartheid and white minority regimes, support for African liberation movements, the propagation of Islam, and enhanced African control over the continent's resources (Libyan Arab Republic 1973a: 19–20; Qaddafi 1975: 93–7, 118–20).

In 1970, Israel had more diplomatic missions in Africa than all of the Arab states combined (Sharawi 1985: 285–8). To neutralize the impact of Israeli diplomacy, Libya established diplomatic relations with a growing number of African states, offered them financial and material support, and then urged them to break relations with Israel (Mattes 1987: 95). At the same time, it moved to reduce Western influence by encouraging African states to close Western military bases and by undermining moderate African governments opposed to Libyan policies. Libya also provided considerable support to African liberation movements, together with radical, anti-Western governments, and it repeatedly denounced the white minority regimes in southern Africa (*JANA*: 9.9.09). In some areas, Libyan foreign policy also took on an Islamic hue, with preference shown for movements that expressed their opposition to the status quo in religious terms; however, Islam was only one factor among many which motivated as well as constrained Libyan policy (Pipes 1981: 19–20; Mertz and Mertz 1983: 89–91, 97–9).

Libyan initiatives in Africa were rewarded by a string of early diplomatic victories. Following his first official visit to Libya, Ugandan President Idi Amin Dada in March 1972 expelled several hundred Israeli advisers and broke diplomatic relations with Israel. When Tanzania invaded Uganda in September 1972, Libya intervened on Uganda's behalf, and in June 1973 Qaddafi praised Amin for transforming Uganda from a satellite of Zionism into a vanguard of states combating apartheid and colonialism (Ronen 2008: 146–8). Following a period of acrimonious relations, Libya resumed diplomatic ties with Chad in April 1972 and, in return for Libyan friendship, the withdrawal of its support for the rival Front de Libération Nationale du Chad (FROLINAT), and promises of aid, Chad broke diplomatic relations with Israel in November 1972. Libya later failed to fulfill its promises, and in 1973 it occupied the Aouzou Strip in northern Chad (Burr and Collins 1999: 92–5). Following these successes, the Libyan diplomatic offensive gained momentum, particularly in the largely Muslim states on the southern edge of the Sahara, and, by early 1974, Libya had largely achieved its central goal in Africa, a sharp reduction in Israeli influence, with Libya often supplanting it (Sharawi 1985: 288–93).

For the remainder of the decade, Libya maintained the anti-Israeli focus of its African policy, but it also sought to advance related goals, such as eliminating colonialism and imperialism and increasing African control over its resources. Qaddafi's condemnation of the white minority regimes in Rhodesia and South Africa, which he grouped with Israel as racist regimes, helped set the stage for a controversial UN General Assembly vote in November 1975 which equated Zionism with racism. Twenty-eight African states voted for the resolution, with 12 abstaining and only five opposing (Sharawi 1985: 307–8). On the other hand, only limited progress was made in increasing African control over the continent's resources in part because Libya's ability to influence mineral producers was largely confined to being an alternative source of capital. In any case, the Libyan focus on African mineral wealth was not entirely disinterested, as its policies in this regard supported its territorial ambitions in Chad and Niger as well as its desire to buy into reserves of strategic minerals in other African states (Mertz and Mertz 1983: 95). With its oil reserves a finite asset, Libya hoped to consolidate its position as an energy supplier by gaining access to natural resources across the continent (Ogunbadejo 1983: 157–8).

Libya was also deeply involved in the Western Sahara throughout much of the 1970s. In addition to promoting popular democracy and the development of a wider Saharan Islamic state, Libyan policy here reflected its overall opposition to colonialism and imperialism. When the Frente Popular para la Liberación de Saguia el-Hamra y Rio de Oro (POLISARIO) launched its campaign in May 1973, Libya proved the only state willing to provide material support (Damis 1983: 39; Jensen 2005: 14). At the same time, Libyan policy in the Western Sahara remained ambiguous as Qaddafi disagreed with select policies of both Algeria and the POLISARIO. As the foremost proponent of Arab unity, he was reluctant to support the POLISARIO goal of an independent state, and Libya did not recognize the Saharan Arab Democratic Republic (SADR) until 1980, four years after its founding. Even then, Qaddafi continued to hope that the SADR would one day merge with Mauritania (Hodges 1983: 325–7).

By the end of the decade, Libyan influence in sub-Saharan Africa was in decline, notably in Uganda and the Central African Republic. In late 1978, Uganda invaded Tanzania in what Amin characterized as a punitive offensive, but, when Tanzania counterattacked, the fighting escalated. Libya had increased its support for the Amin regime after Israeli commandos in July 1976 executed a successful hostage rescue mission at Kampala's Entebbe airport, and in November 1978 it dispatched Libyan troops to Uganda to assist in repelling the invaders (Ronen 2008: 151–3). The Libyan forces suffered a crushing defeat, with Libya enduring the added humiliation of paying a sizeable ransom to secure the release of the survivors (*MEED*: 7.12.79). As for the Central African Republic (Central African Empire, 1976–9), Jean Bedel Bokassa, its self-proclaimed emperor, was in Libya negotiating an aid package when he was deposed in September 1979. Three days later, the official Libyan news agency denounced French involvement in the *coup d'état* as an attempt to thwart the spread of Islam in Africa, but it was clear that what the French really had thwarted was Libyan support for one of the most unsavory regimes on the continent. Even though uncritical support for dictators such as Amin and Bokassa reflected poorly on Libya, its policies here were representative of its broader approach to the continent in the 1970s. For Qaddafi, individual personalities and internal politics seldom mattered as long as governments professed support for Islam and opposed colonialism, imperialism, and Zionism (Fallaci 1979: 121; Wright 1982a: 212–13).

Things fall apart

In the first decade of the revolution, Libyan foreign policy achieved the occasional tactical success but few strategic accomplishments, and after 1980 the situation deteriorated, with Qaddafi's forward policies resulting in a series of setbacks. Most of the difficulties stemmed from Libya's liberal use of force, either against neighboring states or in support of guerrilla terrorist movements; however, a decline in economic fortunes added to its foreign policy woes. As oil revenues dropped sharply in the early 1980s, Libya attempted to meet its offshore debt obligations through unpopular barter deals or counter-trade oil sales, especially in Europe. The continued purchase of sophisticated arms and the mounting costs of its intervention in Chad compounded its constrained economic circumstances. The financial crisis reduced Libya's ability to offer assistance to African states, and it led to massive deportations of foreign workers, mostly from states, such as Egypt and Tunisia, with which Libya had poor diplomatic relations. As the decade progressed, the foreign policy setbacks multiplied, and by the end of the 1980s Libya found itself isolated from much of the outside world.

Testing times in Africa and the Arab world

By 1980, Libyan foreign policy in Africa was under considerable pressure. In the course of the year, nine African states expelled Libyan diplomats, closed Libyan embassies, or broke diplomatic relations with Libya (Haley 1984: 224). Many states were concerned with the intricate nexus of politics, religion, and foreign aid which characterized Libyan foreign policy. While some states resented the use of Islam as an instrument of foreign policy, others with strong Muslim populations or with Muslim populations in one area and Christian or animist populations in another complained that the Libyan emphasis on Islam exacerbated sensitive national cleavages (Mertz and Mertz 1983: 90–3). Libyan recruitment for the Islamic Legion was another source of concern, especially for states located along the southern fringe of the Sahara (Flint and De Waal 2005: 23).

Qaddafi's involvement in Chad, which culminated in a full-scale military intervention in late 1980, was especially concerning because policy-makers in and out of the region feared that success there might encourage similar behavior elsewhere (Nolutshungu 1996: 145–56). Factors driving Libyan policy included the dream of a pan-Islamic African federation, a desire to control the mineral deposits in the Aouzou Strip, and a wish to neutralize Western, especially

French, influence in central Africa (Ogunbadejo 1983: 156–61; Mertz and Mertz 1983: 93–8). In January 1981, Libya announced that it would work with Chad to achieve complete unity, a prospect which provoked strong criticism from nearby states that viewed the Libyan move as more an annexation than a merger. In response, some African nations expelled Libyan diplomats, and members of the Organization of African Unity (OAU) condemned the proposed merger, calling on Libya to withdraw its forces from Chad. Given Qaddafi's history of financing opposition groups in neighboring states and recruiting Muslims from the Sahara and the Sahel into the Islamic Legion, many African states feared that Chad would become a springboard for future Libyan military operations in central and western Africa. After it became known that Libya had forced the union announcement on Chad, the project was shelved, and, in November 1981, Libya withdrew its forces from Chad, except for the Aouzou Strip (Ronen 2008: 162–4).

Over the next 18 months, the most immediate foreign policy issue for Libya was its attempt to convene the nineteenth summit of the OAU in Tripoli with Qaddafi as its chairman. The move was strongly opposed by moderate African states, concerned that their participation in a high-level meeting in Libya would vindicate the latter's policies in Africa. The war in the Western Sahara and the related issue of seating a POLISARIO representative at the summit were also concerns. The summit later convened in Addis Ababa in June 1983 under the chairmanship of the Ethiopian head of state. Qaddafi made a brief appearance but soon departed after being denied the chairmanship and seeing his protégé, the POLISARIO, barred from the meeting. Qaddafi was the first African leader to be denied the OAU chairmanship, a measure of how limited Libyan influence on the continent had become (Wright 1981–2: 14).

In Chad, sporadic outbreaks of fighting led to a renewed intervention by French and Libyan forces in 1983. Libya invaded the northern part of the country and France installed a military force in the southern part, with the United States providing military assistance to the government in Ndjamena. As Libya reinforced its military presence and imposed a civilian administration in northern Chad, Qaddafi defended his right to intervene in African affairs, terming Chad "an extension of Libya" (IHT: 27.4.84). In November 1984, France and Libya announced a mutual phased withdrawal from Chad; however, it soon became clear that a substantial Libyan force remained in the country. Faced with a stalemate, many African states adopted an ambivalent attitude toward the conflict. Concerned about Libya's regional objectives, they were reluctant to support openly a former colonial power against an African state and thus either quietly supported French policy or remained silent (Mertz and Mertz 1983: 98–9).

In January 1987, Chadian units defeated a Libyan force at the oasis town of Fada, and in mid-March they scored an even larger victory at Ouadi Doum, the largest oasis town in northern Chad. The Libyan defeat at Ouadi Doum marked a turning point in the conflict as it rendered untenable the Libyan position at

Faya Largeau, its last strongpoint in Chad (*IHT*: 28–9.3.87). The subsequent Libyan withdrawal from Chad marked a humiliating defeat for the Qaddafi regime and a fatal setback for the Leader's vague plans to create an Islamic federation from Mauritania to Sudan (Burr and Collins 1999: 223–5; Flint and De Waal 2005: 23, 50). After resuming diplomatic relations in 1988, Chad and Libya agreed to submit their dispute over the Aouzou Strip to the International Court of Justice (ICJ). When the ICJ in February 1994 ruled in Chad's favor, Chad and Libya issued a joint communiqué in which Libya agreed to return the Aouzou Strip to Chad, completing the evacuation of Libyan troops in May 1994 (Joffé 2005: 608–9).

Events in Sudan overlapped hostilities in Chad, especially in the Darfur region of northwestern Sudan. Libya and Sudan enjoyed tempestuous contacts after 1969 when military coups put ambitious young officers in charge in both countries. Initially, Qaddafi supported the Sudanese government of Jaafar Muhammad Numayri, but, after Numayri rejected Qaddafi's offer of political union, Libya was involved in several abortive coup attempts. By 1980, Sudan was closely aligned with Egypt and the United States and locked in hostility with Ethiopia and Libya (Lesch 1991: 46–52). After a Transitional Military Council (TMC) replaced the Numayri regime in 1985, Qaddafi again called for political union with Sudan and suggested that Egyptian president Hosni Mubarak would suffer the same fate at Numayri. Although union was never a likely prospect, Qaddafi agreed to provide the new government economic and military aid in return for the use of Darfur as a back door to Chad. With local tensions in the region already high, the presence of thousands of Islamic Legion and Chadian troops in Darfur sparked a conflagration. In the process, the widening Khartoum–Tripoli axis complicated regional relations as linkages between Libyan policies toward Egypt and Sudan, coupled with its ongoing involvement in Chad, further internationalized hostilities (Flint and De Waal 2005: 25, 51; Prunier 2005: 58–67). In mid-1986, Qaddafi renewed his calls for union with Sudan and for subversion against Egypt and the United States, and over the next four years Libya provided economic and military assistance to Sudan. In March 1990, Libya and Sudan concluded a Charter of Integration, which provided for the coordination of military and security forces along with joint efforts to disseminate Arabic language and Arab culture (Lesch 1991: 58–67: Burr and Collins 1999: 246–8, 255–6).

In the second half of the 1980s, sub-Saharan Africa remained a high priority for Libya, but there was little new in its approach to the region. It continued its earlier efforts to reduce Israeli influence while the United States, as part of a wider effort to undermine the Qaddafi regime, actively supported Israeli efforts to restore ties with African states. Libya extended military assistance to some African states, including Burkina Faso, the Central African Republic, Ghana, and Uganda, but others, including Mauritania, Niger, Togo and Zaire, complained of Libyan involvement in their domestic affairs. Libya also continued to recruit for the Islamic Legion, centering its efforts on Burkina Faso, Djibouti,

Ethiopia, Ghana, Mali, Nigeria, and Sudan but not restricting its recruitment efforts to Muslims or to African states (St John 2000: 23–6; Solomon and Swart 2005: 471–3).

Given the strong ideological roots of Libyan foreign policy, it proved ironic that a major problem in Africa was Qaddafi's failure to develop a sound ideological basis for his policies on the continent. Africa was an arena secondary to the Arab world for the promotion of the Libyan position on Palestine, and many Africans concluded that their interests were also subordinate to its global objectives. As a result, whereas the Arab world viewed Qaddafi's ideology as obsolete, most African states viewed it as irrelevant. Another shortcoming of Qaddafi's Africa policy was its negative character. Focused on the immediate goal of destroying Western, especially Israeli, influence, Libya failed to develop longer-term interests and relationships. The negative inspiration of Libyan policy was clear from the start, and it continued even after Libya succeeded in reducing Israeli influence. In a policy with little or no ideological substance, the discrepancy between aid commitments and aid disbursements proved fatal as it reinforced the feeling among African states that Libyan solicitude was insecure and self-serving (St John 1988: 131–6).

Turning to the Arab world, Libya and Syria in September 1980 proclaimed a merger, but one year later, the details of the union remained unclear. Eventually, union plans lapsed because the two states could not agree on operative governmental institutions for the unified state (*MEED*: 28.8.81). In the coming years, Libya and Syria continued union talks; however, no substantive progress was made. Libya would remain at odds with and isolated from the Mashriq for most of the coming two decades (St John 1987a: 61–2). In December 1984, Libya and Morocco concluded a union agreement, known as the Treaty of Oujda, which called for the creation of a federation. Two years later, Morocco declared the agreement null and void after Qaddafi denounced the July 1986 visit of the Israeli prime minister, Shimon Peres, to Morocco (Ronen 2008: 116). Among other issues, Libyan–Moroccan relations in this period were frequently strained by the conflict in the Western Sahara (Damis 1985; Deeb 1989a: 29–31). Efforts to promote Maghrib unity were also hampered by the conflicting priorities of the individual states, with Libya continuing to insist that any movement toward greater Maghrib unity must be viewed only as a step toward the ultimate goal of Arab unity (Joffé 2005: 609–10). In February 1989, Libya joined Algeria, Mauritania, Morocco, and Tunisia in forming the Arab Maghrib Union (Deeb 1989b; Harris 1990). Having emphasized Arab unity for two decades, this was the only union – and it was an imperfect one – to endure.

Support for terrorism

Over the last century, state-sponsored terrorism has often been the weapon of choice for regimes with ambitions in excess of their power base, and Libya was no exception. In the first two decades of the revolution, Libya's association with terrorism, defined as the use by a group for political means of covert violence which is usually directed against a government but may be directed against another group, class or party, led to much adverse publicity. Qaddafi tried to differentiate between terrorism, which he publicly rejected, and revolutionary violence, which he openly advocated, but his efforts were largely unsuccessful (St John 1986: 111). In March 1985, Qaddafi told the General People's Congress (GPC) that the state had the right to liquidate any opponent of the revolution and, in so doing, he compared his critics to contemporary groups practiced in violence, such as the Red Brigades and the Irish Republican Army. Threatening to support such groups if European governments harbored opponents of the regime, Qaddafi also reiterated his support for black and Indian separatist movements in the United States (*Times*: 6.3.85).

The contradictions in the Libyan position on terrorism were apparent in the aftermath of the December 1985 terrorist attacks on the Rome and Vienna airports. Qaddafi denied involvement in the attacks and claimed that there were no Palestinian training camps in Libya but, at the same time, he emphasized his support for the Palestinian people, arguing that such attacks were a part of the struggle to liberate their homeland. In response, PLO chairman Arafat charged that Libya and Syria were behind the recent rash of terrorist attacks in Europe and were using them to discredit the PLO and sideline Arab talks with Israel (*FT*: 2.1.86; *WSJ*: 6.1.86). Thereafter, Qaddafi continued to contradict himself, blurring any distinction between terrorism and wars of national liberation. In early January 1986, he condemned the terrorists who attacked the two airports, but only a week later he told a cheering crowd of Libyans that his government was equipping and training guerrillas for terrorist and suicide missions. Admitting his support for radical Palestinian groups, he went on to describe Libya as a base for the liberation of Palestine (*IHT*: 10.1.86).

In the wake of the April 1986 American attack on Libya and the February 1987 debacle in Chad, Qaddafi focused his efforts on American and French interests in the South Pacific, renewing support for Muslim separatists in the southern Philippines and offering assistance to radical groups on various South Pacific islands, including New Caledonia and Vanuatu (*IHT*: 22.4.87; *Times*: 2.5.87). In April 1987, Libya hosted a conference on anti-colonialism in the South Pacific at which Qaddafi called on the parties in attendance to fight for their freedom. Elsewhere, the Libyan response to the April 1986 attack included the execution of two Britons and one American in Beirut, an attack on a US embassy employee in Sudan, and a missile attack in the direction of a US installation on the Italian island of Lampedusa. In September 1987, the terrorist Abu Nidal, allegedly working for Libya, hijacked Pan Am flight 73, resulting in the death of several Americans (US Department of Defense 1997: 15–16; *WP*: 23.11.09). In mid-1988, the Reagan administration attributed another wave of terrorist attacks to Libya operating under the cover of Japanese and Palestinian terrorist groups (*IHT*: 3.6.88). In December 1988, Pan Am flight 103 blew up over Lockerbie,

Scotland, killing 270 people, and, in September 1989, UTA flight 772 blew up over Niger, killing 171 people.

Confrontation with the United States

The November 1980 election of Ronald Reagan produced a dramatic shift in US policy toward Libya. Where President Carter had pursued a policy of constraint, the Reagan administration carefully orchestrated a systematic increase in diplomatic, economic, and military pressure on Libya. Wrongly considered a Soviet puppet, Qaddafi was viewed by Reagan as an international pariah who should be corralled if not replaced (Wright 1981–2: 13–17). In addition to closing the Libyan People's Bureau in Washington, the Reagan administration began to subject all Libyan visa applications to a mandatory security advisory opinion and advised the US oil companies in Libya to begin an orderly reduction of their American employees. Other elements of the US campaign to isolate Libya included support for governments such as Morocco, Sudan, and Tunisia, which were opposed to Libya, enhanced coordination of US policies with those of its European allies, and the calculated threat of military intervention (St John 2002: 121–7). The United States repeatedly challenged Libyan claims to sovereignty and jurisdiction over the Gulf of Sirte as part of a broader struggle over control of the Mediterranean, a competition reflected in Libyan courtship of Malta in this time frame (Rossi 1986: 5–40). In August 1981, the United States first employed military force against Libya, shooting down two Libyan planes over the Gulf of Sirte (Stanik 2003: 51–6).

In March 1982, the Reagan administration announced an embargo on Libyan oil and imposed an export license requirement on US goods bound for Libya. In addition, it asked its European allies to join the embargo; however, they all declined to participate. In 1984, the United States curtailed the movement of Libyan diplomats accredited to the United Nations, and in November 1985 it banned the import of all Libyan oil products. In the wake of the December 1985 terrorist attacks on the Rome and Vienna airports, the Reagan administration again urged its European allies to join it in imposing sanctions on Libya, and it again received a tepid response (*IHT*: 9.1.86). Four months later, after fresh air and naval engagements in the Gulf of Sirte and the bombing of a West Berlin discothèque, which radio intercepts appeared to suggest was orchestrated from the Libyan embassy in East Berlin, the Reagan administration bombed what it described as centers of terrorist activity and training in Benghazi and Tripoli (Stanik 2003: 176–205).

The news media in the United States widely supported the attack, the first prime-time bombing raid in the nation's history; however, outside the United States, it was generally condemned, especially in the African, Arab, and Islamic worlds. The Non-Aligned Movement denounced the attack as a blatant act of aggression, and OPEC also condemned it, although it quickly rejected a Libyan demand for an oil embargo against the United States (*WSJ*: 16.4.86, 17.4.86,

21.4.86). Inside Libya, a bombing raid intended by the United States to weaken or kill Qaddafi instead strengthened his hold on power. It also embarrassed exiled Libyan opposition groups, undermining their popularity and reducing their already limited capabilities (Anderson 1987: 65; Deeb 1991: 172–3).

Following the attack, the Reagan administration strengthened its sanctions against Libya. In June of that year, all US oil and oil service companies were ordered to halt operations in Libya, and later in the year the United States launched an ill-conceived disinformation campaign, which generated a storm of protest once it became public knowledge (*IHT*: 4–5.10.86). In early 1988, the Reagan administration announced that it intended to maintain economic sanctions against Libya, and in September of that year it repeated charges first made in December 1987 that Libya was building a factory to manufacture chemical weapons (Wiegele 1992: 20–1, 25–6). In early January 1989, less than three weeks before the inauguration of George H. W. Bush, US fighter aircraft downed two more Libyan jets over the Mediterranean (*IHT*: 5.1.89). Largely unsuccessful in modifying Libyan behavior, the policies of the Reagan administration focused attention on a major irony in the American–Libyan relationship. Owing to his esteem for US power and prestige, Qaddafi often betrayed a need for US recognition and confirmation of his importance. In this light, the policies of the Reagan administration encouraged as much as discouraged the behavior it intended to modify because its approach to Libya generated the global attention so desperately craved by the Leader (Orman 1987: 113–14).

Libya and Europe

European leaders recognized Qaddafi's anti-Western behavior, but many of them argued that he was not as dangerous as the Reagan administration claimed. In support of their position, they cited his recent foreign policy failures in Chad and Uganda along with his alienation of a growing number of African and Middle Eastern leaders. Moreover, many Europeans felt that it was a mistake to isolate Libya, in effect putting Qaddafi on a pedestal. Instead, they favored dialog with the Qaddafi regime as the optimum means to protect their interests in Libya (*IHT*: 21.4.86; *WSJ*: 24.4.86). In addition, there was a widespread feeling throughout Europe that the United States continued to address the symptoms of terrorism as opposed to its cause, which most Europeans believed was the Palestinian issue. European leaders also worried that the policies of the Reagan administration would increase the Soviet threat to NATO if it led to a Soviet base at Tobruk or elsewhere on the Libyan coast, a prospect which dimmed as the decade progressed. When a senior Libyan delegation visited Moscow in May 1986, the Soviets refused to extend additional arms credits or to conclude a mutual defense treaty. Instead, they emphasized the confusion that existed in differentiating between Libyan support for revolutionary movements and terrorism (*IHT*: 24.3.87, 7.5.86). With large commercial interests in Libya, several European states, including France, Great Britain, and Italy, also questioned the effectiveness of economic sanctions as well as the commitment of the United States to their progressive application (Joffé 2001: 77–85; Mezran and De Maio 2007: 440–2).

Given the widespread skepticism present in Europe, the foreign policy set-backs of the second Reagan administration simply confirmed in most European capitals the wisdom of pursuing a Libyan policy one step removed from the United States. The ill-conceived American disinformation campaign against Libya damaged the reputation of the Reagan administration, diverted attention from Libyan policies, and exposed a split in US policy toward Libya (*WSJ*: 6.10.86). The Iran–Contra affair was even more damaging as it left the terrorism policy of the United States in total disarray. The sale of arms to Iran, one of the states Washington had most frequently tied to terrorism, contradicted official US policy toward the Iran–Iraq war. To the extent that it was arranging secret deals with radical regimes, the Reagan administration appeared to be guilty of that ambiguity toward state-sponsored terrorism for which in the past it had strongly criticized its European allies.

Years in the wilderness

In mid-November 1991, the United Kingdom and the United States issued indictments against the two Libyan suspects in the bombing of Pan Am flight 103, and later in the month France, the United Kingdom, and the United States issued a tripartite declaration demanding that Libya hand over the two suspects. When it failed to comply, the UN Security Council in March 1992 passed Resolution 748, imposing an air and arms embargo and a reduction in Libyan diplomatic personnel serving abroad. In November 1993, the Security Council passed Resolution 883, which toughened the sanctions in place, freezing Libyan assets overseas, banning the sale of downstream (refining and transportation) oil equipment, and tightening earlier restrictions on commercial air links.

For most of the 1990s, Libyan foreign policy was dominated by issues related to the UN sanctions regime. The United States after 1992 pressed repeatedly for a global boycott of Libyan oil, a move its European allies and many African and Arab states rejected (*FT*: 10.10.96). The European Union (EU) also opposed the Iran and Libya Sanctions Act of 1996, in which the United States imposed penalties on anyone investing $40 million or more in the oil and gas industries of Iran or Libya. In April 1995, the UN relaxed its restrictions on air travel, allowing Libyans to fly to Saudi Arabia for the annual haj pilgrimage. Later in the year, Libya requested permission from the UN Security Council to repatriate more than 1 million African workers, a step it said was prompted by the poor state of the Libyan economy. The UN sanctions had a stronger impact than the US sanctions on Libya, and the Libyan request reflected growing internal unrest in the country. It was also an attempt by Libya to use the imported workforce as a bargaining chip to press the United Nations to ease the embargo (Niblock 2001: 19–94; O'Sullivan 2003: 173–232).

In February 1997, the OAU called for an end to the UN sanctions on the grounds that Libya had taken positive steps toward a resolution of the Lockerbie issue, and by the end of the year the sanctions regime was beginning to crack, with African heads of state taking the lead in opposing it. In October 1997, South African President Nelson Mandela, the first recipient of the Qaddafi International Prize for Human Rights, visited Libya to thank the Leader for his support during the long struggle against white minority rule in South Africa (*IHT*: 23.10.97). During his visit, Mandela called for the sanctions to be lifted, arguing that the Lockerbie case should be dealt with by an international tribunal, an approach the Arab League and the OAU supported (*NYT*: 26.10.97). The presidents of Chad, Eritrea, Gambia, Liberia, Mali, Niger, Tanzania, and Uganda also visited Libya in 1997–8, and, when President Bill Clinton visited South Africa in March 1998, President Mandela publicly defended his ties with Libya (*IHT*: 28–29.3.98; Huliaras 2001: 11–13).

Normalized relations

In August 1998, Libya accepted an Anglo-American proposal to try the two Libyan suspects in the Lockerbie bombing in the Netherlands under Scottish law. Two months later, the UN General Assembly, by a vote of 80 in favor, two opposed (Israel and the United States), and 67 abstentions, adopted a Libyan-sponsored resolution aimed at the United States which called for the repeal of laws imposing unilateral sanctions. In early April 1999, Libya remanded the Lockerbie suspects into UN custody, and the UN suspended its sanctions regime, allowing the resumption of air travel and the sale of industrial equipment. The United States took the opposite tack, retaining its unilateral sanctions on the grounds that the crisis with Libya had not been resolved (*IHT*: 6.4.99).

Focus on Africa

After the United Nations suspended its sanctions package, Qaddafi launched a series of initiatives in Africa. A mix of the old and the new, they reflected a shift in focus from the Middle East to Africa, a change motivated in part by the failure of the Arab states to support Libya during the Lockerbie crisis (Joffé 2005: 613). There was still an anti-Israeli component to Libyan foreign policy; however, Israel was no longer the central concern. Moreover, the issues of colonialism and imperialism were considered passé and were seldom referenced except in a rhetorical context. As for the earlier emphasis on Islam, it continued in a few areas, but, again, its role was much diminished (St John 2000: 28). Instead, Qaddafi repeatedly stressed that the future was for "big spaces," and Libya was part of the big space of Africa (Qaddafi with Jouve 2005: 62–72).

In the subsequent years, Qaddafi involved himself as a regional peace broker and mediator in disputes throughout Africa. He mediated a ceasefire agreement between Congolese President Laurent Kabila and Ugandan President Yoweri

Museveni in 1999, and he also attempted to mediate between the warring factions in Sierra Leone and between Eritrea and Ethiopia. The following year, he promoted a peace initiative to end the civil war in Sudan, and in 2002, he attempted to mediate between the warring factions in Chad. Most of his early efforts as a regional peace broker yielded few immediate results; however, his success rate was no worse than that of most other governments and organizations that attempted to mediate these disputes. Although the Leader often used regional conflicts to promote the geo-strategic ambitions of Libya, his efforts at brokering regional peace were notable for their breath and duration. After 1999, Qaddafi committed untold time, energy, and resources to the mediation of African disputes, especially the intertwined conflicts in Chad, Darfur, and Sudan (*JANA*: 31.8.09, 23.2.10; International Crisis Group 2010).

Libya also revived and expanded bilateral relations with a number of African states, extending financial aid to Ethiopia, Ivory Coast, Mali, Tanzania, Uganda, and Zimbabwe, and it announced joint venture projects in Chad, Ethiopia, Mali, and Tanzania. In the course of the decade, Qaddafi continued to court numerous African states, often resorting to largess to win support for his more controversial policies. The Leader also resurrected his long-time vision for a United States of Africa; however, when the African Union replaced the 35-year-old OAU in 2002, the larger, more influential African states rejected his call for immediate union. In July 2005, Qaddafi repeated calls for greater African unity, citing opportunities in specific areas such as a common defense system and a single monetary zone, and two years later he called for the African Union to be turned into an embryonic federal government (Qaddafi 2005: 1–3; *BBC News*: 4.7.07).

In February 1998, Libya took the lead in establishing the Community of Sahel–Saharan States (COMESSA or CEN-SAD), an initiative which brought to mind Libyan efforts in the 1970s to forge a federation of Saharan and Sahelian states. Headquartered in Tripoli, COMESSA linked 28 African states which were mostly poor but represented over half the population of the continent. COMESSA reflected Qaddafi's long-time interest in regional integration, but it did so without compromising the independence of the member states (Joffé 2005: 613–14). In June 2005, Libya also joined the Common Market for Eastern and Southern Africa (COMESA), a grouping created in 1994 to promote regional integration through trade development. Comprising 19 member states stretching from Egypt to Namibia, COMESA was considered by the African Union to be an important vehicle for the development of the continent's resources (Solomon and Swart 2005: 478).

Libya's involvement in Saharan and Sahelian political affairs raised the possibility of a new pan-Saharan political alliance. In April 2005, Qaddafi told a Tuareg delegation at Oubari in Fezzan that Libya considered itself the protector of the Tuareg and that they should consider Libya their "base and support." Cloaked in ambiguity, his remarks were taken by some observers to constitute a justification for ongoing intervention in Saharan–Sahelian affairs (Keenan

2005: 641–2). As the United States moved to create an African command force, known as US Africa Command (AFRICOM), his comments also served as a warning to the United States to curb its imperial designs in the region.

At one point, Qaddafi also proposed an expansion of the Libyan armed forces to include some 3,000 Tuareg, Tebu, and other Saharan peoples who otherwise might be employed by trans-Saharan smugglers and traffickers. Given the earlier activities of the Islamic Legion, the prospect of a new Libyan-controlled merce- nary force operating in an already volatile area of the world was troublesome to many governments (*NYT*: 24.12.06). Qaddafi also called for the establishment of a Shiite Fatimid state in North Africa after the model of the caliphate that ruled part of the Levant, Egypt, and the Maghrib in the tenth century (Middle East Media Research Institute 2007). After 2007, Qaddafi was deeply involved in efforts to bring peace to the Sahel, especially in Mali and Niger; however, a variety of issues, including the activities of Al-Qaeda in the Islamic Maghrib (AQIM), made sustained progress difficult to achieve (*JANA*: 25.10.09; *WP*: 14.3.10).

In the interim, some of Qaddafi's former protégés were held to account, highlighting the downside of earlier Libyan policies, which emphasized opposi- tion to colonialism and support for Islam while ignoring the personalities and practices of individual regimes. The disgraced former president of Uganda, Idi Amin Dada, died in exile in Saudi Arabia in 2003, and President João Bernado "Nino" Vieira of Guinea-Bissau was assassinated in March 2009 (*FT*: 3.3.09). In Sierra Leone, senior members of the Revolutionary United Front, a rebel fac- tion trained in Libya, were convicted in February 2009 of war crimes and crimes against humanity. When the International Criminal Court in July 2008 charged Sudanese President Omar Hassan al-Bashir with genocide, war crimes, and crimes against humanity, Qaddafi came to his defense, according him a place of honor at the September 2009 celebrations marking the fortieth anniversary of the One September Revolution (*NYT*: 15.7.08; *CSM*: 1.9.09). In 2006, Charles Taylor, the former president of Liberia, was arrested and charged with crimes against humanity in neighboring Sierra Leone, together with related atrocities at home. In the course of a lengthy trial at The Hague, witness testimony detailed his guerrilla training in Libya and his return to Liberia in 1989 as the head of a Libyan-backed resistance group, the National Patriotic Front of Liberia (*FT*: 3.4.06, 15.7.09; *WP*: 15.7.09). Over time, the Ugandan president, Yoweri Museveni, distanced himself from Qaddafi, but the president of Zimbabwe, Robert Mugabe, also accorded a place of honor at the fortieth anniversary cel- ebrations, continued to look to Libya for support (Solomon and Swart 2005: 477; *CSM*: 1.9.09).

In August 2008, more than 200 African kings, traditional leaders, and nota- bles met in Libya at Qaddafi's invitation and bestowed upon him the honorific title "King of Kings." The coronation of the Leader was designed to drum up support for a United States of Africa and to buttress the Leader's nomination to become chairman of the African Union. Over the next two years, Qaddafi met regularly with traditional leaders from around Africa in gatherings that provided him with a forum to promote greater African unity (*JANA*: 28.7.10). Some African states took little notice of these meetings, but others criticized them on the grounds that Qaddafi's designation as King of Kings violated the long-standing independence of traditional leaders. Other states took offense at the emphasis on African unity generally at the center of these gatherings, stressing that foreign policy was the concern of central governments and not traditional leaders.

In February 2009, Qaddafi enjoyed a personal triumph when he was elected to a one-year term as African Union chairman, some 25 years after he was the first and only African leader to be denied the leadership of the OAU. Laying out an ambitious agenda, the Leader said he intended to focus on greater African unity, political unrest in the Congo, Madagascar, and Mauritania, the Eritrea–Ethiopia dispute, and the troubled Darfur region of Sudan, adding that he hoped that the Caribbean states would join the African Union (Qaddafi 2009). Twelve months later, real achievement in most of these policy areas was modest, especially in regards to African unity, Eritrea–Ethiopia, and Darfur, and there was no support for the Caribbean initiative. At the end of his term, Qaddafi hoped to continue for a second year, but the African Union rejected this idea, returning to the long-standing practice of geographical rotation to select a new chairman. In his valedictory address, Qaddafi rebuked his fellow heads of state for choosing to replace him and for failing to push for the creation of a United States of Africa. Charging "the current political elites in Africa lack political awareness," he argued that the current situation "calls for a single African mechanism to face the outside world" and "to confront backwardness in Africa." Concluding on a sour note, Qaddafi claimed that the African Union chairman had no real power and that it was enough for him to be the "King of African Kings and Doyen of African and Arab Rulers" (Qaddafi 2010).

Muddled relations with the Middle East and North Africa

Qaddafi's renewed focus on Africa came at the expense of his long-term concern with the Middle East. He did not attend the Arab League summit in Beirut in March 2002, in part because the Lebanese Shiite community continued to hold him responsible for the disappearance in 1978 of the Iranian-born spiritual leader, Imam Musa al-Sadr. At the fifth ordinary session of the African Union assembly in July 2005, he mocked the very idea of a Middle East, claiming that it was normally considered the "Dirty East" (Qaddafi 2005: 10). Threatening on more than one occasion to pull out of the Arab League, he often used Arab summits, when he chose to attend them, as a forum to berate, cajole, and belittle his fellow members. In the summer of 2004, Saudi Arabia accused Libya of being involved in a plot to assassinate Saudi Crown Prince Abdullah bin Abdulaziz and other members of the Saudi government, adding to his estrangement from the Mashriq (Ronen 2008: 69, 139). A variety of specific issues contributed to the Leader's frustration with the Arab world; however, the central one remained the failure to develop a coherent pan-Arab movement, a Libyan objective from the outset of the One September Revolution (*JANA*: 29.6.10). As for the Palestinian issue, Qaddafi continued to reference it on occasion, but his remarks most often were a mix of ideology and indifference as he distanced himself from an issue that was once central to Libyan foreign policy (St John 2006b: B642). Long an advocate of a military solution to the Israeli–Palestinian dispute, the Leader now advocated a single state solution known as Isratine (Qaddafi with Jouve 2005: 84).

In North Africa, Qaddafi moved to revitalize the moribund Arab Maghrib Union (AMU), hamstrung after 1994 by regional disputes. Libya supported calls for a North African summit which failed to materialize and suggested broadening the scope of the AMU, possibly integrating the newly formed COMESSA grouping; nevertheless, a number of issues, including the conflict over the Western Sahara and domestic politics in the member states, prevented meaningful progress (Darbouche and Zoubir 2009; Zoubir 2007). Consequently, the AMU failed to evolve much beyond its initial framework, and the level of intra-regional trade remained one of the lowest in the world. In lieu of economic reform, AMU member states concentrated on anti-terrorism efforts, tightening border restrictions, reducing commerce, and depressing economic activity (Spencer 2009: 1–14; Zemni and Bogaert 2009). The dispute in the Western Sahara remained the central factor in strained Algerian–Moroccan relations and thus a major obstacle to Maghrib cooperation and integration (Darbouche and Zoubir 2008). AMU officials did agree in 2010 to establish a Maghrib Customs Cooperation Council with headquarters in Algiers and a training center in Casablanca, the most important move toward regional reconciliation in many years (*Economist*: 29.5.10).

Broader ties with Europe and Asia

Throughout the 1990s, the European Union attracted 85 percent of Libyan exports and generated 75 percent of Libyan imports. Germany, Italy, and Spain alone absorbed 80 percent of Libyan exports. Germany and Spain dominated Libyan imports, but the United Kingdom was also a significant exporter to Libya. Following the resolution of the Lockerbie and UTA crises, Libya was expected to undertake a major expansion of its hydrocarbon sector, and the European states hoped to participate. Italy was at the forefront, but France, Spain, and the United Kingdom were not far behind. European companies also anticipated massive opportunities to participate in the redevelopment of Libya's infrastructure (Joffé 2001: 79, 87; Werenfels 2004: 2).

Shortly after the UN sanctions were suspended, Libya became an observer in the Euro-Mediterranean Partnership (EMP) or Barcelona Process. With the conclusion of the Lockerbie trial, the UN sanctions were lifted in September 2003, and in late 2004 Qaddafi visited EU headquarters in Brussels, an important step in his rehabilitation as a world leader. Thereafter, Libya remained an observer in the EMP, but it elected not to seek full membership. Protective of his self-appointed role as an intermediary between Africa and Europe, the Leader refused to become too deeply involved in a regional process with restrictive conditions. With energy exports to Europe not subjected to tariffs, Libya already enjoyed most of the advantages of a free trade regime; therefore, it could achieve most of what it wanted by keeping its hands free. Moreover, Israel was a member of the Barcelona Process, and, although the terms of association stated explicitly that member states had to recognize each other's sovereignty, the terms were such that acceptance of a co-member's right to exist was implicit in the document. Libya also participated in the 5 + 5 Forum, a dialog group formed in 2003 which included five European and five North African states and in which Libya had a larger presence.

EU officials worked with Libya for much of the decade to check the flow of illegal migrants to Europe; nevertheless, the final resolution of this complex issue remained a work in progress (Zoubir 2009a: 409). In July 2005, the European Commission gave Libya €1 million to support its fight against HIV/ AIDS as part of a broader effort to win the release of five Bulgarian nurses and a Palestinian doctor wrongfully accused of infecting children in a Benghazi hospital. After lengthy talks, the six health care workers were finally released in July 2007 (Lutterbeck 2009: 169–71). EU relations with Libya hit another rough spot in the spring of 2010, when Libya temporarily stopped issuing entry visas to the citizens of most European states in retaliation for Switzerland barring entry to senior Libyans, including the Leader and his family. The dispute began in July 2008 when Geneva police arrested one of Qaddafi's sons on a charge of mistreating two domestic employees. Although Libya later painted Switzerland as racist and anti-Islamic, the dispute from the start centered on Qaddafi's concept of family honor. The controversy was not resolved until June 2010, when Switzerland agreed to pay compensation and a Swiss businessman detained by the Libyans was released (*NYT*: 14.6.10).

When French President Nicolas Sarkozy launched the Union for the Mediterranean initiative in July 2008, Qaddafi immediately rejected it on the grounds that it constituted a violation of African Union resolutions, a threat to Arab unity, and a return to colonialism. Of the 44 states invited to Paris to discuss the proposal, the Leader was the only one not to attend. In an October 2009 speech to the General Secretariat of Arab Authors and Writers Union, Qaddafi reiterated his opposition to the Union for the Mediterranean, arguing that the Arab states which had agreed to participate had become "a partner with the Israelis." Concluding on a wistful note, he added that the only thing uniting the contemporary Arab world was Arab culture, language, and literature (*JANA*: 22.10.09).

Italy

With the most trade and investment at stake, Italy was an enthusiastic, early champion of Libyan rehabilitation. The Italian foreign minister traveled to Libya to meet with Qaddafi just one day after the two Libya suspects in the Lockerbie bombing were remanded into UN custody, and the Italian prime minister completed a two-day visit in December 1999. At the time, Libya provided some 25 percent of Italy's total energy imports, and with the completion of the Green Stream pipeline in 2004 its share increased to 30 percent. The end to the UN sanctions regime also invigorated other bilateral economic ties that had slowed but never ceased during the sanctions years (Otman and Karlberg 2007: 26).

In the second half of the decade, bilateral relations centered on two issues, Italian compensation for its occupation of Libya and Libyan cooperation in stemming the flow of illegal immigration to Europe. The two questions were unrelated; however, Libya used the migratory issue to press Italy on the compensation question (Mezran and De Maio 2007: 448–9; Paoletti 2008). In August 2008, the two states concluded a treaty of friendship, partnership, and cooperation in which Italy agreed to make available $5 billion over the next 20 years to pay for Libyan infrastructure projects to compensate for the damage caused by the 32-year Italian occupation. The funds were to come from an increase of up to 4 percent in the corporate income tax of Italian oil and gas companies with a capitalization of more than €20 billion, basically ENI, the giant energy company. Awarded four blocks in the second round of EPSAs, phase four, ENI in 2008 was the largest foreign oil operator in Libya. The 2008 treaty also called for previous agreements on immigration to be implemented and for the patrol of the Libyan coastline by mixed crews on boats provided by Italy. It also provided for surveillance of Libyan land borders by a satellite detection system jointly financed by Italy and the EU. Finally, the treaty was strategic in paving the way for the investment of Libyan sovereign wealth funds in a number of Italian companies, including ENI (Gazzini 2009: 1–13; Ronzitti 2009: 1–10).

Thereafter, Libya and Italy expanded their cooperation and partnership agreements, and Italian investment in Libya, especially in the hydrocarbon sector, increased (*JANA*: 12.6.09). Unfortunately, international criticism of Italian immigration policies also continued to grow, especially the policy of returning migrants and asylum seekers to Libya without screening for refugee status or other vulnerabilities (Human Rights Watch 2009a; Paoletti 2009). In 2009, the Council of Europe's European Committee for the Prevention of Torture and Inhuman or Degrading Treatment or Punishment warned that the return of migrants to Libya was a breach of Italy's obligations under international human rights law as well as EU law (Council of Europe 2009: 42).

United Kingdom

Once Libya had surrendered the two Lockerbie suspects, the British government agreed to restore full diplomatic relations as soon as Libya assumed responsibility for the fatal shooting of Yvonne Fletcher, a London police constable who died in 1984 from shots fired from inside the Libyan People's Bureau. Several Libyans were deported after her murder and the United Kingdom severed diplomatic relations, but Libya failed to cooperate fully in the subsequent investigation and no one was brought to trial (Higgins 1985). Libya quickly agreed to the British stipulations, accepting general responsibility for the actions leading to her death, apologizing to her family, and agreeing to pay compensation and to help investigate her murder. After Libya in late November 1999 paid compensation to Fletcher's family, the new British ambassador to Libya took up his post in December. In the meantime, British Airways in June 1999 introduced a weekly flight from London to Tripoli, the first since 1984, and the British government announced that it was lifting its ban on the export of aircraft, aircraft parts, and flight simulators (*NYT*: 8.7.02; Joffé 2004).

In the wake of Libya's December 2003 renunciation of unconventional weapons and related delivery systems, Prime Minister Tony Blair made the first of several trips to Libya, and bilateral cooperation against global terrorism, which began with the renewal of diplomatic relations in 1999, continued. At the same time, defense cooperation expanded, including training, staff talks, and the provision of defense equipment (Lutterbeck 2009: 174–5). In September 2006, a new British Council opened in Tripoli, including an English language teaching center, and the number of Libyan students studying in British universities continued to grow (Layden 2007). Commercial ties also expanded, with investment in the hydrocarbon sector leading the way. In February 2005, the BG Group, alone or in cooperation with others, was awarded three blocks in the second round of EPSAs, phase four, and, in May 2007, British Petroleum (BP) announced a $900 million contract, returning the British energy giant to Libya over three decades after its assets were nationalized in 1971 (*IHT*: 30.5.07). Rounding out the picture, a joint British–Libyan health task force was established in 2006, and memorandums of understanding were signed in 2009, providing for cooperation in curriculum development, education, and the training of medical personnel (*JANA*: 10.10.09). Later, the Scottish government's release on humanitarian grounds of the only Libyan convicted in the Lockerbie case resulted in a public outcry, especially in the United States; however, it served to strengthen British relations with Libya (*Guardian*: 20.7.09).

France

In March 1999, a Paris court condemned *in absentia* six Libyans to life imprisonment for the 1999 bombing of UTA flight 772, but it did not raise the question of Qaddafi's personal responsibility in the attack. Over the next two years, bilateral relations improved, with the French government promoting French commercial interests in Libya and pressing the latter for support in the war on terrorism. Air links between Paris and Tripoli were resumed in February 2002 after a 10-year halt, and later in the year two French companies were awarded major contracts to support oil and gas development in Libya. In early 2004, Libya agreed to compensate the families of the victims of the UTA bombing, and later that year President Jacques Chirac made an official visit to Libya. Two months later, the French defense minister signed a letter of intent with Libya covering military cooperation and procurement, and in 2005 Total, the French energy giant, was awarded new acreage in Libya in round two of EPSAs, phase four (Otman and Karlberg 2007: 26; Lutterbeck 2009: 173–4). After French President Nicolas Sarkozy and his former wife played a public role in the July 2007 release of the six health care workers held on false HIV/AIDS charges, France and Libya in August 2007 unveiled an arms deal worth approximately €300 million. Later in the year, France announced the endorsement of contracts worth €3.2 billion, and Libya confirmed the purchase of 21 Airbus planes and the conclusion of a nuclear cooperation agreement (Zoubir 2009a: 413).

Germany

German relations with Libya also suffered from outstanding legal proceedings, in this case the 1986 bombing of the La Belle discothèque in West Berlin. After a four-year trial, a German court in November 2001 found four people guilty of planting the bomb that killed three people and injured 229 others, but the prosecution failed to prove either Qaddafi's role or his responsibility in the attack. Although Libya continued to deny any involvement, it agreed in September 2004 to pay compensation to the victims. At the time, Germany was Libya's second largest trading partner, and its commercial interests in Libya increased with the resolution of the La Belle affair. Chancellor Gerhard Schroeder visited Libya in October 2004, meeting with Qaddafi and visiting a site operated by Wintershall, the oil arm of the chemical giant BASF. Wintershall had been active in Libya since 1958, and in 2004 it accounted for 10 percent of Libyan oil production, making it the third largest oil producer in the country (Werenfels 2004: 1–2). Wintershall acquired additional acreage in the EPSAs, phase four, round three, and Germany accounted for a significant portion of Libyan imports and exports in the second half of the decade.

Russia

In 2001–2, a joint commission for cooperation and trade met to explore opportunities for Russian investment in Libya, especially in agriculture, hydrocarbons, nuclear power, and transportation. Issues related to Libya's outstanding post-Cold War debts were also discussed and eventually resolved. In the second half of the decade, bilateral relations focused on arms and energy. The Russian oil and gas company, Tafneft, was awarded a block in round two of the EPSAs, phase four, and three more in round three, while Russia's state-controlled gas company, Gazprom, was awarded blocks in rounds three and four. In mid-2008, Gazprom offered to buy all of Libya's oil and gas exports, a prospect that raised EU concerns that Gazprom was seeking to increase its domination of the European gas market. In the interim, Libya and Russia continued to discuss an arms deal worth an estimated $2 billion, and Libya became the second largest

minority investor in the Russian firm Rusal, the world's largest aluminum producer (*FT*: 10.7.08; *AFP*: 27.1.10).

Asia

In addition to Europe, Qaddafi also moved to expand Libya's relations with
Asia. In mid-2002, a North Korean delegation visited Libya, concluding agreements on scientific and technical cooperation and investment promotion.
Rumors at the time suggested that the visit also included talks related to missile
sales, a possibility which took on new meaning when Libya in December 2003
renounced unconventional weapons and related delivery systems, a decision
North Korea denounced (*NYT*: 2.2.05). In the first visit by a Chinese head of
state, President Jiang Zemin traveled to Libya in April 2002, signing agreements
which included a $40 million deal for a Chinese company to extend Libya's rail
network and a Libyan commitment to open its hydrocarbon sector to Chinese
firms (St John 2008b: 56). In October 2005, the China National Petroleum
Company (CNPC) was awarded an offshore block in the second round of the
EPSAs, phase four, and, in mid-2009, the CNPC quietly withdrew its bid for
Verenex after the NOC signaled its intent to acquire the Libyan holdings of the
Canadian firm. Australia, India, Indonesia, Japan, and Taiwan were also awarded
one or more blocks during the EPSAs, phase four. During a satellite conference
at the Oxford Union Society in May 2007, Qaddafi argued that the Cold War
competition between the Soviet Union and the United States has been replaced
by a competition between China and the United States, with the involvement of
the United States in Africa both more hypocritical and more harmful (Qaddafi
2007).

Normal relations with the United States

In the aftermath of the 9/11 terrorist attacks, Libya was an enthusiastic recruit
to the war on terror, and over the next few months American and British intelligence officials engaged in extensive information-sharing sessions with their
Libyan counterparts. Previously, Libya and the United States had engaged in
secret talks on the subject as early as mid-1999 because Qaddafi recognized that
the Islamist organizations targeted by the White House also represented a threat
to his regime. In recognition of Libyan cooperation, the United States later
added the Libyan Islamic Fighting Group (LIFG) to its official list of terrorist
organizations (St John 2004b: 389–94).

Libya had agreed in 1999 to compensate the families of the victims of the
bombing of UTA flight 772, and in August 2003 it accepted responsibility for the
bombing of Pan Am flight 103 and agreed to pay $2.7 billion in compensation
(Matar and Thabit 2004: 236–44). After a brief delay in which France sought
to increase the amount of the UTA flight 772 payout, the United Nations in

September 2003 lifted its multilateral sanctions. The United States elected to keep its unilateral sanctions in place, citing concerns about Libya's poor human rights record, lack of democratic institutions, destructive role in African conflicts, and pursuit of weapons of mass destruction. Of these concerns, only the pursuit of unconventional weapons had figured in the original US rationale for imposing sanctions on Libya (St John 2008b: 59). Three months later, Libya announced that it had decided of its "own free will" to renounce weapons of mass destruction and related delivery systems. The Libyan announcement was the product of three-party talks held in London under the sponsorship of the British government in which the United States agreed to lift its sanctions in return for the verifiable dismantlement of Libya's unconventional weapons program (St John 2004b: 396–400; Zoubir 2009b: 271–3).

Libya moved quickly to honor its new commitments. In January 2004, it ratified the Comprehensive Nuclear Test Ban Treaty and joined the Chemical Weapons Convention, and in March 2004 it signed the additional protocol to the International Atomic Energy Agency (IAEA) Safeguards Agreement. In the meantime, representatives from the United Kingdom, United States, and concerned international bodies worked to disassemble Libya's unconventional weapons programs. At the same time, the United States began to lift its unilateral sanctions, parts of which had been in place for well over three decades, finally removing Libya from the list of state sponsors of terrorism in May 2006. In the interim, the United States also announced a plan to establish military relations with Libya, and it expressed interest in adding Libya to the Trans-Sahara Counter-Terrorism Partnership (TSCTP), an initiative linking the United States with nine North and West African states working to deny al-Qaeda a sanctuary in the region (St John 2008b: 60).

Although a number of issues were still pending, Libya in May 2006 could be said to have achieved full commercial and diplomatic relations with the United States for the first time in 25 years. And with the installation in December 2008 of the new US ambassador to Libya, Gene A. Cretz, diplomatic relations at the ambassadorial level were restored for the first time in 36 years. In July 2008, the US Congress passed the Libyan Claims Resolution Act, providing a mechanism to resolve the outstanding lawsuits against Libya in US courts, and in September 2008 Secretary of State Condoleezza Rice visited Libya, the first visit by a secretary of state in 55 years (*NYT*: 6.9.08). In December 2008, Ambassador C. David Welch, US Assistant Secretary of State for Near Eastern Affairs, noted that the claims settlement with Libya opened "the horizon to a normal relationship of the kind we might have with any country" (*Reuters*: 27.12.08). His remarks marked the first time an American official had stated publicly the possibility of a normal relationship with Libya since Qaddafi came to power in 1969.

In September 2009, Qaddafi traveled to New York to address the UN General Assembly. In a rambling speech of approximately 100 minutes, six times longer than his allotted time slot but short by Qaddafi standards, the Leader explored issues that had concerned him for years. Referring to the UN Security Council as the "terror council," he called for a thorough reform of the United Nations, adding that the UN headquarters should be removed from New York. Reiterating his long-standing position that the former colonial powers should compensate their former colonies, he suggested that Africa alone was owed compensation of $777 trillion. He also denounced the Ottawa Convention outlawing landmines and repeated his call for a single-state solution to the Israeli–Palestinian problem. Among other proposals, Qaddafi suggested that the UN General Assembly should investigate several assassinations, from Patrice Lumumba to John F. Kennedy to Maurice Bishop, characterized Somali pirates as simple citizens defending their livelihood, and declared that there was no war in Darfur (*JANA*: 23.9.09).

As its relations with Libya normalized, US diplomacy focused on softer issues in a confidence-building strategy (St John 2009: 1–3). The two states concluded an education and culture protocol in 2007, a science and technology agreement in 2008, and a trade and investment pact in 2010 (*WP*: 3.1.08; *JANA*: 20.5.10). They also signed a nonbinding pact on defense cooperation in 2009, which established military-to-military relations, together with collaboration in areas such as peacekeeping, maritime security, and counterterrorism (*FT*: 11.3.09; *AFP*: 27.7.09). At the same time, Libya opposed other US initiatives such as the TSCTP and AFRICOM. In turn, the United States remained concerned about Libyan involvement in the domestic affairs of African states, its goals in the Sahara and Sahel, and its proclivity to play the role of regional peacekeeper.

As Qaddafi continued to complain that Libya had not been sufficiently rewarded by the United States for its renunciation of unconventional weapons, other indications of the fragility of the bilateral relationship surfaced (*FT*: 1.9.09). In August 2009, Abdel Basset al-Megrahi, the only person convicted in the bombing of Pan Am flight 103, was released on compassionate grounds and returned to Libya, a decision heavily criticized by US officials and the families of the victims of the Lockerbie tragedy (*NYT*: 21.8.09). At the time, the UK press depicted his release as a victory for BP, which was finalizing the details of the $900 million contract with Libya announced in May 2007 (*Times*: 15.8.09; *Guardian*: 18.8.09; *BBC News*: 19.8.09). With Megrahi alive almost a year later and BP under intense scrutiny in the United States due to an oil spill in the Gulf of Mexico, the issue raised fresh controversy in mid-2010 when allegations surfaced that BP had lobbied to secure his release (*NYT*: 15.7.10; *WP*: 16.7.10). In the interim, Libya in March 2010 demanded an apology from the United States after a State Department spokesperson made a disparaging statement about the Leader's call for *jihad* against Switzerland, comparing it in a dismissive way to his September 1999 speech at the United Nations (*NYT*: 3.3.10). Before the United States could apologize, Libya called in the local heads of US oil companies and warned them that the diplomatic row could have a negative impact on US business interests in Libya (*JANA*: 15.3.10; *Guardian*: 3.3.10).

Conclusions

Oil revenues created the preconditions for the September 1969 revolution and provided the means for the Revolutionary Command Council (RCC) to reorient Libyan foreign policy; unfortunately, the latter misinterpreted the lessons of its early confrontation with the global hydrocarbon industry. In dealing with the oil companies, the RCC employed a strategy of confrontation to call the bluff of the oil cartels and consuming nations and to wrestle from them pricing and production concessions. Ecstatic with the outcome of this approach, the RCC applied the same principles elsewhere only to find that many of the nation's domestic and foreign policy problems were not amenable to such aggressive solutions. While the hydrocarbon policies of the RCC gave Libya both the impetus and the resources to set radically new foreign policy objectives, most of those goals later proved beyond the demographic, diplomatic, and military resources of the state.

The revolutionary government found it particularly difficult to establish a credible relationship between foreign policy aspirations and real accomplishments. It often addressed complex, long-standing issues with naïve, simplistic solutions, and, in so doing, it grew increasingly frustrated when its policies were greeted by other states with lack of interest or disbelief and widely rejected. In the process, the confrontational nature of Libyan diplomacy garnered the enmity of conservative and radical states alike. Compounding the problem, Qaddafi over time refined his control of the revolutionary government and came to personify Libyan foreign policy. In so doing, a growing fascination with the dress, personality, and manner of the Leader, frequently described in the Western press as bizarre, quixotic, or irrational, often mistook style for substance.

Over the last four decades, Libyan diplomacy has occasionally evidenced a measure of tactical flexibility; nevertheless, the architects of Libyan foreign policy have remained deeply committed to the ideological tenets and central objectives articulated at the outset of the revolution. In the end, this rigidity in the face of ever-changing realities in Africa, the Arab world, and elsewhere has been at the heart of the singular lack of success of Libyan foreign policy, most especially in the first three decades of the revolution. After 1999, change began to trump continuity as a growing pragmatism shook the ideological foundations of Libyan foreign policy. Moreover, the regime from the outset also failed to recognize the full extent to which the means chosen to pursue its foreign policy goals undermined its ability to achieve the ideological objectives upon which they were built. Libyan foreign policy would have likely achieved much more from the start if it had evidenced greater flexibility in responding to changing regional and international realities and been more selective in its choice of means to pursue them.

6

CONCLUSIONS

Successive waves of invaders, from Phoenicians to Greeks to Romans to Arabs to Turks to Italians, left their mark on the landscape and people of Libya. An understanding of the impact of the various stages of history on contemporary Libya is crucial to a broader discussion of its economic, social, and political development. In common with most states, the historical development of Libya combines continuity and change, with continuity dominating some periods and change the predominant theme of others.

Colonial Libya

The Arab invasions, which began in the seventh century and were reinforced by the Hilalian migration in the eleventh century, marked Libya with a distinctive Arab–Islamic character. The Arabs reached Libya earlier than elsewhere in North Africa because Libya was situated closest to the Arabian Peninsula; therefore, the Arabization of the Berbers in Libya occurred sooner than elsewhere in the Maghrib. Moreover, the Arabs and Berbers shared a social system well suited to pastoral nomadism which facilitated intermingling and intermixture, together with the Arabization and Islamization of the Berbers. Arabic and Islam largely replaced the existing languages and religions of the region, and Cyrenaica became the most thoroughly Arabized region outside the Arabian Peninsula, with the Arabization of the remainder of Libya extensive if not as complete.

In the course of 350 years of Ottoman rule, the three regions of modern-day Libya, Cyrenaica, Fezzan, and Tripolitania, developed separate and distinct political economies which have influenced socioeconomic and political practices to the present. Several factors assisted this development, including geography, social development, trade patterns, and the inability of the central government to control the inhabitants of remote areas. The impact of the physiographical character of the area was especially important as the political division of Libya into three provinces mirrored the geographical barriers separating them. With the two largest provinces divided by the Gulf of Sirte and the great Sirte Desert, Cyrenaica before independence tended to look eastward to Egypt and the Mashriq while Tripolitania looked westward to the states constituting the Maghrib. In the south, the remote and isolated Fezzan directed its attention to little beyond the Sahara Desert and the Sahelian states beyond.

The Sublime Porte preserved the territorial unity of Cyrenaica, Fezzan, and Tripolitania, a significant achievement in a time when Europe was carving up the rest of Africa, but its officials were far less successful in creating a sense of national unity among the peoples of the region. The residents of Cyrenaica, Fezzan, and Tripolitania entered the twentieth century with local, tribal, and regional identities dominating the political landscape. In theory, Ottoman nationalism could have been a response to the Italian occupation, but in reality the national concept did not yet enjoy widespread use in the Empire as a whole and certainly not in Libya. Instead, any potential national feeling was undercut by regional, tribal, and sectarian loyalties whose strength and dimensions fluctuated according to region and period, prohibiting the development and growth of a national feeling. The anti-colonial movements in Libya also failed to generate nationwide action; instead, the competition and lack of cooperation between and within regions readily visible in 1911–32 would bedevil the country for decades to come. This failure to develop any real sense of national identity proved highly significant in the subsequent struggle to create a functioning, independent state.

Monarchical Libya

At independence, Libya had no overarching ideology to guide a scattered and diverse population; no set of common traditions to unite the tribesmen of Cyrenaica, the townsmen of Tripolitania, and the nomads of Fezzan; few trained technicians, experienced administrators, or political chieftains knowledgeable in the art of modern government; and a deficit economy wholly dependent on external aid. Within Libya, the background and composition of the political groups supporting independence differed from province to province; however, in all three, they mostly remained concerned with local interests and issues. Consequently, most Libyans after 1951 continued to think of themselves as Cyrenaican, Fezzanese, or Tripolitanian. With a weak sense of statehood, Libyans continued to draw their identity from family, tribe, or region, or, in the widest sense, as members of the broader Islamic community. Given the Libyan experience under both Ottoman and Italian rule, this was understandable; unfortunately, this largely provincial focus hampered the galvanizing of a wider national identity which could be harnessed after independence in support of national goals.

During the first decade of independent life, the monarchy promoted a cohesive national community to give structure and meaning to new state institutions and to enhance and capitalize on feelings of shared experience. With the results of this effort inconclusive owing to existing levels of provincial enmity, observers throughout the 1960s continued to highlight the limited level of national identity or national consciousness found in Libya. In the process, Arab nationalism became the *bête noire* of the monarchy. The Libyan proclamation of statehood coincided with the rise of Arab nationalism in the Middle East, and the monarchy rightly viewed Arabism as inimical to its interests and tried to contain its influence in the kingdom. Earlier, politically aware Libyans had mostly rejected the Arab nationalism that surfaced in the Hijaz during World War I; therefore, it proved ironic that Arab nationalism, 50 years later, would become a significant factor in the overthrow of the monarchy. A relatively small group of Libyan nationalists, which emerged in the second half of the 1960s, constituted a secondary opposition group. Interested in the modernization of the country, they equated nationalism with political freedom, regarding the hereditary monarchy established under the federal union as simply another structure imposed on them by foreign powers.

The disparate and competing political economies of Cyrenaica, Fezzan, and Tripolitania led to the adoption in 1951 of a federal system as an interim step toward more comprehensive national unity. The federal system, which was the latest in a tradition of indigenous political entities that stretched back to the Karamanli dynasty if the early democratic experiments of the Pentapolis are discounted, melded two divergent political legacies, the republic in Tripolitania and the amirate in Cyrenaica, into a reluctant partnership. The Sanusi Amirate had introduced Libya to the benefits of diplomacy and the mechanics of statehood while the Tripoli Republic had initiated the quest for national unity and launched the first bid for indigenous independence. As the process of social integration advanced, a nascent feeling of national purpose and unity supported the creation of a unitary state in 1962–3; nevertheless, there was little evidence to suggest that Libya under the monarchy ever constituted an integrated community.

Revolutionary Libya

A touchstone of Libyan hydrocarbon policy from the beginning and particularly after 1969 was the determination of the state to control the nation's resources, avoiding domination of its oil and gas deposits by the larger oil companies. The 1955 petroleum law provided for the award of a large number of small concessions to avoid domination of the industry by a few large companies or consortiums; consequently, many of the concessions were awarded to smaller, independent oil producers without prospects elsewhere. This policy served the state well, especially in the mid-1980s, when the American oil companies were forced to withdraw. More recently, some observers have suggested that Libya was moving away from this policy, demanding more stringent terms attractive only to larger companies able to bear mounting exploration and development

costs while the National Oil Corporation (NOC) took most of the oil produced. The results of phase four of the exploration and production sharing
agreements (EPSAs), in which 52 contracts were awarded to 36 companies from
19 countries, belie this argument. On the contrary, the wide variety of companies awarded acreage, when tied to the other forms of hydrocarbon agreements
Libya has negotiated in recent years, confirms that diversification of oil and gas
producers remains a core state goal.

Based on the early, hardline policies of the revolutionary government, Libya
has long been considered a price hawk; however, oil pricing is another area
marked by considerable continuity. Following the conclusion of the Tripoli
Agreement in March 1971, the price of Libyan oil was no longer competitive on
world markets, and sales slumped accordingly. In response, the RCC developed
a more conservative – and more competitive – pricing strategy, largely adhering
to OPEC pricing levels for more than a decade. When the OPEC pricing system
collapsed in 1985, Libya joined the remainder of the hydrocarbon industry,
OPEC and non-OPEC producers alike, in pegging its crude oil to the prices set
by the Brent Market. Over the same period, EPSAs became the preferred model
of contractual agreement. The details of the four EPSA phases executed since
1974 have varied slightly, depending on the socioeconomic and political conditions at the time; however, the process itself has remained largely unchanged.

Another notable aspect of hydrocarbon policy is the largely professional and
generally apolitical manner in which the industry has been managed over the
last four decades. For the most part, oil and gas policy has been managed independent of political policy, with the hydrocarbon sector often excluded from the
more radical institutional reforms. Occasionally, politics have impacted directly
on oil and gas policies, but more often than not commercial considerations have
driven major decisions in this economic sector.

In contrast to hydrocarbons, change as opposed to continuity was the
dominant policy pattern in the broader economy after 1969. Intent from the
start on a radical socialization of the economy, the One September Revolution
passed through a brief capitalist phase before the more fundamental aspects of
a socialist regime were implemented in the second half of the 1970s. By the
end of the decade, a large-scale socialist revolution had clearly taken place with
the management of the economy increasingly socialist in intent and effect and
long-standing economic and social structures modified or in the process of
modification.

Under pressure for change, Qaddafi at the end of the 1980s introduced tentative steps in the direction of economic liberalization; however, the so-called
revolution within the revolution was limited in scope, duration, and impact.
With the suspension of UN sanctions in 1999, Libya embarked upon a broader
and deeper process of economic liberalization aimed at the replacement of the
socialist, command economy with a capitalist, free market one. Implemented
in an ad hoc, piecemeal manner, the current phase of economic liberalization
has generated widespread, determined opposition from hardline, conservative

elements within the government; consequently, the direction, pace, and goals of economic liberalization remain unclear. What is clear is that sustained economic reform will require additional legal reform followed by determined political reform, and, if this does not occur, the economic health of Libya in the post-hydrocarbon era is at risk.

In area of social reform, the policies of the Qaddafi regime have been a mix of continuity and change. In the early years of the revolution, regime policies in education, health care, and housing were mostly an expansion and acceleration of policies initiated by the monarchy; however, by the end of the 1970s, policies in these areas, notably housing, had become more radical. Policies related to demonetization, land redistribution, and the elimination of wholesale and retail trade also marked radical departures from earlier approaches. The subsequent introduction of compulsory military training and universal conscription, together with the promotion of a people's army, fall in the same category. Qaddafi's particular emphasis on Islam and his use of Islam for political ends also marked departures from the monarchy, as did a succession of legal reforms leading to an arbitrary and repressive justice system.

Constituted under a very different world order, some elements of the early foreign policy of the revolutionary government have changed whereas others have not. Arab nationalism is no longer central to Libyan foreign policy, and Arab unity is no longer seen as an immediate, realistic goal. Increasingly alienated from the Arab system, the Leader recognized the futility of Arab nationalism in the Nasserite construct with its goal of a unitary Arab state even though he never withdrew completely and irrevocably from the Arab system. Ironically, it was at home that Qaddafi proved most successful in selling Arab nationalism and Arab unity, once considered by him to be two sides of the same coin. The quantitative survey of Libyan university students mentioned earlier found that the regime had been largely successful in creating a national unity grounded in Arab nationalism as opposed to the local or regional identities previously dominant in Libya. The survey also found that most of the respondents were orientated toward Arab unity and believed that Arab nationalism was a means toward Arab unity (Obeidi 2001: 202–9).

The role of *jihad*, the action element of Arab nationalism and once the preferred tool to promote social justice, was also overtaken by events. As the PLO moderated its tactics, other liberation movements supported by Qaddafi went on to achieve success or failure or ignominy. Even as he experienced one setback after another, the Leader persisted in his efforts to distinguish between liberation movements and terrorism, but by the mid-1980s even the Soviet Union could no longer see the difference. After a short decade of UN sanctions, a period in which there is no evidence that Libya supported terrorist activities, Qaddafi became an early and enthusiastic ally of the United States and other governments in the war on terror, largely because Islamist groups were as much a threat to his regime as they were to Western governments. On the other hand, he opposed the creation of US Africa Command (AFRICOM) and refused to join the Trans-Sahara Counter-Terrorism Partnership because both smacked of neocolonialism and neoimperialism.

When faced with a choice between communism or capitalism, Qaddafi searched for a Third Way, but with the implosion of the Soviet Union, the world was reduced to one superpower, rendering positive neutrality in the traditional sense impossible. Having embarked on a program of economic liberalization, ongoing official emphasis on hackneyed concepts such as "people's capitalism," "popular socialism," and "the extension of popular ownership" suggest that Qaddafi is still looking for a hybrid economic system more compatible than a free market with the direct democracy system. His refusal to become a full-fledged member of the Euro-Mediterranean Partnership also reflects his long-time commitment to a Third Way. Finally, his tendency to frame the growing involvement of China in Africa in Cold War terms as a competition with the United States indicates that his concept of positive neutrality may have changed but is not dead.

With the suspension of UN sanctions, Libyan foreign policy in Africa looked to the past as he moved to the future. From the outset of the revolution, Qaddafi emphasized the "third circle"; however, his renewed focus on the African continent after 1999 also reflected his estrangement from the Arab world. In the first two decades of the revolution, Libyan diplomacy in Africa was anti-Israeli, anti-imperial, and anti-colonial in support of wider pan-Arab goals, but the post-1999 approach was broader in scope, less ideological in tone, and more pragmatic. Occasionally, there was still an anti-Israeli element, but Israel was no longer a main concern, and anti-imperialism and anti-colonialism were generally irrelevant. Islam, a central theme in the old days, was still referenced on occasion, but much less so than in the past. Instead, Qaddafi focused on a United States of Africa with himself as its self-appointed head.

Qaddafi claims to have created a unique model of direct democracy, based on an intricate system of congresses and committees, in which power rests in the hands of the people; however, the reality of the situation is very different. As early as 1979, he completed construction of two parallel sectors of power, a people's sector in the form of the direct democracy system and a revolutionary sector, consisting of himself, the remaining members of the RCC, the Free Unionist Officers, and the revolutionary committees. At the same time, he relied – and continues to rely – on an informal network of advisors and confidants, along with relatives and members of the Qaddafi and affiliated tribes. The essential duality of this political structure has not changed since that time although the organization and operation of the revolutionary sector has continued to evolve as the Leader explored new ways to refine his control of the entire political system.

In one sense, Qaddafi after 40 years of tinkering has simply returned the political system to where it was when he ousted the monarchy in 1969. The formal structures of the two governments bear little comparison, but the manner in which power is accumulated, maintained, and dispensed is remarkably similar. Under the monarchy, influential tribes, powerful families, the royal diwan, and Sanusi family members effectively controlled the economic and political system, and under the direct democracy system, influential tribes, powerful families, the Men of the Tent, and Qaddafi family members effectively control the economic and political system. Contemporary Libya remains a largely tribal society operating along informal, cliental lines. Primary allegiances are to the family, clan, and tribe, and the path to advancement is more often than not through nepotism, favoritism, and patronage as opposed to merit, skill, or performance. Basic freedoms, such as freedom of speech, assembly, and the press, do not exist. Effective power rests in the hands of the Leader and a few trusted advisors in a system grounded in family ties and tribal loyalties and buttressed by the military and various intelligence and security organizations.

POST-QADDAFI LIBYA

During the first decade of the twenty-first century, Libya experienced a remarkable international transformation, reestablishing diplomatic ties and expanding commercial relations with the world's powers, including the United States. Inside the country, the regime also sought to move in new directions; however, internal reforms were not as speedy or as far-reaching as its international make-over. Some socioeconomic change occurred, but the full extent, eventual direction, and real permanence of that change remained uncertain. Libyan officials developed expertise in tossing about terms such as accountability, diversification, partnership, and transparency; unfortunately, the reality on the ground was a reform process implemented in a sporadic and incomplete manner with its effectiveness too often compromised by ideological and human capacity constraints. More to the point, there was no meaningful political reform; instead, the Leader continued to trumpet the supposed virtues of the direct democracy system.

Several factors contributed to the modest level of domestic reform implemented in Libya with the most influential one being the gulf that existed between the beliefs, ideas, and myths of the One September Revolution and the economic, social, and political realities they professed to explain. As a small group of reformers continued to advocate for socioeconomic and political reform, they met determined opposition every step of the way from hardline elements who opposed any change that might move Libya away from its highly centralized and authoritarian political system. Old guard elements rightly viewed the introduction of a private sector economy and a more open political system as a threat to their own economic interests as well as to the highly developed patronage networks that underpin the existing political framework. Consequently, conservative and progressive forces continued to struggle over the direction, scope, and pace of reform, a fight whose outcome will influence, if not determine, Qaddafi's successor.

On the succession issue, it is important to recognize at the outset that there is no formal mechanism in place to address succession in Libya. The December

1969 constitutional proclamation, which replaced the 1951 constitution, does not address the issue of succession, and it is unclear if a new constitution, if one is ever adopted, would do so. The first part of *The Green Book* lays out the political philosophy of the revolution, but it makes no reference to a chief executive or head of state. Absent a clear path for succession, the Leader has given every indication that he prefers a dynastic succession as took place in Jordan and Syria, even though he has not yet designated a clearly preferred successor. A number of considerations have impacted in recent years on major policy shifts, for example agreeing to pay compensation to the families of the victims of the Lockerbie bombing and the dismantling of unconventional weapons programs; however, a long-term strategy aimed at securing power for the Leader and his family was likely one of the more influential. When the UN sanctions were suspended, Qaddafi appeared to recognize that a return to the international fold, followed by extensive offshore investment in the oil and gas sector, a central instrument of regime power, offered much better prospects for regime stability than a costly and uncertain arms program and the occasional praise from African and Arab states for anti-Western, anti-status quo behavior.

In the constantly shifting dynamics of Libyan politics, the eventual successor to the Leader remains unclear, but members of Qaddafi's extended family and tribe, who occupy all of the key positions in the higher echelons of the regime, will likely draw on bonds of privilege and kinship in an effort to preserve their collective power. At the same time, the many institutions constituting the people's sector and the revolutionary sector, most of which have distributive as well as security functions, will probably be retained without major overhaul for some time. Consequently, the succession struggle will likely be marked more by continuity than by radical change, at least in the short run, even if it is accompanied by a period of instability as competing factions struggle for supremacy.

As for specific candidates, the liberal-leaning Saif al-Islam al-Qaddafi, the darling of the Western media, has the highest profile among Qaddafi's seven sons and one daughter, but he has no official role beyond heading the Qaddafi International Charity and Development Foundation. Moreover, he appears to lack a power base in the military and security services. In October 2009, the Leader asked senior functionaries to find an official position for Saif, leading to his appointment as general coordinator of the people's social leadership committees (PSLCs), a position thought to be second only to that of the Leader in Libya. At the time, Saif turned down the job on the grounds he could not accept it until democratic reforms had been enacted in Libya. If he later accepts the PSLC appointment and his efforts to adopt a constitution are successful, he will have buttressed his claim to be the most likely successor to the Leader. On the other hand, two other sons, Muatasim Billah al-Qaddafi, the national security adviser, and Khamis al-Qaddafi, a brigade commander in the army, both have strong power bases in the military and security services as well as ties to the more conservative elements in the Libyan power structure. The support that any of these candidates – or other potential candidates – might enjoy within the extended family and tribal structure is a matter of speculation but later could prove highly important. In the end, the one thing that is certain is that the Leader is only in his mid-60s, not old for an Arab head of state, and in relatively good health; therefore, speculation on his eventual successor, which has been going on for 20 years, could easily continue for another decade or more.

With the very nature of the bifurcated political system the main obstacle to economic and social change in Libya, meaningful political reform is on hold and will likely remain so as long as the Leader continues in power. The systematic dismantling of civil society over the last many years has left Libya with few, if any, institutions capable of mobilizing individuals for mass political action. Given the socioeconomic conditions existing in the country, neither modern institutions nor a civil society nor an independent business class can be conjured up over night. As should be obvious from recent experience in places such as Afghanistan and Cambodia, democracy is about far more than elections; it involves education, participation, tolerance, and the creation of independent institutions. Libyans who have grown up under an authoritarian, socialist regime need to learn to think and act for themselves, and this is an extended, involved, and time-consuming process of cultural change. Even in the best of circumstances, it will likely take many years to overcome the negative effects of more than four decades of the One September Revolution.

BIBLIOGRAPHICAL SURVEY OF THE RECENT LITERATURE

This bibliographical survey covers only English-language works published in the last two decades unless there is no recent alternative to an earlier work. The references in the notes have also been restricted to English-language sources. The objective has been to provide English-medium lay readers with easily accessible sources to facilitate further study of Libya.

Wright (1982a) was long the only general history of modern Libya available in English. A more recent addition to the literature, Vandewalle (2006), begins the story in the 1900s but concentrates on the post-1969 political economy. St John (2008a) explores the history of Libya from earliest times to the present with the general reader in mind.

With sources for the ancient period limited, Warmington (1954) and Daniels (1970) are highly recommended. For an introduction to the Phoenicians, see Aubet (1993) and Strong (2002). For the Greeks, Romans, and Byzantines, begin with DiVita and colleagues (1999), MacKendrick (1980), and Raven (1993). The best description of the Islamic conquest of North Africa is Taha (1989). The principal work on the Almohads is Le Tourneau (1969); unfortunately, there is no comparable book in English on the Almoravids. On the Berber dynasties, see Brett and Fentress (1996). For Islam in modern times, begin with Entelis (1997), Joffé (1995), and Ruedy (1996).

For the Ottoman occupation (1551–1911), McCarthy (1997) and Quataert (2000) offer the reader a sound introduction to Ottoman culture, society, and rule. The most comprehensive treatment of the Karamanli dynasty (1711–1835) is Folayan (1979). On corsairing, see Allison (1995), Wheelan (2003), Parker (2004), Lambert (2005), and Zacks (2005). For the second Ottoman occupation (1835–1911), begin with Joffé and colleagues (1982), Pennell (1982), and Anderson (1986a). Ahmida (1994, 2005) explores the state and political economy of post-1830 Libya, especially the impact of Ottoman state centralization, the decline of the Saharan trade, and the penetration of European financial capital. On the Sanusi Order, Evans-Pritchard (1949), Ziadeh (1958), Peters (1990), and Vikor (1995) are recommended. For the troubled history of Libyan Jews, see De Felice (1985), Goldberg (1990), and Simon (1992). On the Italian invasion and occupation, begin with Segré (1974), Anderson (1982), Simon (1987), Childs (1990), and Anderson (1991a). On the Italian colonial experience, see Segré (1987), Jerary (2003), McLaren (2006), and Baldinetti (2009).

On the early days of state formation, see Rivlin (1950), Pelt (1970), and Bills (1995). For the United Kingdom of Libya, the reader is well advised to begin with Khadduri (1963). Villard (1956), Norman (1965), Ziadeh (1967), Ben-Halim (1998), and Sury (2003) are also helpful. De Candole (1990) is a favorable treatment of the monarchy.

The available biographies of Muammar al-Qaddafi, Bianco (1975), Blundy and Lycett (1987), and Tremlett (1993) are dated. The ideology of the revolution is best introduced through a reading of the three slender volumes of *The Green Book*, Qaddafi's socioeconomic and political manifesto, reproduced in Christman (1988). El-Khawas (1986) provides a detailed analysis of the Third Universal Theory, and Ayoub (1987) places the theory in a religious context. St John (1983a, 2008c) explores the changing ideology of the Libyan revolution. Qaddafi with Jouve (2005) is a controversial statement of the Libyan leader's post-1969 ideological journey.

For an introduction to the politics of revolutionary Libya, begin with First (1974) and Davis (1987). Other helpful studies of the politics of the revolution include Cooley (1982), Bearman (1986), Harris (1986), El Saadany (1994), Vandewalle (1995a, 1998, 2008a), El-Kikhia (1997), Obeidi (2001), and St John (2008b). El Fathaly and colleagues (1977) and El Fathaly and Palmer (1980a) explore early revolutionary political structures. Deeb and Deeb (1982) examine the role of women, education, and Islam.

The economy of contemporary Libya, especially the hydrocarbon sector, has been examined in several detailed studies, including Waddams (1980), Allan (1981), Gurney (1996), and Otman and Karlberg (2007). Selected aspects of the economy are also discussed in Allan (1982), Khader and El-Wifati (1987), Joffé and McLachlan (1982), Buru and colleagues (1985), and St John (2007, 2008b, 2008d, 2008e).

Aspects of the international relations and foreign policy of Libya have attracted considerable attention. For a broad analysis of Libyan foreign policy, see St John (1987a) and Ronen (2008). Haley (1984), ElWarfally (1988), Davis (1990), St John (2002), and Stanik (2003) discuss selected aspects of the lengthy and often difficult bilateral relationship with the United States. On the long and involved history of Libyan involvement in Africa, see Lemarchand (1988), Wright (1989a), Burr and Collins (1999), and Deeb (1991).

On the art and architecture of Libya, see Barbar (1979), Brandily (1982),

Cresti (2003), and McLaren (2006). The body of Libyan literature available in the English language is small but growing: Qaddafi (1998), Fagih (2000a, 2000b, 2000c, 2000d, 2000e), Matar (2007), Al-Koni (2002, 2008), and Chorin (2008a).

Only the most relevant books on Libya have been discussed in this brief bibliographical survey. In addition, there are hundreds of significant and worthwhile articles, some of which are listed in the following bibliography. Unpublished PhD dissertations are another valuable source material. The internet has also become an increasingly important and useful source of information, especially for current affairs. For the reader eager to delve into all aspects of the socio-economic and political life of contemporary Libya, the most extensive available bibliography is found in St John (2006a).

GLOSSARY

amir	independent chieftain
dinar	unit of currency in Libya
diwan	court (of a ruler)
hadith	traditions or collected sayings of the Prophet Muhammad
haj	pilgrimage to Mecca, fifth pillar of Islam
ijma	use of consensus to establish agreed Islamic doctrine
imam	religious leader or expert on Islamic law and theology
jabal	mountain
jihad	holy war
Koran	sacred book of Muslims
Maghrib	western Islamic world, traditionally Algeria, Morocco, and Tunisia
mahdi	envoy sent by God to complete work of Prophet Muhammad
Mashriq	eastern Islamic World
Sahel	western stretch of the Sahara Desert bordering on the Atlantic Ocean
Sayyid	honorific title
sharia	Islamic law
Sharif	descendant of Muhammad through his daughter, Fatima
sheik	arbiter, elder, religious teacher, or spiritual leader
Sidi	honorific title
sunna	reported deeds and sayings of the Prophet
ulama	religious leaders and scholars
wadi	river or dry riverbed

BIBLIOGRAPHY

Books, articles, reports, and papers

Abou-El-Haj, Rifaat (1983) "Agenda for Research in History: The History of Libya between the Sixteenth and Nineteenth Centuries," *International Journal of Middle East Studies*, 15 (2, August): 305–19.

Ahmida, Ali Abdullatif (1994) *The Making of Modern Libya: State Formation, Colonization, and Resistance, 1830–1932*, Albany: State University of New York Press.

—— (2005) *Forgotten Voices: Power and Agency in Colonial and Postcolonial Libya*, London: Routledge.

Ajami, Fouad (1978/79) "The End of Pan-Arabism," *Foreign Affairs*, 57 (2, Winter): 355–73.

Alexander, Nathan [Ronald Bruce St John] (1981a) "Libya: The Continuous Revolution," *Middle Eastern Studies*, 17 (2, April): 210–27.

—— (1981b) "The Foreign Policy of Libya: Inflexibility amid Change," *Orbis*, 24 (4, Winter): 819–46.

Allan, John Anthony (1981) *Libya: The Experience of Oil,* London: Croom Helm.

—— (1982) "Capital Has Not Substituted for Water in Agriculture," in J. A. Allan (ed.) *Libya since Independence: Economic and Political Development*, London: Croom Helm, pp. 25–35.

—— (1983) "Libya Accommodates to Lower Oil Revenues: Economic and Political Adjustments," *International Journal of Middle East Studies*, 15 (2, August): 377–85.

—— (1987) "Water for Agriculture in the 1990s: Another Phase in Libya's Agricultural Development," in Bichara Khader and Bashir El-Wifati (eds.) *The Economic Development of Libya*, London: Croom Helm, pp. 124–33.

—— (1988) "The Great Man-Made River: Progress and Prospects of Libya's Great Water Carrier," *Libyan Studies*, 19: 141–6.

—— (1989) "Water Resource Evaluation and Development in Libya, 1969–1989," *Libyan Studies*, 20: 235–42.

Allison, Robert J. (1995) *The Crescent Obscured: The United States and the Muslim World, 1776–1815*, New York: Oxford University Press.

Anderson, Lisa S. (1982) "The Tripoli Republic, 1918–1922," in E. G. H. Joffé and K. S. McLachlan (eds.) *Social & Economic Development of Libya*, Wisbech, Cambridgeshire: Middle East & North African Studies Press, pp. 43–65.

—— (1984) "Nineteenth-Century Reform in Ottoman Libya," *International Journal of Middle East Studies*, 16 (3, August): 325–48.

—— (1985a) "Assessing Libya's Qaddafi," *Current History*, 84 (502, May): 197–200, 226–7.

—— (1985b) "Qadhdhafi and the Kremlin," *Problems of Communism*, 34 (September–October): 29–44.

—— (1986a) *The State and Social Transformation in Tunisia and Libya, 1830–1980*, Princeton, NJ: Princeton University Press. H N 784 . A8 A53 1986

—— (1986b) "Qadhdhafi and his Opposition," *Middle East Journal*, 40 (2, Spring): 225–37.

—— (1987) "Libya's Qaddafi: Still in Command?," *Current History*, 86 (517, February): 65–8, 86–7.

—— (1990) "Tribe and State: Libyan Anomalies," in P. S. Khoury and J. Kostiner (eds.) *Tribes and State Formation in the Middle East*, Berkeley: University of California Press, pp. 288–302.

—— (1991a) "The Development of Nationalist Sentiment in Libya, 1908–1922," in R. Khalidi, L. S. Anderson, M. Muslih, and R. S. Simon (eds.) *The Origins of Arab Nationalism*, New York: Columbia University Press, pp. 225–42.

—— (1991b) "Legitimacy, Identity, and the Writing of History in Libya," in E. Davis and N. Gavrielides (eds.) *Statecraft in the Middle East: Oil, Historical Memory, and Popular Culture*, Miami: Florida International University Press, pp. 71–9.

—— (2006) "Rogue Libya's Long Road," *Middle East Report*, 241 (Winter): 42–7.

Ansell, Meredith O. and Al-Arif, Ibrahim Massaud (1972) *The Libyan Revolution: A Sourcebook of Legal and Historical Documents, v. 1, 1 September 1969, 30 August 1970*, Stoughton, WI: Oleander Press.

Appleton, Leonard (1979) "The Question of Nationalism and Education in Libya under Italian Rule," *Libyan Studies*, 10: 29–33.

Arab Petroleum Research Centre (1985) *Arab Oil and Gas Directory*, Paris: Arab Petroleum Research Centre.

Ashiurakis, Ahmed M. (1976) *A Concise History of the Libyan Struggle for Freedom*, Tripoli: General Publishing, Distributing & Advertising Co.

Aubet, Maria Eugenia (1993) *The Phoenicians and the West: Politics, Colonies and Trade*, Cambridge: Cambridge University Press.

Ayoub, Mahmoud Mustafa (1987) *Islam and the Third Universal Theory: The Religious Thought of Mu'ammar al-Qadhadhafi*, London: KPI.

Baldinetti, Anna (2003) "Libya's Refugees, Their Places of Exile, and the Shaping of Their National Idea," *Journal of North African Studies*, 8 (1, Spring): 72–86.

—— (2009) *The Origins of the Libyan Nation: Colonial Legacy, Exile and the Emergence of a New Nation State*, London: Routledge.

Barbar, Ashil M. (1979) *Islamic Architecture in Libya*, Monticello, IL: Vance.

Barker, Paul and McLachlan, Keith S. (1982) "Development of the Libyan Oil Industry," in J. A. Allan (ed.) *Libya since Independence: Economic and Political Development*, London: Croom Helm, pp. 37–54.

Bearman, Jonathan (1986) *Qadhafi's Libya*, London: Zed Books.

Ben-Halim, Mustafa Ahmed (1998) *Libya: The Years of Hope: The Memoirs of Mustafa Ahmed Ben-Halim,* London: AAS Media Publishers.

Benkhial, A. S. and Bukechiem, A. A. (1989) "Irrigated Farming in the Jebel el Akhdar: Prospects and Problems," in J. A. Allan, K. S. McLachlan, and M. M. Buru (eds.)

Libya: State and Region, A Study of Regional Evolution, London: School of Oriental & African Studies, University of London, pp. 73–93.

Bennett, Valerie Plave (1975) "Libyan Socialism," in H. Desfosses and J. Levesque (eds.) *Socialism in the Third World*, New York: Praeger Publishers, pp. 99–120.

Bianco, Mirella (1975) *Gadafi: Voice from the Desert*, London: Longman Group.

Bills, Scott L. (1995) *The Libyan Arena: The United States, Britain, and the Council of Ministers, 1945–1948*, Kent, OH: Kent State University Press.

Birks, J. Stace and Sinclair, Clive A. (1979) "The Libyan Arab Jamahiriya: Labour Migration Sustains Dualistic Development," *Maghreb Review*, 4 (3, June–July): 95–102.

—— (1984) "Libya: Problems of a Rentier State," in R. Lawless and A. Findlay (eds.) *North Africa: Contemporary Politics and Economic Development*, London: Croom Helm, pp. 241–75.

Bleuchot, Hervé (1982) "The Green Book: Its Context and Meaning," in J. A. Allan (ed.) *Libya since Independence: Economic and Political Development*, London: Croom Helm, pp. 137–64.

Blundy, David and Lycett, Andrew (1987) *Qaddafi and the Libyan Revolution*, London: Weidenfeld & Nicolson.

Bosworth, R. J. B. (2006) *Mussolini's Italy: Life under the Fascist Dictatorship, 1915–1945*, New York: Penguin.

Bounenni, Bassam (2008) "Mediterranean Summit: Between French Hopes and Arab Realities," *Arab Reform Bulletin*, 6 (6, July): 1–2.

Brandily, Monique (1982) "Music and Social Change," in E. G. H. Joffé and K. S. McLachlan (eds.) *Social and Economic Development of Libya*, Wisbech, Cambridgeshire: Middle East & North African Studies Press, pp. 207–14.

Brett, Michael and Fentress, Elizabeth (1996) *The Berbers*, Oxford: Blackwell.

Burgat, François (1987) "The Libyan Economy in Crisis," in B. Khader and B. El-Wifati (eds.) *The Economic Development of Libya*, London: Croom Helm, pp. 213–27.

—— (1995) "Qadhafi's Ideological Framework," in D. Vandewalle (ed.) *Qadhafi's Libya, 1969 to 1994*, New York: St. Martin's Press, pp. 47–63.

Burr, J. Millard and Collins, Robert O. (1999) *Africa's Thirty Years' War: Chad, Libya, and the Sudan, 1963–1993*, Boulder, CO: Westview.

Buru, M. M., Ghanem, S. M. and McLachlan K. S. (eds.) (1985) *Planning and Development in Modern Libya*, Wisbech, Cambridgeshire: Middle East & North African Studies.

Cachia, Anthony J. (1945) *Libya under the Second Ottoman Occupation (1835–1911)*, Tripoli: Government Press.

Carvely, Andrew (1973) "Libya: International Relations and Political Purposes," *International Journal*, 28 (4, Autumn): 707–28.

Cecil, Charles O. (1965) "The Determinants of Libyan Foreign Policy," *Middle East Journal*, 19 (1, Winter): 20–34.

Childs, Timothy W. (1990) *Italo-Turkish Diplomacy and the War over Libya, 1911–1912*, Leiden: E. J. Brill.

Chorin, Ethan D. (2008a) *Translating Libya: The Modern Libyan Short Story*, London: Saqi.

—— (2008b) "The Future of the US–Libyan Commercial Relationship," in D. Vandewalle (ed.) *Libya since 1969: Qadhafi's Revolution Revisited*, New York: Palgrave Macmillan, pp. 153–71.

Christman, Henry M. (ed.) (1988) *Qaddafi's Green Book: An Unauthorized Edition*, Buffalo, NY: Prometheus.

Cooley, John K. (1982) *Libyan Sandstorm: The Complete Account of Qaddafi's Revolution*, New York: Holt, Rinehart and Winston.

Council of Europe (2009) "20 Years of Combating Torture: 19th General Report of the European Committee for the Prevention of Torture and Inhuman or Degrading Treatment or Punishment, 1 August 2008–31 July 2009," Strasbourg: Council of Europe Publishing.

Cresti, Federico Cresti (2003) "City and Territory in Libya during the Colonial Period: Sources and Research Documents," in A. Baldinetti (ed.) *Modern and Contemporary Libya: Sources and Historiographies*, Rome: Istituto Italiano per L'Africa e L'Oriente, pp. 141–68.

Cricco, Massimiliano (2002) "The Image of Colonel Qaddafi in American and British Documents (1969–1971)," *Journal of Libyan Studies*, 3 (2, Winter): 32–40.

Cumming, Duncan (1968) "Libya in the First World War," in Fawzi F. Gadallah (ed.) *Libya in History*, Benghazi: University of Libya, pp. 383–92.

Damis, John (1983) "Prospects for Unity/Disunity in North Africa," *American–Arab Affairs*, 6 (Fall): 34–58.

—— (1985) "Morocco, Libya and the Treaty of Union," *American–Arab Affairs*, 13 (Summer): 44–55.

Daniels, Charles (1970) *The Garamantes of Southern Libya*, Stoughton, WI: Oleander Press.

Darbouche, Hakim and Zoubir, Yahia H. (2008) "Conflicting International Policies and the Western Sahara Stalemate," *International Spectator*, 43 (1, March): 91–105.

—— (2009) "The Algerian Crisis in European and US Foreign Policies: A Hindsight Analysis," *Journal of North African Studies*, 14 (1): 33–55.

Davis, Brian L. (1990) *Qaddafi, Terrorism, and the Origins of the US Attack on Libya*, New York: Praeger.

Davis, John (1987) *Libyan Politics: Tribe and Revolution*, London: I.B. Tauris.

Dearden, Ann (1950) "Independence for Libya: The Political Problems," *Middle East Journal*, 4 (4, October): 395–409.

De Candole, E. A. V. (1990) *The Life and Times of King Idris of Libya*, published privately.

Deeb, Marius (1996) "Militant Islam and Its Critics: The Case of Libya," in J. Ruedy (ed.) *Islamism and Secularism in North Africa*, New York: St. Martin's Press, pp. 187–97.

Deeb, Mary-Jane (1989a) "Inter-Maghribi Relations since 1969: A Study of the Modalities of Unions and Mergers," *Middle East Journal*, 43 (1, Winter): 20–33.

—— (1989b) "The Arab Maghrib Union in the Context of Regional and International Politics," *Middle East Insight*, 6 (5, Spring): 42–6.

—— (1990) "New Thinking in Libya," *Current History*, 89 (546, April): 149–52, 177–8.

—— (1991) *Libya's Foreign Policy in North Africa*, Boulder, CO: Westview.

—— (1992) "Militant Islam and the Politics of Redemption," *Annals of the American Academy of Political and Social Science*, 524 (November): 52–65.

—— (1999) "Political and Economic Developments in Libya in the 1990s," in Yahia H. Zoubir (ed.) *North Africa in Transition: State, Society, and Economic Transformation in the 1990s*, Gainesville: University Press of Florida, pp. 77–89.

—— (2000) "Qadhafi's Changed Policy: Causes and Consequences," *Middle East Policy*, 7 (2, February): 146–53.

Deeb, Marius K. and Deeb, Mary-Jane (1982) *Libya since the Revolution: Aspects of Social and Political Development*, New York: Praeger.

De Felice, Renzo (1985) *Jews in an Arab Land: Libya, 1835–1970*, Austin: University of Texas Press.

Del Boca, Angelo (2003) "The Myths, Suppressions, Denials, and Defaults of Italian Colonialism," in P. Palumbo (ed.) *A Place in the Sun: Africa in Italian Colonial Culture from Post-Unification to the Present*, Berkeley: University of California Press, pp. 17–36.

DiVita, Antonino, DiVita-Evrard, Ginette, and Bacchielli, Lidiano (1999) *Libya: The Lost Cities of the Roman Empire*, Cologne: Könemann.

Djaziri, Moncef (1995) "Creating a New State: Libya's Political Institutions," in D. Vandewalle (ed.) *Qadhafi's Libya, 1969–1994*, New York: St. Martin's Press, pp. 177–200.

Dris-Aït-Hamadouche, Louisa and Zoubir, Yahia (2007) "The Maghreb: Social, Political, and Economic Developments," *Perspectives on Global Development and Technology*, 6 (1–3): 261–90.

Dupree, Louis (1958) "The Non-Arab Ethnic Groups of Libya," *Middle East Journal*, 12 (1, Winter): 33–44.

Energy Information Administration (2004) *Libya: Country Analysis Briefs*, Washington, DC: Department of Energy, January (accessed at http://www.eia.doe.gov).

—— (2005) *Libyan Reserves, Geology, Companies: Country Analysis Briefs*, Washington, DC: Department of Energy, February (accessed at http://www.eia.doe.gov).

Entelis, John P. (ed.) (1997) *Islam, Democracy, and the State in North Africa*, Bloomington: Indiana University Press.

Epstein, Edward Jay (1996) *Dossier: The Secret History of Armand Hammer*, New York: Random House.

Evans-Pritchard, E. E. (1949) *The Sanusi of Cyrenaica*, Oxford: Oxford University Press.

Fagih, Ahmed (2000a) *Charles, Diana and Me and Other Stories*, London: Kegan Paul International.

—— (2000b) *Gazelles and Other Plays*, London: Kegan Paul International.

—— (2000c) *Valley of Ashes*, London: Kegan Paul International.

—— (2000d) *Who's Afraid of Agatha Christie? and Other Stories*, London: Kegan Paul International.

—— (ed.) (2000e) *Libyan Stories: Twelve Short Stories from Libya*, London: Kegan Paul International.

Fallaci, Oriana (1979) "Iranians Are Our Brothers: An Interview with Col. Muammar el-Qaddafi of Libya," *New York Times Magazine*, December 16: 40–41, 116–28.

Farley, Rawle (1971) *Planning for Development in Libya: The Exceptional Economy in the Developing World*, New York: Praeger.

El Fathaly, Omar I. (1977) "Libya: The Social, Economic, and Historical Milieus," in O. I. El Fathaly, M. Palmer, and R. Chackerian (eds.) *Political Development and Bureaucracy in Libya*, Lexington, MA: D.C. Heath, pp. 9–31.

El Fathaly, Omar I. and Abusedra, Fathi S. (1977) "The Impact of Sociopolitical Change on Economic Development in Libya," in O. I. El Fathaly, M. Palmer, and R. Chackerian (eds.) *Political Development and Bureaucracy in Libya*, Lexington, MA: D.C. Heath, pp. 33–44.

El Fathaly, Omar I. and Chackerian, Richard (1977) "Leadership, Institutionalization, and Mass Participation in Libya," in O. I. El Fathaly, M. Palmer, and R. Chackerian (eds.) *Political Development and Bureaucracy in Libya*, Lexington, MA: D.C. Heath, pp. 91–102.

El Fathaly, Omar I. and Palmer, Monte (1977a) "Political Development among Rural Libyans," in O. I. El Fathaly, M. Palmer, and R. Chackerian (eds.) *Political Development and Bureaucracy in Libya*, Lexington, MA: D.C. Heath, pp. 47–73.

—— (1977b) "Opposition to Social Change among Traditional Libyan Elites," in O. I. El Fathaly, M. Palmer, and R. Chackerian (eds.) *Political Development and Bureaucracy in Libya*, Lexington, MA: D.C. Heath, pp. 75–90.

—— (1980a) *Political Development and Social Change in Libya,* Lexington, MA: D.C. Heath.

—— (1980b) "Opposition to Change in Rural Libya," *International Journal of Middle East Studies*, 11 (2, April): 247–61.

—— (1982a) "The Transformation of the Elite Structure in Revolutionary Libya," in E. G. H. Joffé and K. S. McLachlan (eds.) *Social & Economic Development of Libya*, Wisbech, Cambridgeshire: Middle East & North African Studies, pp. 255–79.

—— (1982b) "The Transformation of Mass Political Institutions in Revolutionary Libya: Structural Solutions to a Behavioral Problem," in E. G. H. Joffé and K. S. McLachlan (eds.) *Social & Economic Development of Libya*, Wisbech, Cambridgeshire: Middle East & North African Studies, pp. 233–53.

—— (1995) "Institutional Development in Qadhafi's Libya," in D. Vandewalle (ed.) *Qadhafi's Libya, 1969 to 1994*, New York: St. Martin's Press, pp. 157–76.

El Fathaly, Omar I., Palmer, Monte, and Chackerian, Richard (eds.) (1977) *Political Development and Bureaucracy in Libya*, Lexington, MA: D.C. Heath.

Field, James A. (1969) *America and the Mediterranean World, 1776–1882*, Princeton, NJ: Princeton University Press.

First, Ruth (1974) *Libya: The Elusive Revolution*, Harmondsworth, Middlesex: Penguin.

Flint, Julie and De Waal, Alex (2005) *Darfur: A Short History of a Long War*, London: Zed Books.

Folayan, Kola (1979) *Tripoli during the Reign of Yusuf Pasha Qaramanli*, Ile-Ife, Nigeria: University of Ife Press.

Gazzini, Claudia (2009) "Assessing Italy's Grande Gesto to Libya," *Middle East Report Online*, 14 March (accessed at http://www.merip.org).

Ghanem, Shukri (1975) *The Pricing of Libyan Crude Oil*, Valletta, Malta: Adams Publishing House.

—— (1982) "The Libyan Economy before Independence," in E. G. H. Joffé and K. S. McLachlan (eds.) *Social & Economic Development of Libya*, Wisbech, Cambridgeshire: Middle East & North African Studies, pp. 141–59.

—— (1985a) "The Libyan Role within OPEC," in M. M. Buru, S. M. Ghanem, and K. S. McLachlan (eds.) *Planning and Development in Modern Libya*, Wisbech, Cambridgeshire: Middle East & North African Studies, pp. 158–77.

—— (1985b) "Changing Planning Policies in Libya," in M. M. Buru, S. M. Ghanem, and K. S. McLachlan (eds.) *Planning and Development in Modern Libya*, Wisbech, Cambridgeshire: Middle East & North African Studies, pp. 220–9.

—— (1987) "The Oil Industry and the Libyan Economy: The Past, the Present, and the Likely Future," in Bichara Khader and Bashir El-Wifati (eds.) *The Economic Development of Libya*, London: Croom Helm, pp. 58–72.

—— (2004) "Libya: Vision for the Future," paper presented at Arab Strategy Forum: The Arab World in 2020, 14 December.

Goldberg, Harvey E. (1990) *Jewish Life in Muslim Libya: Rivals & Relatives*, Chicago: University of Chicago Press.

Golino, Frank Ralph (1970) "Patterns of Libyan National Identity," *Middle East Journal*, 24 (3, Summer): 338–52.

Goudarzi, Gus H. (1970) *Geology and Mineral Resources of Libya: A Reconnaissance*, Washington, DC: US Government Printing Office.

Gurney, Judith (1996) *Libya: The Political Economy of Oil*, Oxford: Oxford University Press.

Haines, C. Grove (1947) "The Problem of the Italian Colonies," *Middle East Journal*, 1 (4, October): 417–31.

Haley, P. Edward (1984) *Qaddafi and the United States since 1969*, New York: Praeger.

Hardy, Paula (2002) *Libya*, Richmond, Surrey: Zerzura Editions.

Harris, Lillian Craig (1986) *Libya: Qadhafi's Revolution and the Modern State*, Boulder, CO: Westview.

—— (1990) "North African Union: Fact or Fantasy?," *Arab Affairs*, 12: 52–60.

Hersh, Seymour M. (1981) "The Qaddafi Connection," *New York Times Magazine*, June 14: 52–68, 72.

Hesnawi, Habib (2003) "Italian Imperial Policy towards Libya, 1870–1911," in A. Baldinetti (ed.) *Modern and Contemporary Libya: Sources and Historiographies*, Rome: Istituto Italiano per L'Africa e L'Oriente, pp. 49–62.

Higgins, Rosalyn (1985) "The Abuse of Diplomatic Privileges and Immunities: Recent United Kingdom Experience," *American Journal of International Law*, 79 (3, July): 641–51.

Hodges, Tony (1983) *Western Sahara: The Roots of a Desert War*, Westport, CT: Lawrence Hill & Company.

Huliaras, Asteris (2001) "Qadhafi's Comeback: Libya and Sub-Saharan Africa in the 1990s," *African Affairs*, 100 (398, January): 5–25.

Human Rights Watch (2006a) "Words to Deeds: The Urgent Need for Human Rights Reform," 18 (1, January): 1–83.

—— (2006b) "A Threat to Society? The Arbitrary Detention of Women and Girls for 'Social Rehabilitation'," 18 (2, February): 1–39.

—— (2006c) "Stemming the Flow: Abuses against Migrants, Asylum Seekers and Refugees," 18 (5, September): 1–139.

—— (2009a) "Pushed Back, Pushed Around: Italy's Forced Return of Boat Migrants and Asylum Seekers, Libya's Mistreatment of Migrants and Asylum Seekers," September: 1–98.

—— (2009b) "Truth and Justice Can't Wait: Human Rights Developments in Libya amid Institutional Obstacles," December: 1–77.

IMF (2005) *Socialist People's Libyan Arab Jamahiriya 2004 Article IV Consultation – Staff Report; Staff Statement; and Public Information Notice on the Executive Board Discussion*, IMF Country Report No. 05/83, March (accessed at http://www.imf.org).

—— (2006) *The Socialist People's Libyan Arab Jamahiriya: 2005 Article IV Consultation – Staff Report; and Public Information Notice on the Executive Board Discussion*, IMF Country Report No. 06/136, April (accessed at http://www.imf.org).

—— (2007) *The Socialist People's Libyan Arab Jamahiriya: 2006 Article IV Consultation – Staff Report; Staff Statement; Public Information Notice on the Executive Board Discussion; and Statement by the Executive Director for the Socialist People's Libyan Arab Jamahiriya*, IMF Country Report No. 07/149, May (accessed at http://www.imf.org).

—— (2008a) *Socialist People's Libyan Arab Jamahiriya: 2008 Article IV Consultation – Staff Report; Public Information Notice on the Executive Board Discussion; and Statement by the Executive Director for the Socialist People's Libyan Arab Jamahiriya*, IMF Country Report No. 08/302, September (accessed at http://www.imf.org).

—— (2008b) *Socialist People's Libyan Arab Jamahiriya: Statistical Appendix*, IMF Country Report No. 08/301, September (accessed at http://www.imf.org).

—— (2009) *Socialist People's Libyan Arab Jamahiriya: 2009 Article IV Consultation – Staff Report; Public Information Notice on the Executive Board Discussion; and Statement by the Executive Director for the Socialist People's Libyan Arab Jamahiriya*, IMF Country Report No. 09/294, September (accessed at http://www.imf.org).

International Crisis Group (2010) *Libya/Chad: Beyond Political Influence* [*Libye/Tchad: au-delà d'une politique d'influence*], Africa Briefing 71, 23 March (accessed at http://www.crisisgroup.org).

Irwin, Ray W. (1931) *The Diplomatic Relations of the United States with the Barbary Powers, 1776–1816*, Chapel Hill: University of North Carolina Press.

Jensen, Erik (2005) *Western Sahara: Anatomy of a Stalemate*, Boulder, CO: Lynne Rienner.

Jerary, Mohammed Taher (2003) "The Libyan Cultural Resistance to Italian Colonization: The Consequences of Denying the Values of Others," in A. Baldinetti (ed.) *Modern and Contemporary Libya: Sources and Historiographies*, Rome: Istituto Italiano per L'Africa e L'Oriente, pp. 17–36.

Joffé, E. G. H. (1988) "Islamic Opposition in Libya," *Third World Quarterly*, 10 (2, April): 615–31.

—— (1990) "Relations between Libya, Tunisia and Malta up to the British Occupation of Malta," *Libyan Studies*, 21: 65–73.

—— (1995) "Qadhafi's Islam in Local Historical Perspective," in D. Vandewalle (ed.) *Qadhafi's Libya, 1969 to 1994*, New York: St. Martin's Press, pp. 139–54.

—— (2001) "Libya and Europe," *Journal of North African Studies*, 6 (4, Winter): 75–92.

—— (2004) "Libya: Who Blinked, and Why," *Current History*, 103 (673, May): 221–5.

—— (2005) "Libya's Saharan Destiny," *Journal of North African Studies*, 10 (3–4, September–December), 605–17.

—— (2008) "Prodigal or Pariah? Foreign Policy in Libya," in D. Vandewalle (ed.) *Libya since 1969: Qadhafi's Revolution Revisited*, New York: Palgrave Macmillan, pp. 191–213.

—— (2009) "Political Dynamics in North Africa," *International Affairs*, 85 (5, September): 931–49.

Joffé, E. G. H. and McLachlan, K. S. (eds.) (1982) *Social & Economic Development in Libya*, Wisbech, Cambridgeshire: Middle East & North African Studies Press.

Keenan, Jeremy (2005) "Waging War on Terror: The Implications of America's 'New Imperialism' for Saharan Peoples," *Journal of North African Studies*, 10 (3–4, September): 619–47.

Khadduri, Majid (1963) *Modern Libya: A Study in Political Development*, Baltimore, MD: Johns Hopkins University Press.

Khader, Bichara (1987) "Libyan Oil and Money," in B. Khader and B. El-Wifati (eds.) *The Economic Development of Libya*, London: Croom Helm, pp. 195–212.

Khader, Bichara and El-Wifati, Bashir (eds.) (1987) *The Economic Development of Libya*, London: Croom Helm.

El-Khawas, Mohamed (1986) *Qaddafi: His Ideology in Theory and Practice*, Brattleboro, VT: Amana.

El-Kikhia, Mansour O. (1997) *Libya's Qaddafi: The Politics of Contradiction*, Gainesville: University Press of Florida.

Al-Koni, Ibrahim (2002) *The Bleeding of the Stone*, New York: Interlink Books.

—— (2008) *Gold Dust*, Cairo: American University in Cairo Press.

Lambert, Franklin (2005) *The Barbary Wars: American Independence in the Atlantic World*, New York: Hill & Wang.

Laroui, Abdallah (1977) *The History of the Maghrib: An Interpretative Essay*, Princeton, NJ: Princeton University Press.

Latham, John S. (1985) "A Rationale for a 'Green River' to Supply the Jifarah Plain of North West Libya," in M. M. Buru, S. M. Ghanem, and J. S. McLachlan (eds.) *Planning and Development in Modern Libya*, Wisbech, Cambridgeshire: Middle East & North African Studies Press, pp. 138–50.

Layden, Anthony (2007) "Recent Developments in Libya," *Libyan Studies*, 38: 3–11.

Lemarchand, René (ed.) (1988) *The Green and the Black: Qadhafi's Policies in Africa*, Bloomington: University of Indiana Press.

Lenczowski, George (1974) "Popular Revolution in Libya," *Current History*, 73 (February): 57–61, 86.

Lesch, Ann Mosley (1991) "Sudan's Foreign Policy: In Search of Arms, Aid, and Allies," in J. O. Voll (ed.) *Sudan, State and Society in Crisis*, Bloomington: Indiana University Press, pp. 43–70.

Le Tourneau, Roger (1969) *The Almohad Movement in North Africa in the Twelfth and Thirteenth Centuries*, Princeton, NJ: Princeton University Press.

Lewis, William H. (1970) "Libya: The End of Monarchy," *Current History*, 58 (January): 34–48.

Lewis, William H. and Gordon, Robert (1954) "Libya after Two Years of Independence," *Middle East Journal*, 8 (1, Winter): 41–53.

Libyan Arab Republic, Ministry of Information and Culture (1973a) *Aspects of First of September Revolution*, Tripoli: General Administration for Information.

—— (1973b) *The Revolution of 1st September: The Fourth Anniversary*, Benghazi: General Administration for Information.

—— (1973c) *The Third International Theory: The Divine Concept of Islam and the Popular Revolution in Libya*, Tripoli: General Administration for Information.

—— (1974) *The Fundamentals of the Third International Theory*, Tripoli: General Administration for Information.

Liverani, Mario (2000) "The Garamantes: A Fresh Approach," *Libyan Studies*, 31: 17–28.

Lombardi, P (1982) "Italian Agrarian Colonization during the Fascist Period," in E. G. H. Joffé and K. S. McLachlan (eds.) *Social & Economic Development of Libya*, 95–116, Wisbech, Cambridgeshire: Middle East & North African Studies Press.

Lutterbeck, Derek (2009) "Migrants, Weapons and Oil: Europe and Libya after the Sanctions," *Journal of North African Studies*, 14 (2, June): 169–84.

McCarthy, Justin (1997) *The Ottoman Turks: An Introductory History to 1923*, London: Longman.

MacKendrick, Paul (1980) *The North African Stones Speak*, Chapel Hill: University of North Carolina Press.

McLachlan, Keith S. (1982) "Strategies for Agricultural Development in Libya," in J. A. Allan (ed.) *Libya since Independence: Economic and Political Development*, London: Croom Helm, pp. 9–24.

—— (1989a) "Libya's Oil Resources," *Libyan Studies*, 20: 243–50.

—— (1989b) "Al-Khalij, the Libyan Oil Province: A Review of Oil and Development," in J. A. Allan, K. S. McLachlan, and M. M. Buru (eds.), *Libya: State and Region, A Study of Regional Evolution*, London: School of Oriental & African Studies, University of London, pp. 47–61.

McLaren, Brian L. (2006) *Architecture and Tourism in Italian Colonial Libya: An Ambivalent Modernism*, Seattle: University of Washington Press.

Mahmud, Mustafa Bakar and Russell, Alex (1999) "An Analysis of Libya's Revenue per barrel from crude oil upstream activities, 1961–93," *OPEC Review*, 23 (3, September): 213–49.

El Mallakh, Ragaei (1969) "The Economics of Rapid Growth," *Middle East Journal*, 23 (3, Summer): 308–20.

Malone, Dumas (1970) *Jefferson and the Rights of Man, Jefferson and His Time*, Vol. 2, Boston, MA: Little, Brown.

Martinez, Luis (2007) *The Libyan Paradox*, New York: Columbia University Press.

Mason, John P. (1982) "Qadhdhafi's 'Revolution' and Change in a Libyan Oasis Community," *Middle East Journal*, 36 (3, Summer): 319–35.

Matar, Hisham (2007) *In the Country of Men*, New York: Dial Press.

Matar, Khalil I. and Thabit, Robert W. (2004) *Lockerbie and Libya: A Study in International Relations*, Jefferson, NC: McFarland & Company.

Mattes, Hanspeter (1987) "Libya's Economic Relations as an Instrument of Foreign Policy," in B. Khader and B. El-Wifati (eds.) *The Economic Development of Libya*, London: Croom Helm, pp. 81–123.

—— (1995) "The Rise and Fall of the Revolutionary Committees," in D. Vandewalle (ed.) *Qadhafi's Libya, 1969–1994*, New York: St. Martin's Press, pp. 89–112.

—— (2004) "Challenges to Security Sector Governance in the Middle East: The Libyan Case," Geneva Centre for the Democratic Control of Armed Forces, Working Paper No. 144, Geneva, August.

—— (2008) "Formal and Informal Authority in Libya since 1969," in D. Vandewalle (ed.) *Libya since 1969: Qadhafi's Revolution Revisited*, New York: Palgrave Macmillan, pp. 55–81.

Mayer, Ann Elizabeth (1978) "Developments in the Law of Marriage and Divorce in Libya since the 1969 Revolution," *Journal of African Law*, 22 (1, Spring): 30–49.

—— (1979) "The Regulation of Interest Charges and Risk Contracts: Some Problems of Recent Libyan Legislation," *International and Comparative Law Quarterly*, 28 (October): 541–59.

—— (1980) "Libyan Legislation in Defense of Arabo-Islamic Sexual Mores," *American Journal of Comparative Law*, 28: 287–313.

—— (1982) "Islamic Resurgence or New Prophethood: The Role of Islam in Qadhdafi's Ideology," in A. E. Hillal Dessouki (ed.) *Islamic Resurgence in the Arab World*, New York: Praeger, pp. 196–220.

—— (1990) "Reinstating Islamic Criminal Law in Libya," in D. H. Dwyer (ed.) *Law and Islam in the Middle East*, New York: Bergin & Garvey, pp. 99–114.

—— (1995) "In Search of Sacred Law: The Meandering Course of Qadhafi's Legal Policy," in D. Vandewalle (ed.) *Qadhafi's Libya, 1969–1994*, New York: St. Martin's Press, pp. 113–37.

Mertz, Robert Anton and Mertz, Pamela MacDonald (1983) *Arab Aid to Sub-Saharan Africa*, Munich: Kaiser Verlag.

Mezran, Karim and De Maio, Paola (2007) "Between the Past and the Future: Has a Shift in Italian–Libyan Relations Occurred?," *Journal of North African Studies*, 12 (4, December): 439–51.

Middle East Media Research Institute (2007) "In Overture to Iran, Qaddafi Declares North Africa Shi'ite and Calls for Establishment of New Fatimid State," *Middle East Media Research Institute*, no. 1535, April 6.

Monastiri, Taoufik (1982) "The Organization of Primary, Preparatory and Secondary Teaching in Libya from 1969 to 1979," in E. G. H. Joffé and K. S. McLachlan (eds.) *Social & Economic Development of Libya*, Wisbech, Cambridgeshire: Middle East & North African Studies Press, pp. 315–30.

—— (1995) "Teaching the Revolution: Libyan Education since 1969," in D. Vandewalle (ed.) *Qadhafi's Libya, 1969 to 1994*, New York: St. Martin's Press, pp. 67–88.

Monitor Group and Cambridge Energy Research Associates (2006) *National Economic Strategy: An Assessment of the Competitiveness of the Libyan Arab Jamahiriya*, Tripoli: General Planning Council of Libya.

Muscat, Frederick (1980) *My President, My Son*, 2nd edn.., Valletta, Malta: Edam Publishing House.

Nassar, Hala Khamis and Boggero, Marco (2008) "Omar al-Mukhtar: The Formation of Cultural Memory and the Case of the Militant Group that Bears His Name," *Journal of North African Studies*, 13 (2, June): 201–17.

National Democratic Institute for International Affairs (2006) "The Libyan Political System and Prospects for Reform: A Report from NDI's 2006 Delegation (April 17–25)," Washington, DC: National Democratic Institute for International Affairs.

Niblock, Timothy C. (2001) *"Pariah States" & Sanctions in the Middle East: Iraq, Libya, Sudan*, Boulder, CO: Lynne Rienner.

Nolutshungu, Sam C. (1996) *Limits of Anarchy: Intervention and State Formation in Chad*, Charlottesville: University Press of Virginia.

Norman, John (1965) *Labor and Politics in Libya and Arab Africa*, New York: Bookman Associates.

Obeidi, Amal (2001) *Political Culture in Libya*, Richmond, Surrey: Curzon.

—— (2008) "Political Elites in Libya since 1969," in D. Vandewalle (ed.) *Libya since 1969: Qadhafi's Revolution Revisited*, New York: Palgrave Macmillan, pp. 105–26.

Ogunbadejo, Oye (1983) "Qaddafi's North African Design," *International Security*, 8 (1, Summer): 154–78.

OPEC (1980, 2008) *Annual Statistical Bulletin*, Vienna: Organization of the Petroleum Exporting Countries.

Orman, John (1987) *Comparing Presidential Behavior: Carter, Reagan, and the Macho Presidential Style*, New York: Greenwood Press.

O'Sullivan, Meghan L. (2003) *Shrewd Sanctions: Statecraft and State Sponsors of Terrorism*, Washington, DC: Brookings Institution Press.

Otman, Waniss and Karlberg, Erling (2007) *The Libyan Economy: Economic Diversification and International Repositioning*, New York: Springer.

Pajak, Roger F. (1976) "Soviet Arms Aid to Libya," *Military Review*, 7 (July): 82–7.

—— (1980–1) "Arms and Oil: The Soviet–Libyan Arms Supply Relationship," *Middle East Review*, 13 (2, Winter): 51–6.

Paoletti, Emanuela (2008) "Readmission Agreements between Italy and Libya: Relations among Unequals?," paper presented at 9th Mediterranean Research Meeting, Montecatini Terme, March.

—— (2009) "A Critical Analysis of Migration Policies in the Mediterranean: The Case of Italy, Libya, and the EU," RAMSES2 Working Paper 12/09, European Studies Centre, University of Oxford, April.

Pargeter, Alison (2000) "Anglo-Libyan Relations and the Suez Crisis," *Journal of North African Studies*, 5 (2, Summer): 41–58.

—— (2006) "Libya: Reforming the Impossible?," *Review of African Political Economy*, 33 (108, June): 219–35.

—— (2008) "Qadhafi and Political Islam in Libya," in D. Vandewalle (ed.) *Libya since 1969: Qadhafi's Revolution Revisited*, New York: Palgrave Macmillan, pp. 83–104.

Parker, Richard B. (2004) *Uncle Sam in Barbary: A Diplomatic History*, Gainesville: University Press of Florida.

Pelt, Adrian (1970) *Libyan Independence and the United Nations: A Case of Planned Decolonization*, New Haven, CT: Yale University Press.

Pennell, C. R. (1982) "Political Loyalty and the Central Government in Precolonial Libya," in E. G. H. Joffé and K. S. McLachlan (eds.) *Social and Economic Development of Libya*, Wisbech, Cambridgeshire: Middle East & North African Studies Press, pp. 1–18.

—— (1989) "Work on the Early Ottoman Period and Qaramanlis," *Libyan Studies*, 20: 215–19.

Peters, Emrys L. (1990) *The Bedouin of Cyrenaica: Studies in Personal and Corporate Power*, Cambridge: Cambridge University Press.

Pim, R. H. and Binsariti, A. (1994) "The Libyan Great Man-Made River Project Phase I: The Water Resource," *Proceedings of the Institution of Civil Engineers: Water, Maritime, and Energy*, June: 123–45.

Pipes, Daniel (1981) "No One Likes the Colonel," *American Spectator*, 14 (3, March): 18–22.

Prunier, Gérard (2005) *Darfur: The Ambiguous Genocide*, Ithaca, NY: Cornell University Press.

Qaddafi, Muammar (1970) "The Libyan Revolution in the Words of Its Leaders: Proclamations, Statements, Addresses, Declarations and Interviews from September 1 to Announcement of the Counter-Plot (December 10)," *Middle East Journal*, 24 (2, Spring): 203–19.

—— (1973a) "A Visit to Fezzan," in I. William Zartman (ed.) *Man, State, and Society in the Contemporary Maghrib*, New York: Praeger, pp. 131–6.

—— (1973b) *Delivered by Col. Mo'ammar el-Gadhafi: 1. The Broadlines of the Third Theory; 2. The Aspects of the Third Theory; 3. The Concept of Jihad; 4. The Divine Concept of Islam,* Tripoli: General Administration for Information.

—— (1975) *Discourses*, Valetta, Malta: Adam Publishing House.

—— (1976) *The Green Book, Part I: The Solution of the Problem of Democracy: The Authority of the People,* London: Martin Brian & O'Keefe. DT2ϟ. 62444\`3

—— (1978) *The Green Book, Part II: The Solution of the Economic Problem: "Socialism,"* London: Martin Brian & O'Keefe.

—— (1979) *The Green Book, Part III: The Social Basis of the Third Universal Theory*, Tripoli: Public Establishment for Publishing, Advertising and Distribution.

—— (1998) *Escape to Hell and Other Stories*, Montréal: Stanké.

—— (2005) "Statement by Brother Leader of the Revolution on the Occasion of the Opening of the Fifth Ordinary Session of the Assembly of the African Union, Sirte, Libya," 4 July (accessed at http://www.africa-union.org).

—— (2007) "The Brother Leader Addresses the Students of Oxford University on Africa in the 21st Century," 16 May (accessed at http://www.algathafi.org).

—— (2009) "Leader of the Revolution, African Union Chairman, Asserts Most Important Decision Taken by 2009 Sirte Summit Is the Transformation of the Commission into an Authority," 4 July (accessed at http://www.jananews.ly).

—— (2010) "Leader of the Revolution, Doyen of African Leaders: Current Political Elites in Africa Lack Political Awareness and Will to Achieve Continent's Unitary Transformation," 10 February (accessed at http://www.jananews.ly).

Qaddafi [Gaddafi], Muammar with Jouve, Edmond (2005) *My Vision,* London: John Blake.

Quataert, Donald (2000) *The Ottoman Empire, 1700–1922*, Cambridge: Cambridge University Press.

Raven, Susan (1993) *Rome in Africa*, 3rd edn., London: Routledge.

Rinehart, Robert (1979) "Historical Setting," in H D. Nelson (ed.) *Libya: A Country Study*, 3rd edn., Washington, DC: US Government Printing Office, pp. 1–57.

Rivlin, Benjamin (1949) "Unity and Nationalism in Libya," *Middle East Journal*, 3 (1, January): 31–44.

—— (1950) *The United Nations and the Italian Colonies*, New York: Carnegie Endowment for International Peace.

Rogan, Eugene (2009) *The Arabs: A History*, New York: Basic Books.

Ronen, Yehudit (2002) "Qadhafi and Militant Islamism: Unprecedented Conflict," *Middle Eastern Studies*, 38 (4, October): 1–16.

—— (2008) *Qaddafi's Libya in World Politics*, Boulder, CO: Lynne Rienner.

Ronzitti, Natalino (2009) "The Treaty on Friendship, Partnership, and Cooperation between Italy and Libya: New Prospects for Cooperation in the Mediterranean?," paper presented at Mediterranean Strategy Group Conference on Is Regional Cooperation in the Maghrib Possible? Implications for the Region and External Actors, Genoa, 11–12 May.

Rossi, Enzo (1986) *Malta on the Brink: From Western Democracy to Libyan Satellite*, European Security Studies 5, London: The Institute for European Defence & Strategic Studies.

Roumani, Jacques (1973) "Libya and the Military Revolution," in I. William Zartman (ed.) *Man, State, and Society in the Contemporary Maghrib*, New York: Praeger, pp. 344–60.

—— (1983) "From Republic to Jamahiriya: Libya's Search for Political Community," *Middle East Journal*, 37 (2, Spring): 151–68.

Ruedy, John (ed.) (1996) *Islamism and Secularism in North Africa*, New York: St. Martin's Press.

El Saadany, Salah (1994) *Egypt and Libya from Inside, 1969–1976: The Qaddafi Revolution and the Eventual Break in Relations, by the Former Egyptian Ambassador to Libya*, Jefferson, NC: McFarland.

St John, Ronald Bruce (1981) "Libya's Foreign and Domestic Policies," *Current History*, 80 (470, December): 426–9, 434–5.

—— (1982) "The Soviet Penetration of Libya," *The World Today*, 38 (4, April): 131–8.

—— (1983a) "The Ideology of Mu'ammar al-Qadhdhafi: Theory and Practice," *International Journal of Middle East Studies*, 15 (4, November): 471–90.

—— (1983b) "The Determinants of Libyan Foreign Policy," *Maghreb Review*, 8 (3–4, May–August): 96–103.

—— (1983c) "Libya's 'New' Foreign Policy," *Contemporary Review*, 243 (1410, July): 15–18.

—— (1986) "Terrorism and Libyan Foreign Policy, 1981–1986," *The World Today*, 42 (7, July): 111–15.

—— (1987a) *Qaddafi's World Design: Libyan Foreign Policy, 1969–1987*, London: Saqi.

—— (1987b) "Whatever's Happened to Qaddafi?," *The World Today*, 43 (4, April): 58–9.

—— (1988) "The Libyan Debacle in Sub-Saharan Africa: 1969–1987," in R. Lemarchand (ed.) *The Green and the Black: Qadhafi's Policies in Africa*, Bloomington: Indiana University Press, pp. 125–38.

—— (1993) "Qaddafi's World Design Revisited," *Global Affairs*, 8 (1, Winter): 161–73.

—— (2000) "Libya in Africa: Looking Back, Moving Forward," *Journal of Libyan Studies*, 1 (1, Summer): 18–32.

—— (2002) *Libya and the United States: Two Centuries of Strife*, Philadelphia: University of Pennsylvania Press.

—— (2003a) "Round Up the Usual Suspects: Prospects for Regime Change in Libya," *Journal of Libyan Studies*, 4 (1, Summer): 5–21.

—— (2003b) "Libya Foreign Policy: Newfound Flexibility," *Orbis*, 47 (3, Summer): 463–77.

—— (2004a) "Libya: Coming In from the Cold, Ties Re-established in Europe and Africa," in C. Legum (ed.), B621–35, *Africa Contemporary Record* 27 (1998–2000), New York: Africana Publishing Company.

—— (2004b) "Libya Is Not Iraq: Preemptive Strikes, WMD, and Diplomacy," *Middle East Journal*, 58 (3, Summer): 386–402.

—— (2006a) *Historical Dictionary of Libya*, 4th edn., Lanham, MD: Scarecrow.

—— (2006b) "Libya: Lockerbie Trial Ends, Sparking New Libyan Initiatives," in C. Legum (ed.), B634-48, *Africa Contemporary Record* 28 (2001–2002), New York: Africana Publishing Company.

—— (2006c) "Libya and the United States: The Next Steps," Atlantic Council Issue Brief, March.

—— (2007) "Libya's Oil & Gas Industry: Blending Old and New," *Journal of North African Studies*, 12 (2, June): 239–54.

—— (2008a) *Libya: From Colony to Independence*, Oxford: Oneworld.

—— (2008b) "Libya: Reforming the Economy, Not the Polity," in Y. H. Zoubir and H. Amirah-Fernández (eds.), *North Africa: Politics, Region, and the Limits of Transformation*, London: Routledge, pp. 53–70.

—— (2008c) "Redefining the Libyan Revolution: The Changing Ideology of Muammar al-Qaddafi," *Journal of North African Studies*, 13 (1, March): 91–106.

—— (2008d) "The Changing Libyan Economy: Causes and Consequences," *Middle East Journal*, 62 (1, Winter): 75–91.

—— (2008e) "The Libyan Economy in Transition: Opportunities and Challenges," in Dirk Vandewalle (ed.) *Libya since 1969: Qadhafi's Revolution Revisited*, New York: Palgrave Macmillan, pp. 127–51.

—— (2008f) "Libya and the United States: A Faustian Pact?," *Middle East Policy*, 15 (1 Spring): 133–48.

—— (2008g) "Qaddafi's Old Theories Facing New Realities," *Arab Reform Bulletin*, December (accessed at http://www.carnegieendowment.org/arb).

—— (2009) "A New US Relationship with Libya?," *Foreign Policy in Focus*, March 27: 1–3 (accessed at http://www.fpif.org).

—— (2010) "The Slow Pace of Reform Clouds the Libya Succession," Real Instituto Elcano de Estudios Internacionales y Estratégicos, 12 March (accessed at http://www.realinstitutoelcano.org).

Salem, Salem F. (1996) "The Health Care Delivery System in Libya with Special Emphasis on Public Health Care Services in Benghazi," *Libyan Studies*, 27: 99–123.

Seale, Patrick and McConville, Maureen (1974) *The Hilton Assignment*, London: Fontana/Collins.

Segrè, Claudio G. (1974) *Fourth Shore: The Italian Colonization of Libya*, Chicago, IL: University of Chicago Press.

—— (1982) "Italian Development Policy in Libya: Colonialism as a National Luxury," in E. G. H. Joffé and K. S. McLachlan (eds.) *Social & Economic Development of Libya*, Wisbech, Cambridgeshire: Middle East & North African Studies Press, pp. 81–93.

—— (1987) *Italo Balbo: A Fascist Life*, Berkeley: University of California Press.

Sharawi, Helmy (1985) "Israeli Policy in Africa," in K. El-Din Haseeb (ed.) *The Arabs & Africa*, London: Croom Helm, pp. 285–319.

Simon, Rachel (1987) *Libya between Ottomanism and Nationalism: The Ottoman Involvement in Libya during the War with Italy (1911–1919)*, Berlin: Klaus Schwarz Verlag.

—— (1992) *Change within Tradition among Jewish Women in Libya*, Seattle: University of Washington Press.

Simons, Geoff (2000) "The Great Man-Made River Project: Technology, Evaluation, Politics," *Journal of Libyan Studies*, 1 (2, Winter): 28–40.

Slouschz, Nahum (2005) "Nahum Slouschz," in J. Wright (ed.) *Travellers in Libya*, London: Silphium Books, pp. 226–31.

Solomon, Hussein and Swart, Gerrie (2005) "Libya's Foreign Policy in Flux," *African Affairs*, 104 (416, July): 469–92.

Spencer, Claire (2009) "North Africa: The Hidden Risks to Regional Stability," Chatham House briefing paper 2009/01: April.

Stanik, Joseph T. (2003) *El Dorado Canyon: Reagan's Undeclared War with Qaddafi*, Annapolis, MD: Naval Institute Press.

Strong, Anthony (2002) *The Phoenicians in History and Legend*, Bloomington, IN: AuthorHouse.

Sury, Salaheddin Hasan (1982) "The Political Development of Libya, 1952–1969: Institutions, Policies and Ideology," in J. A. Allan (ed.) *Libya since Independence: Economic and Political Development*, London: Croom Helm, pp. 121–36.

—— (2003) "A New System for a New State: The Libyan Experiment in Statehood, 1951–1969," in A. Baldinetti (ed.) *Modern and Contemporary Libya: Sources and Historiographies*, Rome: Istituto Italiano per L'Africa e L'Oriente, pp. 179–94.

Taha, Dhanun (1989) *The Muslim Conquest and Settlement of North Africa and Spain*, London: Routledge.

Takeyh, Ray (1998) "Qadhafi and the Challenge of Militant Islam," *Washington Quarterly*, 21 (3, Summer): 159–72.

—— (2000) "Qadhafi's Libya and the Prospect of Islamic Succession," *Middle East Policy*, 7 (2, February): 154–64.

Terrill, W. Andrew (1994) "Libya and the Quest for Chemical Weapons," *Conflict Quarterly*, 14 (1, Winter): 47–61.

Tremlett, George (1993) *Gadaffi: The Desert Mystic*, New York: Carroll & Graf.

US Department of Defense (1997) *The Defense Science Board 1997 Summer Study Task Force on DOD Responses to Transnational Threats, Volume 1, Final Report*, October, mimeograph.

US Department of State (2010) *2009 Country Reports on Human Rights Practices*, March 11 (accessed at http://www.state.gov).

Vandewalle, Dirk (1991) "Qadhafi's 'Perestroika': Economic and Political Liberalization in Libya," *Middle East Journal*, 45 (2, Spring): 216–31.

—— (1995a) "The Failure of Liberalization in the Jamahiriyya," in D. Vandewalle (ed.) *Qadhafi's Libya, 1969 to 1994*, New York: St. Martin's Press, pp. 203–22.

—— (1995b) "The Libyan Jamahiriyya since 1969," in Dirk Vandewalle (ed.) *Qadhafi's Libya, 1969 to 1994*, New York: St. Martin's Press, pp. 3–46 .

—— (1998) *Libya since Independence: Oil and State-Building*, Ithaca, NY: Cornell University Press.

—— (2006) *A History of Modern Libya*, Cambridge: Cambridge University Press.

—— (2008a) "Libya's Revolution in Perspective: 1969–2000," in D. Vandewalle (ed.) *Libya since 1969: Qadhafi's Revolution Revisited*, New York: Palgrave Macmillan, pp. 9–53.

—— (2008b) "Libya in the New Millennium," in D. Vandewalle (ed.) *Libya since 1969: Qadhafi's Revolution Revisited*, New York: Palgrave Macmillan, pp. 215–37.

Vikor, Knut S. (1995) *Sufi and Scholar on the Desert Edge: Muhammad b. Ali al-Sanusi and his Brotherhood*, Evanston, IL: Northwestern University Press.

Villard, Henry Serrano (1956) *Libya: The New Arab Kingdom of North Africa*, Ithaca, NY: Cornell University Press.

Waddams, Frank C. (1980) *The Libyan Oil Industry*, London: Croom Helm.

ElWarfally, Mahmoud G. (1988) *Imagery and Ideology in US Policy toward Libya, 1969–1982*, Pittsburgh, PA: University of Pittsburgh Press.

Warmington, B. H. (1954) *The North African Provinces from Diocletian to the Vandal Conquest*, Cambridge: Cambridge University Press.

Werenfels, Isabelle (2004) "How to Deal with the 'New Qaddafi'?," Berlin, Stiftung Wissenschaft und Politik (SWP) Comments 29, October: 1–4.

—— (2008) "Qadhafi's Libya: Infinitely Stable and Reform-Resistant?," Berlin, Stiftung Wissenschaft und Politik (SWP) Research Paper, July: 1–31.

Wharton, Barrie (2003) "'Between Arab Brothers and Islamist Foes': The Evolution of the Contemporary Islamist Movement in Libya," *Journal of Libyan Studies*, 4 (1, Summer): 33–48.

Wheelan, Joseph (2003) *Jefferson's War: America's First War on Terror, 1801–1805*, New York: Carroll & Graf.

Wiegele, Thomas C. (1992) *The Clandestine Building of Libya's Chemical Weapons Factory: A Study in International Collusion*, Carbondale: Southern Illinois University Press.

World Bank (2006) "Socialist People's Libyan Arab Jamahiriya: Country Economic Report," Report No. 30295-LY, July (accessed at http://www.worldbank.org).

Wright, Claudia (1981–2) "Libya and the West: Headlong into Confrontation?," *International Affairs*, 58 (1, Winter): 13–41.

Wright, John (1982a) *Libya: A Modern History*, Baltimore, MD: Johns Hopkins University Press.

—— (1982b) "Libya: Italy's 'Promised Land'," in E. G. H. Joffé and K. S. McLachlan (eds.) *Social & Economic Development of Libya*, Wisbech, Cambridgeshire: Middle East & North African Studies Press, pp. 67–79.

—— (1985) "Italian Fascism and Libyan Human Resources," in M. M. Buru, S. M. Ghanem, and K. S. McLachlan (eds.) *Planning and Development in Modern Libya*, Wisbech, Cambridgeshire: Middle East & North African Studies Press, pp. 46–56.

—— (1987) "Mussolini, Libya and the 'Sword of Islam'," *Maghreb Review*, 12 (1–2, January–April): 29–33.

—— (1989a) *Libya, Chad and the Central Sahara*, London: C. Hurst.

—— (1989b) "Colonial and Early Post-Colonial Libya," *Libyan Studies*, 20: 221–334.

—— (1990) "British and Italians in Libya in 1943," *Maghreb Review*, 15 (1–2, January–April): 31–6.

—— (2003) "Sayyid Ahmad al-Sharif and the First World War," *Journal of Libyan Studies*, 4 (1, Summer): 63–75.

Yergin, Daniel (1991) *The Prize: The Epic Quest for Oil, Money, and Power*, New York: Free Press.

Zacks, Richard (2005) *The Pirate Coast: Thomas Jefferson, the First Marines, and the Secret Mission of 1805*, New York: Hyperion.

Zemni, Sami and Bogaert, Koenraad (2009) "Trade, Security and Neoliberal Politics: Whither Arab Reform? Evidence from the Moroccan Case," *Journal of North African Studies*, 14 (1, March): 91–107.

Ziadeh, Nicola A. (1958) *Sanusiyah: A Study of a Revivalist Movement in Islam*, Leiden: E. J. Brill.

—— (1967) *The Modern History of Libya*, London: Weidenfeld and Nicolson.

Zoubir, Yahia H. (2007) "Stalemate in Western Sahara: Ending International Legality," *Middle East Policy*, 14 (4, Winter): 158–77.

—— (2009a) "Libya and Europe: Economic Realism at the Rescue of the Qaddafi Authoritarian Regime," *Journal of Contemporary European Studies*, 17 (3, December): 401–15.

—— (2009b) "The United States and Libya: The Lengthy Road to Reconciliation," in R. Looney (ed.) *Handbook of US–Middle East Relations: Formative Factors and Regional Perspectives*, London: Routledge, pp. 262–80.

Internet sources

All Africa. Accessed at http://allafrica.com.

Community of Sahel-Saharan States. Accessed at http://www.cen-sad.org.

Gaddafi International Charity and Development Foundation. Accessed at http://gdf.org.ly.

Al Gathafi Speaks. Accessed at http://www.algathafi.org.
Great Man-Made River Authority. Accessed at http://www.gmmra.org.
Green Book Studies. Accessed at http://www.greenbookstudies.com.
Libya Forum. Accessed at http://www.libyaforum.org.
Libya Our Home. Accessed at http://www.libya-watanona.com.
Libyan Constitutional Union. Accessed at http://www.libyanconstitutionalun-ion.net.
Libyan Investment. Accessed at http://www.libyaninvestment.com.
Libyan Jamahiriya Broadcasting Corporation (LJBC). Accessed at http://www.ljbc.net.
Libyan Remembrance. Accessed at http://www.libyaalwafa.com.
Libyan Tmazight Congress. Accessed at http://www.alt-libya.org.
Middle East Online. Accessed at http://www.middle-east-online.com.
National Conference of the Libyan Opposition. Accessed at http://libya-nclo.com.
National Oil Corporation. Accessed at http://www.noclibya.com.ly.
Transparency – Libya. Accessed at http://www.transparency-libyaonline.com.

Newspapers, news agencies, and magazines

Agence France-Presse (AFP), Paris
Bloomberg, New York
BBC News, London
Business Week (BW), New York
Christian Science Monitor (CSM), Boston
The Economist, London
Financial Times (FT), London
Forbes, New York
Guardian, London
Houston Chronicle, Houston
International Herald Tribune (IHT), Paris
Jamahiriya Arab News Agency (JANA), Tripoli
Middle East Economic Digest (MEED), London
New York Times (NYT), New York
Reuters, New York
The Times, London
The Tripoli Post, Tripoli
Wall Street Journal (WSJ), New York
Washington Post (WP), Washington, DC.

INDEX